The Effects of the Global Pandemic Process on the Social and Economic Structure
and Public Policies in Combating the Pandemic

Murat Demir & Ali Burak Aksungur (Eds.)

The Effects of the Global Pandemic Process on the Social and Economic Structure and Public Policies in Combating the Pandemic

**Bibliographic Information published by the
Deutsche Nationalbibliothek**
The Deutsche Nationalbibliothek lists this publication in the Deutsche Nationalbibliografie; detailed bibliographic data is available online at http://dnb.d-nb.de.

Library of Congress Cataloging-in-Publication Data
A CIP catalog record for this book has been applied for at the Library of Congress.

ISBN 978-3-631-85656-7 (Print)
E-ISBN 978-3-631-85728-1 (E-PDF)
E-ISBN 978-3-631-85976-6 (EPUB)
DOI 10.3726/b18800

© Peter Lang GmbH
Internationaler Verlag der Wissenschaften
Berlin 2021
All rights reserved.

Peter Lang – Berlin · Bern · Bruxelles · New York · Oxford · Warszawa · Wien

All parts of this publication are protected by copyright. Any utilisation outside the strict limits of the copyright law, without the permission of the publisher, is forbidden and liable to prosecution. This applies in particular to reproductions, translations, microfilming, and storage and processing in electronic retrieval systems.

This publication has been peer reviewed.

www.peterlang.com

Preface

The coronavirus first appeared at the end of 2019 and quickly spread across the globe, has infected tens of millions of people, and has caused more than three million people to die around the world. During this period, all countries have taken several measures to reduce the spread of the coronavirus pandemic. Therefore, the COVID-19 pandemic has a wide range of economic, political and social consequences.

As a result of the spread of the coronavirus around the world, countries have imposed shutdowns and quarantines. These measures have damaged both industrialized and developing economies. The economic downturn has been exacerbated by falling demand, weakening productivity, and worsening expectations. In 2020, a lot of countries experienced negative growth rates.

Beyond economic consequences, the coronavirus pandemic also has some political consequences. Some governments are regarded as successful since they manage this process better. On the other hand, in countries where process management has gotten out of control people will discuss government failures.

The social consequences of the pandemic are also noteworthy. Staying at home and reducing social interactions and activities have been bringing significant changes in people's social lives. The way of doing business, working and communicating transform the social life during the pandemic period.

These consequences and disruptions have been attempted to be mitigated by the introduction of several fiscal policies, monetary policies, health policies, and public management policies. These policy instruments are intended to mitigate the coronavirus's negative effects on economic and social life, as well as protect society from the negative consequences of these preventive measures.

During the pandemic period, countries have also improved their public health infrastructure, enacted some regulations to protect the workforce, increased their social expenditures, and social inclusion, implemented proactive measures to protect the supply chain, and tried to increase the quality of the online education infrastructure. It is also worth noting that the degree to which the countries implement such policies depend on whether the country can afford the costs of these policies.

In this context, this book discusses and analyzes the economic and social effects of the pandemic from a broader perspective. Therefore, this book stands out as a resource for students, academicians, and policymakers to benefit from the deep analyzes and discussions about the consequences of the coronavirus pandemic.

Prof. Erdal Tanas Karagol
Associate Member of the Turkish Academy of Sciences

Introduction

The COVID-19 outbreak, which was first detected in the last months of 2019 in Wuhan, Hubei province of China, was declared a global pandemic by the World Health Organization on March 11, 2020 due to its rapid spread. COVID-19, which infected millions all over the world and claimed the lives of hundreds of thousands of people within a year, has become a priority for almost all countries due to its direct and indirect effects on the social, economic, financial, and political structures. Countries, on the one hand have tried to combat the pandemic, and on the other hand, worked towards developing and managing new legal arrangements in many fields from consumption to social order, and the working conditions of the new normal. There are undoubtedly many challenges here. The main challenges are the identification of the new administrative, financial, economic, and social normals, how to make sure that the society adopts them, and how to finance the change in circumstances burdened by high public funding due to declining revenues and increasing costs.

Beyond its impact on public health, the pandemic has also affected education and healthcare services, public order, urban life, and national and global economic and financial systems. This effect of the pandemic has made it difficult to fight the pandemic, as well as requiring public policies.

The pandemic and the measures adopted have negatively affected countries and societies, businesses and other organizations, families and individuals in various aspects. Measures that restricted people's mobility contracted and halted the operations of many businesses, leading to economic stagnation and shrinking. As a result of a significant fall in the demand of goods or services, particularly in durable goods, tourism, travel, accommodation, and automotive sectors, factories suspended activities, and many countries experienced economic and employment-related contractions and increasing unemployment.

Curfews and lockdowns imposed during the COVID-19 pandemic, which is considered to be the deepest crisis experienced by the world economy since the 1929 depression, disrupted distribution chains and brought production to a standstill in some industries such as tourism. Disruptions in the distribution chain affected total supply through the real sector, and when combined with demand contraction, led countries to a deflationary process. Developed countries have supported households through unemployment benefits while this support has been limited in developing countries with higher rates of informal employment.

Restrictions imposed to prevent the spread of the pandemic also negatively affected social life, social relationships and the psychology of individuals. With the COVID-19 pandemic, social life has been suspended in cities, domestic and international travels have been restricted, curfews have been imposed upon certain age groups and those with chronic illnesses, lockdowns have been introduced, and schools have been closed. Many industries have adopted flexible working arrangements and cultural, art, and sports events have been suspended. Without a doubt, all these problems affect cities deeply.

Public policies and policy tools determined by the public have been the main driver of the response against the pandemic in almost every country. The success of measures adopted to combat the pandemic has been an area widely discussed recently. Similar measures in many countries have differed significantly. While some countries have been able to prevent deepening the crisis by managing the pandemic successfully, others have not been able to succeed despite adopting the same public policies, deepening the crisis.

The greatest expectation from public financial management and fiscal policies in combating the pandemic has been the contribution to the manageability of the crisis. It is extremely difficult to introduce a policy that can completely eliminate the effects of the pandemic before it is completely over. It is important to develop and adopt policy sets and tools that will minimize the effects of the pandemic and ensure that it can be managed without turning into a financial, economic and social crisis.

The fact that this global pandemic has ended in developed countries in the West does not mean that it has ended and the problems are over. If the fight in question is not carried out with the same determination in underdeveloped countries, the pandemic, which will continue to spread from underdeveloped countries to the whole world with new variants, will also open the success achieved so far up for discussion. On the other hand, in the context of social justice, it is necessary to offer relevant assistance, from health benefits to social and financial support, including vaccination programs to the rest of the world. Globalization should be considered as such.

The effects of the pandemic on the social and economic structure and public policies are analyzed under seven headings.

In the first chapter, Demir and Geyik analyzes the fiscal policies adopted in response to the pandemic by comparing Turkey with selected countries under the heading "Fiscal Policies Adopted during the Global Pandemic and Their Effectiveness." The study emphasizes the importance of the economic and financial strength of countries in the effectiveness of public policies and that countries that implement the measures adopted in response to the pandemic with determination had been more successful. Policies and measures adopted in countries subject to review have been effective in maintaining the activities of the private sector to a limited extent, responding to the need for additional funding for the healthcare system, supporting commercial activities through tax concessions, and keeping the income loss of households at a minimum via rent support and unemployment benefits. This indicates that these countries (China, US, Germany, UK, Turkey, Spain) have been able to manage the pandemic before it turned into major economic, fiscal, or social crises.

In the second chapter titled "Impact of the Global COVID-19 Pandemic on Human Resource Management Practices of Businesses" that covers the employment policies of businesses during the pandemic, Acar and Demir touches upon the impact of the COVID-19 pandemic and related restrictions on the economy and businesses and then focuses on human resource management, an important function of businesses and organizations. Within this framework, the current and possible changes the pandemic caused on staffing, training, career planning, performance management, and wage management-related policies, activities, and practices of human resource management are analyzed. As expected, the Coronavirus crisis has also negatively affected businesses and public and private organizations operating in most industries, with the exception of some lines of work. At the micro level, businesses and other organizations suffered a major decline in business and employment volumes and income. In this context, there have also been declines and losses in the working conditions and income of the self-employed and paid workers. In addition, new working arrangements, especially the dissemination of remote and flexible work, have been quite influential. In the dissemination of remote/flexible working arrangements, smart communication and information technologies have been decisive and the effects of COVID-19 have been accelerating and deepening. As a result, there has been a significant rise in the use of electronic(e-) or digital forms of business and work. In terms of HRM policies and practices, the crisis has impacted staffing, career management, training, performance, and wage management aspects the most. The contraction in the work and employment volume of businesses has led to significant changes in human resource management policies and practices, reducing the working time, leading to paid and unpaid leave, and the introduction of flexible working arrangements such as remote working.

In the third chapter titled "Effects of Covid-19 on Turkish Higher Education," Sarıoğlu and Efe analyzes the impact of the global pandemic on the education industry using a case study. According to the findings, distance education has negatively impacted students who have a number of challenges before accessing and using distance education tools. This has also been reflected in the level of learning and success of these students and revealed the importance of public support and policies in eliminating the challenges posed by the pandemic on educational services. The public nature of educational services also makes this support mandatory. This problem deepens inequality of opportunity between regions in a country and on a global level, between developed and underdeveloped countries. At the national level, governments and educational systems, and at the global level, multinational organizations and developed countries are responsible for ensuring the access of students living in less developed regions to the educational network to benefit from educational services. Because these problems will lead to many others, especially income distribution problems in the medium and long term.

In the fourth chapter titled "The Global Economy during COVID-19 Pandemic: Realizations and Predictions," Sever and Ay analyze the impact of the COVID-19 pandemic on the global growth performance, financial markets, labor market, and international trade activities and touch upon predictions. Financial support packages offered by governments in response to the pandemic and monetary policy decisions adopted by central banks have played a pivotal role in the recovery of economies. Central banks have fought the pandemic through asset purchases, liquidity support to financial institutions, swap deals and credit flows. Especially in developing countries, economies have been intervened through treasury bills, state-guaranteed bonds, and mortgage-based support packages. When developed and developing economies were examined, it was seen that all countries adopted monetary expansionary policies despite future inflation pressures. While developed economies have not experienced inflation, emerging and developing economies, such as India and Turkey, witnessed signs of inflation. Contractions in supply and demand due to various reasons, such as uncertainty and containment measures, had a negative impact on international trade in goods and services. The importance of global cooperation in eliminating supply chain disruptions and reducing risks for the future has been made very clear. Experience in remote working and the advancing technological infrastructure have also led to significant changes in the way people work. The educated and skilled workforce has started to shift to new lines of business. After these developments, the income gap between the qualified and unqualified workforce has grown even more.

In the fifth chapter titled "The COVID-19 Pandemic and Its Effects on Urban Life," Karasu analyzes the impact of the COVID-19 pandemic from four aspects, namely cultural and psychosocial, economic, architectural and design, and technology. With the COVID-19 outbreak, social life in cities is suspended, travels within and between countries are restricted, movements of certain age groups and individuals with chronic diseases are restricted, partial or complete curfews are imposed, education in schools are suspended, working hours are made flexible, or working from home is preferred. Cultural, art, and sports events are suspended and production is paused in factories. Without a doubt, all these problems affect cities deeply. Unfair income distribution in cities, growing inequality, ignoring the principle of public interest in planning, urban building density created for the purpose of rent, social segregation and racism, privatization of education and healthcare services, and neoliberal policies that promote growth despite the environment have become untenable in the face of the pandemic. As in COVID-19, solving pandemics before they create critical consequences requires an urban society that is more environmentally friendly, has social concerns, is open to participation, and targets quality of life instead of growth. Smart city technologies should contribute to this goal. Zoning plans should not be used for brand city competitions or grand flashy projects but for the sake of public interest and the future of society. Cities should be transformed into areas where there is quality of life for all.

In the sixth chapter titled "Administrative Measures Adopted in Response to the COVID-19 Pandemic and Their Effects," Çelik and Aksungur take a look at the administrative measures adopted in response to the pandemic and their effectiveness. Upon the detection of the first case in Turkey, a number of administrative measures were adopted rapidly. In-person education gave way to distance education, curfews were imposed, and restrictions were introduced for travel. Public areas such as shopping centers, market places, and recreational areas were shut down and mass gatherings were postponed. Measures were adopted in public transportation vehicles to maintain social distance. Wearing masks was made mandatory everywhere. The recommendations produced by the Coronavirus Scientific Committee, which was established quite early on, following the developments in the world and the course of the disease within the country, were quickly transformed into policies under the coordination of the president and ministers. The pandemic showed the important role of digital services in striking a balance between protecting public health and ensuring the continuity of public services. The setting caused by the pandemic allowed digital services to improve quickly, and progress that would normally take years took a very short time. Thanks to digitalization in health, data could easily be transformed, allowing the prompt adoption of necessary measures according to the course of the pandemic. In a process where social and economic life is restricted and the availability of public services is difficult, the government took steps to ensure the continuity of public services much faster than usual and introduced many services. The COVID-19 pandemic is of great importance as it reminds us again of the importance of healthcare and social security systems and social state practices. Turkey, on the one hand, introduced administrative measures to treat patients, prevent the spread of the disease and contain the pandemic, and on the other hand, resorted to measures to support social and economic life, which have been deeply impacted. Thus, a balance point was sought between protecting public health and maintaining social and economic life.

In the final chapter of the study titled "Public Financial Management Responses to the COVID-19: General Overview and Policy Practices in Turkey," Akdemir analyzes the role and effectiveness of fiscal management in managing the problems brought on by the pandemic. Pressures on financial capacity and coordination failures, especially in developing countries, have made the fight against COVID challenging. For this reason, the crisis has deepened in many countries, leading to a contraction in economic activity. During the pandemic, decline in public revenues and increase in public expenditures have deepened public financing issues, while additional funds have been activated or additional budget was created. Thanks to the financial and monetary measures adopted to mitigate the adverse impact of the COVID-19 pandemic, healthcare services have become more sustainable. In this context, while countries with robust public financial management have had more opportunity to combat the pandemic, developing countries with structural public financing problems have had a much more difficult time in fighting the pandemic and assumed a heavy burden. In this process, liquidity support provided by Turkey has included semi-fiscal transactions such as equity funding, loans, asset purchase or debt assumption, guarantees and debt deferral. In this context, the Wealth Fund of Turkey was also assigned to offer capital support to companies affected by COVID-19. Public banks deferred and refinanced principal and interest payments of companies whose cash flows were negatively affected by the pandemic by at least three months. During the pandemic, the payback period for credit card debt was extended, low-interest loan packages were offered for low-income households, payback of shopkeepers for the months of April, May, and June was deferred penalty-free, low-interest loan options and credit cards with longer payback periods were offered for shopkeepers, and loan packages were offered for companies that abstained from layoffs under the leadership of state-owned banks. Increases in the debt burden and comprehensive support programs have the potential to create problems in the functioning of the central government budget in the coming years, and fiscal consolidation may be an issue after the pandemic. Uncertainties in vaccination programs and the extent to which the vaccine will protect against the mutated virus can delay economic recovery. Moreover, the fact that the vaccine is not the silver bullet and the need to continue vaccination at regular intervals can put countries, especially low-income and developing countries, under a burden that they cannot deal with. Given that health or vaccination are global challenges, developing effective solutions against COVID-19 requires broader partnerships and joint response. This also requires strengthening public financial management systems to improve the effectiveness of potential fiscal consolidation steps that will be taken during post-pandemic recovery.

Prof. Murat Demir

Table of Contents

Murat Demir and Osman Geyik
Fiscal Policies Adopted during the Global Pandemic and Their
Effectiveness 17

Rıza Demir and Ahmet Cevat Acar
Impact of the Global COVID-19 Pandemic on Human Resource
Management Practices of Businesses 37

Fatih Sarıoğlu and Gözde Nalbant Efe
Effects of COVID-19 on Turkish Higher Education 91

Erşan Sever and Merve Ay
The Global Economy during COVID-19 Pandemic: Realizations and
Predictions 125

Mithat Arman Karasu
The COVID-19 Pandemic and Its Effects on Urban Life 153

Abdullah Çelik and Ali Burak Aksungur
Administrative Measures Adopted in Response to the COVID-19
Pandemic and Their Effects 175

Tekin Akdemir
Public Financial Management Responses to the COVID-19: General
Overview and Policy Practices in Turkey 197

Murat Demir*
Osman Geyik**

Fiscal Policies Adopted during the Global Pandemic and Their Effectiveness

Abstract The outbreak, which was mostly regional and had limited effects at the beginning, soon became a pandemic on a global scale, affecting the entire world. The fact that COVID-19 has been a global pandemic, without a doubt, caused its social and economic outcomes to also be experienced on a global scale.

The fact that the pandemic has been threatening public health, as well as economic systems and functions, has made it difficult to fight it, making it a requirement to adopt public policies. Public policies and policy tools determined by the public have been the main driver of the response against the pandemic in almost every country. The success of measures adopted to combat the pandemic has been an area widely discussed recently. Similar measures in many countries have differed significantly. While some countries have been able to prevent deepening the crisis by managing the pandemic successfully, others have not been able to succeed despite adopting the same public policies, deepening the crisis. This study evaluates the COVID-19 pandemic and analyzed the fiscal policies adopted in China, the US, Germany, the UK, Turkey, and Spain to counter the pandemic and the effectiveness of these policies.

Keywords: Global pandemic, health services, fiscal policies in combating global pandemic, effectiveness of fiscal policies

INTRODUCTION

As the COVID-19 pandemic became global and started to affect social and economic functions, governments took action and adopted a number of decisions to prevent the spread of the virus and mitigate its effects. The public economy and the market economy have been intervened via measures such as allocating the necessary resources and supplying the additional medical devices and supplies to the healthcare industry, especially for vaccination efforts, supporting the

---

* Prof., Harran University, Faculty of Economics and Administrative Sciences, Department of Public Finance, mdemir@harran.edu.tr
** Dr., Dicle University, Faculty of Economics and Administrative Sciences, Department of Public Finance, osmangeyik@gmail.com

industries and employees impacted by the pandemic economically, adopting administrative measures to prevent the spread of the virus, and offering low-interest rate loans to the private sector.

In this process, the need to use fiscal policies effectively to prevent social welfare losses and mitigate the impact of the COVID-19 pandemic has become a necessity. A considerable part of public policies adopted by states has been shaped and implemented through basic fiscal policy tools such as taxes and public expenditures. In this context, the fiscal policy tools in question can be considered as the most important weapon to mitigate the loss of those impacted by COVID-19.

The decline in employment and the stagnation of economic activities have negatively affected all macroeconomic indicators, while also putting great pressure on public finance. Such a conjuncture, in which fiscal discipline is extremely difficult to maintain, also adversely affects debt indicators, especially in developing countries where financial depth is shallow, further increasing the debt burden through high interest rates. During this period, the increase in poverty and the deepening of the injustice in income distribution made it necessary for states to be involved in the process, especially in terms of social transfers.

The pandemic has deeply affected and continues to affect national and global economies socially, financially, and economically. In an economy where employment is contracting and the economy is shrinking, declining tax revenues, rising public spending and debt burdens, as well as public finances and the public economy are also directly affected. As in previous pandemics, the role of public policies in combating the COVID-19 pandemic is, without a doubt, very important. The basic question here is: what should be the composition of fiscal policies, which is an essential item that will guide public policies in this process? While it is extremely difficult to introduce a set of fiscal policies that will meet the expectations of the private sector, society and the state in solving existing economic and financial problems, especially in developing countries with a number of structural problems, such as Turkey, it will undoubtedly not be easy to develop a set of fiscal policies that will also solve the problems brought about by the pandemic.

Pandemics, which have the potential to cause a major economic crisis, are difficult for public and private sectors to manage as they lead to internal and external uncertainties by means of direct and indirect effects. The pandemic affects public and private sectors differently; there are also different levels of effect at different sections of sectors. This level of effect will surely be shaped by how successfully the pandemic is managed.

The pandemic can be contained without deepening it through public interventions with timely and correct policy instruments. However, delayed public policies that are adopted with the wrong policy instruments deepen the crisis, disrupt the functioning of the social and economic structure, and impose a heavy burden on the private sector.

1. Global Pandemic as a Public Matter

In terms of its economic and social effects, the COVID-19 pandemic has become quite destructive. The COVID-19 pandemic has a very different nature compared to previous ones (Atkeson, 2020). The pandemic has first threatened public health and then damaged the economy, which forced states to introduce comprehensive policies. The COVID-19 pandemic is infectious both in terms of economic problems and health-related problems (Baldwin and Mauro, 2020). The fact that states have had to introduce comprehensive policies to combat the pandemic has imposed more burden on budgets, leading to more economic problems. Tight relationships among countries and difficulty in controlling human mobility due to globalization have made it a challenge to respond to the pandemic. The fact that the pandemic has threatened public health and disrupted the functioning of the economy has turned it into a public problem and made comprehensive public policies necessary. Both the International Monetary Fund (IMF) and the World Health Organization (WHO) have made comprehensive analyses on the pandemic, looking at its global impact. The report, published by the IMF (2020), noted that the COVID-19 pandemic has not only represented a global public health emergency but has also brought about an international economic emergency due to its negative impact on public finances. COVID-19 is more fatal than seasonal flu and at least ten times more contagious than SARS. For this reason, it has great potential to harm public health by rapidly spreading in both developed and developing countries (WHO, 2020; Wilder-Smith et al., 2020).

2. Social and Economic Effects of the Global Pandemic

The COVID-19 pandemic, which has affected the entire world, has a much different effect than other outbreaks, as it has led to not only health-related problems but also economic problems. Expectations that the pandemic would cause a global recession have been realized, and there has been a significant contraction in the global economy (Chakraborty and Thomas, 2020). In particular, countries leading the world economy, such as China and the United States, have been significantly affected by this pandemic, which has led to disruptions in supply chains, which, in turn, has indirectly affected other countries. For the first quarter of 2020, it is estimated that the contraction in GDP growth of China and the United States will be much worse than in 2008 (Goldman, 2020). Developments and macroeconomic indicators have shown that the economic and financial effects of COVID-19 are much heavier than those of the 2008 global financial crisis and that a global recession is possible in 2020 (Anderson et al. 2020).

A study conducted by Gopinath (2020) and Furman (2020) concluded that COVID-19 caused supply and demand shocks, leading to a decline in work opportunities for individuals and production capacities of companies. Identifying the appropriate monetary and fiscal policies to combat the new economic and fiscal symptoms that will emerge after COVID-19, especially the economic recession, will be the areas of work that economic administrations will first focus on and the issues that will be the most challenging. The restrictions imposed by the pandemic have led to a decrease in all sectors of the national and global economy and the labor force, and many people have lost their jobs (Nicola et al., 2020).

The ongoing COVID-19 pandemic has also caused widespread destruction in the world's advanced economies. For this reason, governments all over the world have been introducing stimulus packages to help protect households and balance sheets of companies. The shock caused by the pandemic has also led to a considerable rise in the rate of unemployment. Faria-e Castro developed a simulation to measure the effectiveness of fiscal policies. In the study, the service industry, which was suddenly closed during the pandemic, was included in the modeling, and it was found that the closure of the service industry deeply affected others. It was also found that the contraction in the real economy affected the financial sector, which, in turn, had reverberations in real economy. When the expansion of unemployment insurance coverage, tax cuts, unconditional transfers and wage support provided in the service sector were included in the simulation, it was concluded that the increase in unemployment disrupted the financial balances and the recession could not be avoided despite intensive public support. Liquidity support for firms has shown to yield more positive results in terms of balancing income and employment (Faria-e Castro, 2021).

Economic restrictions imposed due to the COVID-19 pandemic have led to considerable income losses for low-income households. Those with low income have also been the ones most negatively affected in terms of employment (Auderbach et al., 2020).

Many studies have shown the importance of public support in mitigating the effects of the pandemic, especially in developing countries. In some of these studies, it was found that transfers to households had more impact on social structures, while transfers to companies had more impact on financial structures and are decisive in preventing the deepening of the crisis (Fairlie, 2020).

Restrictions imposed due to COVID-19 have had unwanted consequences on the income of households and an unexpected increase in the cost of businesses. The effects of cost increases in an economic structure with shrinking demand have negatively impacted all macroeconomic sizes. There is no doubt that state intervention is a necessity in managing such a process in which many economic variables are impacted (Goolsbee and Syverson, 2020).

Any failure to manage the response to the COVID-19 pandemic has the potential to cause industries to collapse (for example, airline, tourism and accommodation services) by putting pressure on the real sector through financial crises. Economic and financial crises brought about by the pandemic will affect the entire global economy at micro and macroeconomic levels and with economic, financial, social, and political aspects, representing in the form of welfare loss in developed countries, and of increase in poverty in developing countries (Furman, 2020; Galí, 2020; Odendahl and Springford, 2020).

Pandemic response takes place under much more difficult conditions in developing countries that have problems with public financing, financing growth and development, and have basic structural economic issues such as inflation and unemployment. As is known, such countries experience significant difficulties in combating private sector savings deficits, public sector deficits, and foreign trade deficits. The contraction of the economy due to the pandemic and public policies adopted to reduce the losses caused by this contraction is putting heavy pressure on public finances. In a contracting economy, there is a reduction in all public revenues, especially tax revenues, and social transfers to households and sectors negatively affected by the pandemic are rapidly increasing public spending. This process, which disrupts the balance of public finance, creates new financing problems, increasing the borrowing requirement of the public sector and raising borrowing costs through interest rates.

Fighting the pandemic undoubtedly has many dimensions. Social demands and expectations of the public affected by the pandemic, demands and expectations of industries affected by the pandemic, and demands, expectations, priorities of the state having to mitigate the impact of the pandemic on public finances have required multidimensional measures against the pandemic. In addition, it is safe to say that things are much more difficult for countries that already deal with macroeconomic structural problems. Under these critical conditions, it is extremely difficult to manage the social and economic structure without being affected by the pandemic. What is important here is the ability to manage the crisis without deepening it.

Besides the problems it poses, the pandemic also offers a number of opportunities, albeit at a more limited level. For example, economic challenges experienced by China due to the global pandemic and their reflection on the global supply chain have provided Turkey with important opportunities. During this period, Turkey has become an important supplier of EU countries, especially for the manufacturing sector. Turkey's unexpected growth rate of 1.8 % for 2020 can be tied to the growth in the manufacturing industry. Sectors created because of the pandemic, such as remote working models, especially distance education, have been important investment areas of this new period.

Although expectations for 2021 suggest that a recovery will take place with the global pandemic under control, this will not be easy. The most important issue here is the necessity to control the pandemic with the same effectiveness and determination all across the world. Vaccination programs and other preventive healthcare services that will be provided only in developed countries will not be sufficient to combat this global pandemic. Inadequate vaccination programs and preventive healthcare services in less developed countries and developing countries will cause the pandemic to continue with newer variants of the virus. No doubt, in such a case, measures adopted by developed countries will also become controversial, and new variants of the virus will reduce the effectiveness of the entire response.

COVID-19 vaccines, which have been developed faster than expected, are used in many OECD countries under vaccination schemes set by the public sector. However, it is possible that demand for vaccines will surpass supply for some time. Current developments show that vaccination is performed in favor of developed countries while developing and less developed countries have significant challenges and limitations accessing vaccines. Eliminating this discrepancy and achieving vaccine justice have an important role in the response to the pandemic. It is important that measures adopted to combat a pandemic that can travel across borders are implemented in all countries with the same determination and content in terms of controlling the rate of spread of the pandemic and the effectiveness of the measures. Governments must therefore provide the necessary logistical and healthcare infrastructure by reallocating vaccines to areas where it is most needed, regardless of international borders (OECD, 2021).

3. Fiscal Policy Measures Adopted during the Global Pandemic

There is intense debate over the effectiveness of conventional fiscal policies and fiscal policy instruments to combat COVID-19. COVID-19 affects almost every sector and every income level, creating direct and indirect effects on the economic, financial and social structure. Therefore, to combat COVID-19, many countries push the boundaries of fiscal policy, trying out new policies and policy instruments (Auerbach et al., 2020).

The implementation of fiscal policies, which have a pivotal role in combatting the global pandemic, causes additional burden on the budget, while the lack of such policies will deepen the economic and social impacts of the pandemic. A state's deficiencies in the field of health or lack of investment during outbreaks cause people with low income to not adequately benefit from healthcare services. In this case, the state will not be able to meet social demands and expectations and fulfill the requirements of being a social state at a time when individual efforts are vain (Stiglitz, 1994).

Taken into consideration the countries analyzed under this study, it was concluded that fiscal policies adopted by states are concentrated in certain fields and show similarities. Although measuring the effects of these policies is not possible in the short term, it is possible to evaluate some of their effects. The goal of the fiscal policies adopted during this period has been to prevent sudden drops in employment, eliminate the problem of paying rent for business owners, who have had to suspend economic activities, prevent layoffs, and eliminate challenges before tax payment and loss of household income loss. In addition, allocating additional budget to finance increased health spending is also a priority of fiscal policies to counter the pandemic.

The question of how to develop a set of fiscal policies to counter the problems that arise during the pandemic is difficult to answer. There are differences as well as similarities between financial packages introduced by countries. One similar aspect of policy measures adopted by countries to support businesses has been the fact that they focused on tax deferrals and short-time working allowances. However, there have been significant differences between measures adopted to support households according to the level of development of countries (OECD, 2020).

The effects of the pandemic vary in almost every country. Some of the variables that influence the effectiveness of the pandemic response are the economic structures of countries, their average income levels, sectoral distribution of GDP, public financing structures, regimes, social cohesion and functions, public order, the roles and responsibilities of states in the overall economic structure, the roles and responsibilities of states in the healthcare industry, characteristics of private health insurance schemes, and demographic indicators.

While it was projected that more resource would be allocated for pandemic response and fiscal policies would be implemented more successfully in developed countries, where the macroeconomic structure and public finance indicators are robust, considerable decline has been experienced by many developed countries, including the US and the UK, in terms of growth and employment. In these countries, poor adherence to containment measures has rapidly increased the number of cases, and strict restrictions, especially curfews, have brought their economies to a standstill.

In many countries, the focal point of pandemic-time fiscal policies has been managing financing problems caused by declined public revenues and increased public spending. Without a doubt, the ability to manage the crisis, and the composition of resources to be provided to victims and the way these resources are provided have been priority areas. Determining which sector is affected by the crisis, how the sectors affected by the crisis affect others, and their impact on employees and foreign trade are among the issues that policy-makers have had difficulty dealing with during the pandemic.

Even in countries where the most liberal policies are in place, the state steers economic and social life as a producer and consumer, in addition to its role as a regulator and supervisor. The fluctuating course of the pandemic has been another issue that suppressed the effectiveness of fiscal policies. Usual delays in fiscal policies, combined with the uncertainty about the course of the pandemic have weakened the effectiveness of measures.

Table 1 shows that the average unemployment rate for OECD countries has increased by 30 % from 5.39 % in 2019 to 7.11 % in 2020. Developed OECD countries have managed to prevent layoffs by preventing the crisis to impact employment figures through unemployment funds and short-term work allowances. Of course, success here is closely related to the depth of the unemployment fund, the financial structure of social security systems and the state of public funding. It is safe to say that developing OECD countries that lack the sufficient depth in these areas are much more affected by the employment crisis.

In particular, unemployment rates have significantly risen during the pandemic in Chile, Estonia, Mexico, and Hungary. In some developed and developing countries, there has been an increase in unemployment rates due to working from home and flexible working arrangements.

Table 2 shows that a significant contraction due to the pandemic has revealed itself in growth figures. The average growth rate for the Eurozone, which was

Table 1: Employment Figures (2018–2020)

Countries	2018	2019	2020
Austria	4.86	4.51	5.39
Belgium	5.96	5.37	5.63
Canada	5.89	5.73	9.56
Chile	7.38	7.22	10.78
Czech Republic	2.27	2.02	2.55
Denmark	5.12	5.06	5.64
Estonia	5.38	4.40	6.79
Finland	7.36	6.69	7.76
France	9.03	8.45	8.02
Germany	3.40	3.15	4.18
Hungary	3.59	3.30	4.13
Italy	10.62	9.97	9.12
Japan	2.44	2.35	2.77
Korea	3.83	3.78	3.94
Mexico	3.33	3.49	4.44
Netherlands	3.84	3.40	3.83
New Zealand	4.33	4.10	4.60
Poland	3.86	3.28	3.17
Portugal	7.05	6.55	7.00
Spain	15.27	14.11	15.54
Sweden	6.33	6.77	8.29
Turkey	10.97	13.70	13.20
United Kingdom	4.08	3.83	4.48
United States	3.90	3.67	8.0
Euro area (19 countries)	8.20	7.57	7.92
OECD - Total	5.48	5.39	7.11

Source: IMF Fiscal Monitoring Reports April 2021

1.6 % in 2019, was 6.2 % in 2020. China and Turkey have been the only two countries in the world economy that grew in 2020 by 2.3 % and 1.8 %, respectively. China and Turkey have been the winners of the pandemic, when production of the US and EU economies have fallen considerably. In particular, Turkey has turned the crisis into an opportunity when China's supply chain was disrupted and tried to meet the demands of EU countries thanks to its production structure that is mainly focused on manufacturing.

Table 2: Growth Figures (2018–2020)

Countries	2018	2019	2020
China	6.7	6.1	2.3
Ireland	8.5	5.6	3.4
Turkey	3.0	0.9	1.8
Lithuania	3.9	4.3	−0.8
Norway	1.1	0.9	−0.8
Luxembourg	3.1	2.3	−1.3
Poland	5.4	4.5	−2.7
Sweden	2.0	1.4	−2.8
Estonia	4.4	5.0	−2.9
Finland	1.3	1.3	−2.9
Switzerland	3.0	1.1	−2.9
Denmark	2.2	2.8	−3.3
Netherlands	2.4	1.7	−3.8
Romania	4.5	4.1	−3.9
Bulgaria	3.1	3.7	−4.2
Germany	1.3	0.6	**−4.9**
Hungary	5.4	4.6	−5.0
Belgium	1.8	1.7	−6.4
Austria	2.6	1.4	−6.6
Malta	5.2	5.5	−7.0
Portugal	2.8	2.5	−7.6
France	1.8	1.5	**−8.1**
Greece	1.6	1.9	−8.2
Italy	0.9	0.3	−8.9
Spain	2.4	2.0	−11.0
United Kingdom	1.3	1.4	:
European Union – 27 countries	2.1	1.6	-6.2
Euro area - 19 countries	1.9	1.3	-6.6

Source: IMF Fiscal Monitoring Reports April 2021

The effectiveness of fiscal policies cannot be measured by only looking at these figures. The course of the pandemic, the burden imposed by the pandemic, and the level of social adherence to containment measures differ in each country. The composition and effectiveness of the fiscal policy that each country will adopt in combating the pandemic, which has different effects at regional, national and global levels, will undoubtedly be unique. The success or effectiveness is being able to develop fiscal policies that well-manage and timely meet the demands and expectations of the society, can meet the needs of the private sector, and can allocate resources for all demands and expectations by overcoming the burden and financial challenges imposed by declining public revenue and increasing public spending and to identify the policy instruments to achieve these goals.

For developing countries such as Turkey, which suffer from significant structural problems, this process is much more difficult to manage and finance. For developed countries that have solved a significant part of these structural problems, the process is much easier to manage, especially with their size of the financing. For underdeveloped countries that lack a vaccination program, it is possible to say that the economic and social destruction will be dramatic.

The pandemic and pandemic response serve as global public goods. In other words, overlooking the response in Africa while fighting the pandemic in the EU would also be a failure for the fight in the EU. At this point, intensive global cooperation on fiscal policies, public health policies and other public policies is needed to counter the pandemic.

During the pandemic, problems experienced by the health industry have shown once again the important of public healthcare institutions. Structural problems and disruptions in the health industry of Italy and Spain have brought rapid privatization of healthcare structures in these countries up for discussion. A health policy that limits public healthcare services to preventive healthcare services has proven to be disastrous during the pandemic.

CONCLUSION

Nowadays, when the economic and social effects of the COVID-19 pandemic are heavily discussed, the composition and nature of measures and policies to be adopted to combat it are of vital importance. The social, economic, and financial structures of countries and level of adherence to social rules mandated by the pandemic are the main variables that guide the effectiveness of the response.

Almost every country has had to face the direct or indirect impact of the pandemic. What matters in this context is the ability to manage the problems brought about by the pandemic before they deepen. Of course, managing such a process is extremely challenging. During the pandemic, public revenues declined rapidly, while public spending increased in a contracting economy, leading to problems in the balance of public financing. The financial burden imposed by new borrowing schemes and how to distribute them have been

Table 3: Fiscal Policies Adopted by Countries

Country	Policy goal	Policy tool	Conclusion
Fiscal Policy Measures Adopted in China	Preventing the pandemic, preventing the increase in unemployment, keeping household income losses at a minimum, preventing the deepening of the economic bottleneck and preventing economic recession	An estimated 4.8 trillion Chinese Yuan (RMB) (4.7 % of GDP) has been allocated for discretionary fiscal measures. Key measures include: (I) expenditures for pandemic prevention and control measures, (ii) production of medical equipment, (iii) rapid payment and expansion of unemployment insurance coverage, (iv) tax cuts and waiver of social security premiums, and (v) additional public investment expenditures. A loan guarantee of 400 billion Yuan (0.4 % of GDP) has been provided for SMEs. The rate of transfer payments for pensions has been increased from 3 % to 4 %. Toll fees has been cancelled as of February 17 and some service fares collected by airports and railways have been restricted. Electricity prices have been reduced by 5 % by the end of 2020 (excluding sectors that have high energy consumption). Railway logistics fee has been reduced by 50 % by the end of June. SMEs in the service sector have been made exempt from paying rent for public goods for three months. Social security payments of businesses have been deferred for six months. Insurance premiums of 2019 have been refunded to businesses that have not laid of their employees or have made minimum layoffs. The scope of unemployment benefits has been expanded. VAT exemptions have been introduced for goods and services used in pandemic control, and VAT rate has been reduced from 3 % to 1 % by the end of the year (IMF, 2021b; IMF, 2021c)	It is safe to say that policies and measures adopted by countries have not been sufficient from the perspective of employees and sectors. These policies, which have been introduced to prevent the deepening of economic and social problems brought about by the pandemic, have provided the cash flow support necessary for producers operating in some sectors to sustain their activities, and prevented the welfare loss of households to a limited extent.

Table 3: Continued

Country	Policy goal	Policy tool	Conclusion
Fiscal Policy Measures Adopted in the United States	Preventing the pandemic, preventing the increase in unemployment, keeping household income losses at a minimum, preventing the deepening of the economic bottleneck and preventing economic recession	An estimated USD 2.3 trillion (about 11 % of GDP) has been earmarked for use under the CARES act. USD 475 billion have been allocated for the treatment of COVID-19 patients, drug and public health measures, payments of hospitals, disease control centers, vaccine development, medical equipment costs, additional medical expenses, testing, and vaccine tracking systems. Extended unemployment insurance and loan programs for small-size businesses have been introduced. Following the expiration of unemployment support, an additional USD 300 has been provided on a weekly basis. A total of USD 263.7 billion has been allocated for household support, support for businesses, education, child care and other support packages. USD 382.5 billion has been earmarked for tax breaks and loans targeting employers hit by the pandemic to prevent them from laying off employees. Income tax declaration has been extended by 90 days (IMF, 2021b; IMF, 2021c).	The United States has tried to prevent the loss of income that will arise because of the pandemic by offering direct cash transfers to low and middle-income households and support to businesses. It would not be wrong to say that the impact of these measures has been limited considering employment and growth figures.
Fiscal Policy Measures Adopted in Germany	Preventing the pandemic, preventing the increase in unemployment, keeping	To combat the COVID-19 crisis and support recovery afterwards, two additional budgets have been adopted by the government- EUR 156 billion (4.9 % of GDP) in March 2020 and EUR 130 billion (4 % of GDP) in June. It was planned to allocate EUR 218.5 billion to finance the package of measures to be adopted. Medical equipment, hospital capacity and R&D (vaccine) expenses, subsidy to increase access to short-term work to sustain	Measures were adopted to increase household cash flow. The impact of the measures has been limited,

(continued on next page)

Table 3: Continued

Country	Policy goal	Policy tool	Conclusion
	household income losses at a minimum, preventing the deepening of the economic bottleneck and preventing economic recession	the income of companies and employees (Kurzarbeit), increased access to basic income support by low-income families and the self-employed, EUR 50 billion loan to small-business owners and the self-employed hit hard by the COVID-19 pandemic, and interest-free tax deferral for up to one year have been among measures adopted (IMF, 2021b; IMF, 2021c).	but their effectiveness has been increased with the adoption of additional budgets.
Fiscal Policy Measures Adopted in the United Kingdom	Preventing the pandemic, preventing the increase in unemployment, keeping household income losses at a minimum, preventing the deepening of the economic bottleneck and preventing economic recession	The estimated cost of COVID-19 support measures is £ 280 billion. For 2021 and 2022, the government has allocated £ 55 billion. The COVID-19 job retention scheme to subsidize the wages of employees on leave and social security contributions of businesses has been extended until March 2021. Income support for the self-employed has been extended by six months. Paid sick leave for self-isolating individuals, compensation for up to two weeks for small-sized businesses, and support programs for self-isolating low-income individuals have been introduced. Direct grant and rent support have been provided to small-sized companies in retail hardest hit by the pandemic. International support has been provided by offering a £ 150 million loan to IMF's Disaster Relief Fund and £ 2.2 billion to IMF Poverty Reduction and Growth Trust to help low-income countries. £ 110.8 billion has been earmarked for funding the National Health Service, including increasing the number of hospital beds, medical staff and equipment. About £ 2.2 billion has been waived by removing VAT and customs duties on the import of medical devices to be used to counter the pandemic. Property tax and accommodation tax have been reduced, and VAT and income tax imposed upon the self-employed have been deferred. Deferred interest opportunities have been offered to SMEs and commercial enterprises (IMF, 2021b; IMF, 2021c).	The fact that the measures have been adopted for a certain period of time also rendered their impact limited. Other measures are likely to have a temporary impact on the budget, as deferred taxes are expected to be paid later on.

Table 3: Continued

Country	Policy goal	Policy tool	Conclusion
Fiscal Policy Measures Adopted in Turkey	Preventing the pandemic, preventing the increase in unemployment, keeping household income losses at a minimum, preventing the deepening of the economic bottleneck and preventing economic recession	As of the beginning of October, it is estimated that the entire financial support package will be worth TRY 646 billion (12.9 % of GDP) in 2020. Of this, approximately TRY 173 billion (3.5 % of GDP) is made up of budgetary measures. Basic financial measures consist of the following: i) loan guarantees granted to companies and households (GDP, 6.4 % of GDP); ii) loan deferral of state-owned banks (2.6 % of GDP); iii) tax deferral for businesses (1.4 % of GDP); iv) equity capital support for public banks (0.5 % of GDP); and v) short-term work program re-introduced in December and extended until February 2021 (0.4 % of GDP). The VAT rate has been reduced on some goods (food and accommodation services) until May 2021. Finally, in addition to the short-term employment scheme, the nationwide ban on layoffs has been extended until March 2021. TRY 1.4 billion has been earmarked for COVID-19 treatment, TRY 5 billion for new hospitals, and TRY 6 billion for performance pay for healthcare workers. Minimum cash assistance was provided to families in need. VAT on operating lease for the service sector has been reduced until the end of 2020. Tax deferral has been made possible for the self-employed and those over 65 or with chronic illness. In addition to the issuance of withholding and VAT declarations, payment of social security premiums in some sectors (e.g., retail/shopping malls, iron and steel, automotive, logistics and transportation sectors) has been postponed. The corporate tax rate has been reduced from 22 % to 20 % (IMF, 2021b; IMF, 2021c).	The goal of the fiscal policies and measures adopted have been to offer cash flow support, prevent a sudden decline in employment, and to compensate for the income loss incurred by households whose economic activities have come to a standstill. These measures have had a positive effect on indicators. The fact that these limited measures were intended for a certain period of time will also cause their economic benefits to be limited.

(continued on next page)

Table 3: Continued

Country	Policy goal	Policy tool	Conclusion
Fiscal Policy Measures Adopted in Spain	Preventing the pandemic, preventing the increase in unemployment, keeping household income losses at a minimum, preventing the deepening of the economic bottleneck and preventing economic recession	EUR 40.6 billion has been allocated for unemployment benefits for workers temporarily laid off due to COVID-19, exemption of employing companies from insurance premiums, exemption of businesses that suspend economic activities from social insurance premiums, payments for infected or quarantined workers, and those having difficulty paying rent. Payment of social security contributions has been postponed for the self-employed and companies in selected industries, tax incentives have been offered for property owners that reduce rent on properties used as hotels, restaurants, and in tourism activities (EUR 324 million), tax deferrals have been offered for small and medium sized business owners and the self-employed (interest-free for the first three to four months), tax declaration and self-assessment deadlines for SMEs and the self-employed have been extended, income tax and VAT installments of SMEs and the self-employed have been calculated based on de facto profit in 2020 (EUR 200 million), income tax and VAT reduction (EUR 117 million), VAT rate on purchasing COVID-19-related medical supplies, COVID-19 tests, and vaccines (EUR 70 million) have been zeroed temporarily, VAT rate has been reduced from 21 to 4 % in digital publications (EUR 5 million) (IMF, 2021b; IMF, 2021c).	These policies, which have been introduced to prevent the deepening of economic and social problems brought about by the pandemic, have provided the cash flow support necessary for producers operating in some sectors to sustain their activities, and prevented the welfare loss of households to a limited extent.

Source: IMF, Policy-Responses to COVID-19 and COVID-19 policy tracker.

particularly challenging for economy administrations with structural problems. All these developments have narrowed the extent of fiscal policy instruments and opened the effectiveness of public policies up for discussion.

These restrictions on fiscal policies in the fight against the pandemic have led countries to monetary policies. Countries' efforts to counter the pandemic through monetary expansion have led to inflationary pressure during the recession, especially in developing countries, including Turkey, guiding countries back to fiscal policies.

A number of fiscal policy measures have been put in place due to the increased spread of the pandemic and to minimize the damage caused by it. Preferred policy measures by states are expenses for pandemic prevention and control efforts, supporting medical production processes, social transfers to prevent household income loss due to disruptions to economic activities, support to employers, tax cuts and deferrals, additional healthcare expenditures, and rent support. In addition, countries have tried to prevent the economic and social problems that may arise during and after the pandemic by adopting various measures depending on their level of economic development.

The economic and financial structures of countries are decisive in determining the size of budgets to be allocated for these policies. The policies and measures adopted by countries analyzed under this study seem to be insufficient in terms of employees and sectors. These policies, which have been designed to prevent the deepening of economic and social problems brought about by the pandemic, have provided the cash flow support necessary for producers operating in some sectors to sustain their activities and prevented the welfare loss of households to a limited extent.

The pandemic can negatively affect a sector in a country, while offering a number of opportunities for another sector, leading to the formation of new sectors. It is extremely important to support these new sectors when introducing fiscal policies.

In 2020, the most striking indicator about the world economy was a significant contraction and low economic growth figures all over the world, except for China and Turkey. While the entire world, especially the US and EU economies, has experienced a contraction of up to 7 %, this has not been reflected in unemployment. An effort has been made to manage the process somehow by way of policy instruments such as unemployment insurance and working allowance. Turkey has been able to grow by 1.8 % in 2020 by filling the gaps in the global supply chain through its dynamic and economic functioning.

Policies and measures adopted in countries subject to review have been effective in maintaining the activities of the private sector to a limited extent, responding to the need for additional funding for the healthcare system, supporting commercial activities through tax concessions, and keeping the income loss of households at a minimum via rent support and unemployment benefits. This indicates that these countries have been able to manage the pandemic before it turned into major economic, fiscal, or social crises. Resources to be earmarked to national and global vaccination efforts and the success of vaccination programs will contribute to the sustainability of the achievements. Without a doubt, all of these public policies are based on fiscal policies funded by public resources. The pandemic has once again shown how important the role of the state is in the overall economic structure and functioning. Even countries that are clearly advocating for liberal management have taken on a proactive role, transferring resources directly to both the private economy and the public economy and managing the process.

The most fundamental public policies of the new era will be to develop vaccines to contain the pandemic, establish global cooperation on this matter, distribute available doses to all countries, and monitor vaccination programs with the same determination and competence in every country, whether it be less developed or developed. If the pandemic is not contained, the sustainability and effectiveness of a fiscal policy focused only on compensating for the devastation caused by the pandemic in the medium and long term are questionable. Developed countries that can compensate for the 7 to 8 % contraction in 2020 with a strong public financing balance have limited ability to cover major economic contractions that can take place in the following years. Long delays in controlling the pandemic will undoubtedly lead to greater costs for underdeveloped and developing countries, and existing structural economic problems will deepen.

REFERENCES

Anderson, R. M., Heesterbeek, H., Klinkenberg, D., & Hollingsworth, T. D. (2020). How will country-based mitigation measures influence the course of the COVID-19 epidemic? *The Lancet*, 395(10228), 931–934. Retrieved May 18, 2021, from DOI: https://doi.org/10.1016/S0140-6736(20)30567-5.

Atkeson, A. (2020). *What will be the economic impact of COVID-19 in the US? Rough estimates of disease scenarios (No. w26867)*. National Bureau of Economic Research. Retrieved May 6, 2021, from DOI: https://doi.org/10.3386/w26867.

Auerbach, A. J., Gorodnichenko, Y., & Murphy, D. (2020). *Fiscal policy and covid19 restrictions in a demand-determined economy* (No. w27366). National Bureau of Economic Research.

Baldwin, R., & Di Mauro, B. W. (2020). Economics in the time of COVID-19: A new eBook. *VOX CEPR Policy Portal.*

Chakraborty, L., & Thomas, E. (2020). COVID-19 and macroeconomic. *Economic & Political Weekly*, 55, 15.

Fairlie, R. W. 2020. The Impact of COVID-19 on Small Business Owners: The First Three Months after Social-Distancing Restrictions. *NBER Working Paper No. 27462.*

Faria-e-Castro, M. (2021). Fiscal policy during a pandemic. *Journal of Economic Dynamics and Control.* Retrieved March 1, 2021, from https://doi.org/10.1016/j.jedc.2021.104088

Furman, J. (2020). Protecting people now, helping the economy rebound later. Baldwin, R., & Di Mauro, B. W. (Eds.), *Mitigating the COVID Economic Crisis: Act Fast and Do Whatever It Takes*, pp. 191–196. Center for Economic Policy and Research. Washington, DC: CEPR Press.

Galí, J. (2020). Helicopter money: The time is now. Baldwin, R., & Di Mauro, B. W. (Eds.), *Mitigating the COVID Economic Crisis: Act Fast and Do Whatever It Takes*, pp. 57–62. Center for Economic Policy and Research. Washington, DC: CEPR Press.

Goldman, S. (2020). US daily: A sudden stop for the US economy. Retrieved May 18, 2021, from https://www.goldmansachs.com/insights/pages/us-daily-20-march-2020.html.

Goolsbee, A., and Syverson, C. (2020). Fear, Lockdown, and Diversion: Comparing Drivers of Pandemic Economic Decline. University of Chicago, Becker Friedman Institute for Economics Working Paper.

Gopinath, G. (2020). Limiting the economic fallout of the coronavirus with large targeted policies. Baldwin, R., & Di Mauro, B. W. (Eds.), *Mitigating the COVID Economic Crisis: Act Fast and Do Whatever It Takes*, pp. 41–48. Center for Economic Policy and Research. Washington, DC: CEPR Press.

IMF (2020). IMF's Georgieva: COVID-19 economic outlook negative, but rebound in 2021. Retrieved May 6, 2021, from https://www.imf.org/external/mmedia/view.aspx?vid=6144138845001.

IMF (2021a). Fiscal monitoring reports. Retrieved May 18, 2021, from https://www.imf.org/en/Publications/FM/Issues/2021/03/29/fiscal-monitor-april-2021

IMF (2021b). Policy-responses to COVID-19. Retrieved May 20, 2021, from https://www.imf.org/en/Topics/imf-and-covid19/Policy-Responses-to-COVID-19.

IMF (2021c). COVID19 policy tracker. Retrieved March 21, 2021, from https://www.imf.org/COVID19policytracker.

Nicola, M., Alsafi, Z., Sohrabi, C., Kerwan, A., Al-Jabir, A., Iosifidis, C., ... & Agha, R. (2020). The socio-economic implications of the Coronavirus and COVID-19 pandemic: A review. *International Journal of Surgery*, 78, 185–193. Retrieved May 11, 2021, from DOI: https://doi.org/10.1016/j.ijsu.2020.04.018.

Odendahl, C., & Springford, J. (2020). Bold policies needed to counter the coronavirus recession. Baldwin, R., *& Di Mauro, B. W. (Eds.), Mitigating the COVID Economic Crisis: Act Fast and Do Whatever It Takes*, pp. 145–150. Center for Economic Policy and Research. Washington, DC: CEPR Press.

OECD (2020). Tax and fiscal policy in response to the coronavirus crisis: Strengthening confidence and resilience. Retrieved March 27, 2021, from http://www.oecd.org/coronavirus/en/.

OECD (2021). Access to COVID-19 vaccines: Global approaches in a global crisis. Retrieved May 10, 2021 from https://read.oecd-ilibrary.org/view/?ref=1069_1069384-ewmqrw9sx2&title=Access-to-COVID-19-vaccines-Global-approaches-in-a-global-crisis

Stiglitz, J. E. (1994). The role of the state in financial markets. *Bruno, M., & Pleskovic, B. (Eds.), Proceedings of the World Bank Annual Conference on Development Economics, 1993: Supplement to the World Bank Economic Review and the World Bank Research Observer*, pp. 19–52. Washington, DC: World Bank.

WHO. (2020). Similarities and differences – COVID-19 and Influenza. Retrieved May 21, 2021 from https://www.who.int/news-room/q-a-detail/q-a-similarities-and-differences-COVID-19-andinfluenza.

Wilder, S. A., Chiew, C. J., & Lee, V. J. (2020). Can we contain the COVID-19 outbreak with the same measures as for SARS? *The Lancet Infectious Diseases*. Retrieved May 21, 2021 from https://doi.org/10.1016/S1473-3099(20)30129-8.

Rıza Demir[*]
Ahmet Cevat Acar[**]

Impact of the Global COVID-19 Pandemic on Human Resource Management Practices of Businesses

Abstract The COVID-19 pandemic, which first emerged in Wuhan, China's Hubey province, in the last months of 2019 and rapidly spread across the world, has had a significant impact on countries' health systems as well as their economies, social lives, and social relations, creating many uncertainties and problems. Undoubtedly, the areas most affected by the measures taken due to the pandemic are the economy and businesses which are the basic elements of the economy. As a result of the quarantines and curfews imposed due to the pandemic, many businesses had to cease their activities, resulting in an unprecedented trade cut in many industries. Due to a substantial drop in demand for products and services in sectors such as durable consumer goods, tourism, transport, accommodation, and automotive, economic growth has slowed and unemployment has risen in many countries.

The COVID-19 pandemic has significantly affected human resources management practices as well as activities for the basic functions of businesses such as sales-marketing, production, and finance. The main effects of the pandemic on human resource management are cost reduction by reducing all employee expenses, a short-term and rapid transition from regular employment to flexible work programs, and widespread use of digitalization in employee management practices. Although the pandemic may have some impacts on various human resource management functions and issues, some practices within the framework of human resource management functions may also play an important role in both managing the crisis and taking advantage of any opportunities that may occur after the pandemic.

The general effects of the COVID-19 pandemic on the economy, businesses and human resource management of organizations will be the subject of this section of the book. The current and potential changes caused by the pandemic on the policies, activities, and practices related to human resources management functions such as staffing, training (training-development), career planning and development, performance management, and pay management will be examined.

---

[*] Asst. Prof., Istanbul University, Faculty of Business Administration, rdemir@istanbul.edu.tr
[**] Prof., Istanbul University, Faculty of Business Administration, acara@istanbul.edu.tr

Keywords: COVID-19, pandemic, human resource management, flexible, digitalization, performance, training

INTRODUCTION

The COVID-19 outbreak, which was first detected in the last months of 2019 in Wuhan, Hubei province of China, was declared a global pandemic by the World Health Organization on March 11, 2020 due to its rapid spread. COVID-19 infected millions and claimed the lives of hundreds of thousands of people from all over the world in only a year and has become one of the most influential outbreaks in history. As of April 5, 2021, there are approximately 132 million confirmed COVID-19 cases, 106 million recovered individuals, and 2.9 million deaths (Worldometers, 2021).

The global pandemic of COVID-19 not only affected people's physical and psychological health, but also adversely impacted countries, societies, businesses, organizations, individuals, and families in various ways. Measures that restricted people's mobility contracted and halted the operations of many businesses, leading to economic stagnation and shrinking. Significant fall in the demand of goods or services, particularly in durable goods, tourism, travel, accommodation, and automotive sectors, contracted the economy and employment in many countries and increased unemployment. Restrictions imposed to prevent the spread of the pandemic also negatively affected social life, social relationships and the psychology of individuals. Postponement/cancellation of visits, cultural and art events, sports events, and mass gatherings due to the pandemic minimized social interaction, while limitation of social relations negatively affected solidarity in society. The negative effects of deprivation of social interaction due to isolation are expected to continue in society for a long time after the pandemic. The higher occurrence of domestic violence, conflicts between neighbors, and firearms sales today is thought to be related to the pandemic (Campbell, 2020). Social problems caused by the pandemic undoubtedly affect the psychology of individuals in a negative way. Studies have shown that feeling of loneliness caused by isolation causes poor cognitive performance, feelings of negativity and depression, and increases sensitivity to social threats (Donthu and Gustafsson, 2020: 285). A study conducted in Germany during the pandemic found that anxiety and stress disorders were more common in areas with more cases, and that the pandemic caused more negative psychological effects in people between the ages of 20 and 40 and women younger than 40 (Deutsche Welle, 2020).

The effects of the COVID-19 pandemic, which poses significant risks for humanity, are thought to persist for a long time even after vaccination is completed successfully. An important prediction is that nothing will be the same after the pandemic, and people will continue to live within the new normal (Karakaş, 2020: 541). According to these predictions, it is safe to say that many issues, approaches, understanding, and methods in the fields of economy, politics, social relations, business management, etc. will be questioned, leading to concrete changes.

In this chapter of the book, the effects of the COVID-19 pandemic and related measures on the economy and businesses will be addressed, and their impacts on human resource management, which is one of the important functions of businesses and other organizations, will be discussed. Within this framework, the current and possible changes the pandemic caused on staffing, training and development, career planning and management, performance management, and pay management-related policies, activities, and practices of human resource management will be analyzed.

1. Overall Impact of the Pandemic on the Economy and Businesses

Without a doubt, the global COVID-19 pandemic and related measures affected economies and businesses the most. The main effects of the pandemic on the economy and businesses are economic contractions, reduced employment, change in forms of employment, increased unemployment, and the fact that businesses in certain industries had to change their business and employment strategies, policies, and practices due to restricted movement and lower demand for goods and services (Acar, 2020; Asmelash and Cooper, 2020; Balcı and Çetin, 2020: 40; Eke and Eke, 2020: 43; Petzer, 2020: 6; Supardi et al., 2020: 1265; Ting, Ling and Hwa, 2020: 4; Tucker, 2020).

1.1. Impact of the Pandemic on Economic Growth

The main economic impact of the global COVID-19 pandemic has been the disruption of production that started in Asia and soon spread to supply chains around the world, reducing the growth rates of countries and plunging many countries into economic stagnation. The impact of the pandemic on growth is due to a decline in production and service delivery, which has resulted from

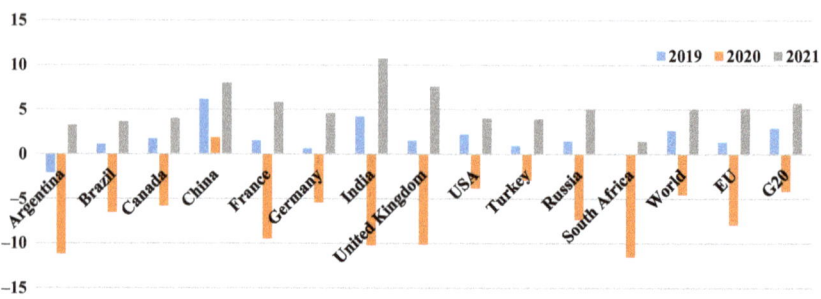

Chart 1: 2019 Growth Rates and 2020 and 2021 Growth Estimations of Countries

the fact that activities in almost all industries have come to a standstill due to restrictions, uncertainty, and a sense of panic (Balcı and Çetin, 2020: 43). As seen in Chart 1, the OECD estimates that in 2020, all of the G20 countries except China will experience a recession, the world economy will see a contraction of 4.5 % in 2021, and there will be a fragile recovery in 2021 even though the growth at the end of 2021 will be way lower than 2019 and projections made before the pandemic in many countries. The realized growth rate in 2019 and estimated rates for 2020 and 2021 of selected countries are shown in Chart 1 (OECD, 2021a).

As seen from the chart, the pandemic has caused further economic recession in Argentina, France, India, the United Kingdom and South Africa. It is noteworthy that the growth rate in China, the country of origin of the pandemic, has not gone in a negative direction. In addition, compared to other countries, it is safe to say that the negative impact of the pandemic on growth in Turkey has remained limited. India, the UK, China, France, and Russia are at the forefront of growth estimations for 2021.

Although the effect of the pandemic on growth rates has been negative as seen above, the economic effects for each industry have not been the same. Durable goods, transportation, accommodation and some parts of the service industry have been negatively affected by the pandemic much more, while healthcare and medical equipment production, cleaning products, food distribution, e-commerce, remote meeting platforms, etc. have experienced a positive period (Donthu and Gustafsson, 2020). Similarly, it is believed that not all industries will recover and grow the same after the pandemic.

1.2. Impact of the Pandemic on Employment and Unemployment

The economic contraction caused by the global COVID-19 pandemic has inevitably led to a decline in employment and increased unemployment. The report released by OECD shows significant differences in the rate of employment between 2019 and 2020 and 2021. For example in the US, the employment rate, which was 71.6 % in December 2019, fell to 60.3 % in April 2020, which can be described as the period of shock when the pandemic was quite influential over economic indicators and social life. The rate, which rose to 68 % by the end of 2020, was around 68 % by February 2021. The pandemic changed employment rates by 10 % for male employees and 12 % for female employees in the US. Between December April 2019 and April 2020, the total employment rate decreased by 2 % in Japan, 3.5 % in Australia, 2 % in France, 1 % in the UK and 6 % in Turkey. Employment rates as of February 2021 are 68.3 % in the US; 77.6 % in Japan; 74.4 % in Australia; 65.6 % in France; 75 % in the UK and 43.8 % in Turkey (OECD, 2021b; TurkStat, 2021).

The International Labor Organization also predicted at the beginning of the pandemic that unemployment will increase considerably due to the pandemic. In this report of ILO, it was estimated that 5.3, 13, and 24.7 million people will become unemployed because of the pandemic according to low, medium, and high scenarios, respectively (ILO, 2020b: 3). The rates of unemployment between the years of 2018 and 2021 according to the statistics of OECD and other organizations are shown in Table 1 (OECD, 2021c; Statista, 2020; TurkStat, 2021).

As shown in the table, especially within the first six months after March 2020, when the effects of the pandemic became clearer than ever, the unemployment rate increased considerably in almost every country. The increase in the rate of unemployment slowed down starting from September 2020. This can also be associated with lowered participation in labor force due to the prolonged crisis. The unemployment increased the most in Canada, India, the US, and Argentina due to the pandemic. It is also clear from the unemployment rates that China recovered relatively quickly from the trauma caused by the pandemic. It is safe to say that the pandemic has not increased unemployment in Turkey as much as it has in other countries.

Another effect of the pandemic on the economy has been the increase in underemployment. The pandemic revealed tens of thousands of employees, who have had to work under their status or capacity, despite possessing the required education, experience, and skills, and have suffered income loss. Compared to the fourth quarter of 2019, the estimated total working hour loss in the second quarter of 2020 amounted to 17 % (equivalent to 495 million full-time jobs).

Table 1: Unemployment Rates of Countries (%)

Countries	2018	2019	2020						2021	
			January	March	May	July	September	November	January	February
Argentina	9.2	9.7	-	8.9	-	-	13.1	10.9	10.1	-
Brazil	11.6	11.0	11.2	12.2	12.9	13.8	-	14.4	14.3	14.1
Canada	5.7	5.6	5.5	7.8	13.7	10.9	9.0	8.8	9.4	8.2
China	4.9	5.2	5.3	5.9	5.9	5.7	5.4	5.2	5.4	5.5
France	8.8	8.2	8.1	7.5	6.9	7.1	7.9	8.1	7.8	7.9
Germany	3.3	3.3	3.4	3.8	4.2	4.5	4.5	4.6	4.6	-
India		7.6	7.2	8.8	21.7	7.4	6.7	6.5	6.5	6.9
UK	3.8	3.7	3.9	3.8	3.7	4.3	-	5.1	4.9	5
USA	3.9	3.5	3.6	4.4	13.3	10.2	7.9	6.7	6.3	6.2
Turkey	12.8	13.1	12.6	12.9	14.0	13.8	-	12.6	12.2	-
Russia	4.9	4.6	4.7	4.7	6.1	6.3	6.3	6.1	5.8	5.7
S. Africa	26.9	28.2	-	-	-	-	30.8	23.3	32.5	-
OECD	5.5	5.2	5.3	5.6	8.7	8.0	7.3	6.9	6.79	-
EU	7.8	7.4	7.4	7.2	7.6	8.1	8.3	7.3	7.3	-

Working hour loss was 7.2 % (equivalent to 205 million full-time jobs) in the third quarter of 2020 and 4.6 % (equivalent to 130 million full-time jobs) in the last quarter (ILO, 2021). This loss in working hours has also led to a significant loss in labor income. Estimates for the loss of labor income (regardless of income support measures) point to a global decline of 10.7 % in the first three quarters of 2020 compared to the first three quarters of 2019. This decrease amounts to about USD 5 trillion, or 5.5 % of total global gross product for the first three quarters of 2019. The labor income loss is the highest in middle-income countries while being around 15 % in lower-middle-income countries and 11 % in upper-middle-income countries (ILO, 2020a: 1). The loss of labor income due to the decline in economic activity further strains workers who are near or below the poverty line. Together with the ever-increasing number of unemployed and employees close to or below the poverty line due to loss of labor income due to the pandemic, millions of people worldwide (between 20 and 35 million employees according to ILO's medium and bad scenarios) are projected to fall into poverty (ILO, 2020c: 5). This situation puts the elderly with health conditions, young people, and women, who already had employment problems before the pandemic, self-employed, short-time, or temporary workers, and migrant workers in a more vulnerable position, further deepening the existing inequality between the sections of society.

1.3. Impact of the Pandemic on the Policies and Practices of Businesses

Naturally, the COVID-19 pandemic has also negatively affected businesses on a micro level, other organizations, as well as their policies and practices. Pandemic-related isolation, change in the priorities and consumption habits of people staying at home, and income loss due to increased unemployment and underemployment have decreased demand for goods and services in certain industries, leading to a significant reduction in consumption and spending. Well-known and long-established businesses in many industries are expected to go bankrupt (Tucker, 2020). Tourism has been one of the industries most affected by the pandemic. In the US, 80 % of hotel rooms have been vacant (Asmelash and Cooper, 2020); most airlines have reduced their workforce by 90 %. Large companies producing automobiles, trucks and buses, as well as electronic products, have also been forced to suddenly halt their activities due to the pandemic. Although these businesses resumed production to some extent afterward, they faced a serious supply and price increase issue. Also, the cancellation or postponement of formal education at all levels, museum, art, exhibition, conference, and sports events put businesses that directly or indirectly operate in these fields into a difficult situation. Similarly, the closure of movie theaters, sports halls, restaurants, and hairdressers and the fall in the demand for mass or individual transport services due to lockdowns have brought about major economic hardships for those operating in these fields.

The COVID-19 pandemic has also significantly affected the education industry and its activities worldwide. Because of the pandemic, educational institutions, from preschool to higher education, were immediately closed and over a billion students worldwide were removed from their conventional educational environment (Özer, 2020). To fill this gap, educational activities are sustained remotely or using hybrid methods in Turkey, as in the rest of the world. Around 77 % (13.9 million) of 18.2 million students (1.6 million in preschool, 5.3 million in primary, 5.7 million in secondary, and 5.6 million in high-school education) in Turkey took courses using the Education Information Network (EBA) between March 2020 and April 2021 (Ministry of National Education, 2021; NTV, 2020). Within the same period, a total of 14.560 hours of broadcast were delivered via three different channels over EBA and 213 million hours of live lessons were delivered. These educational methods are often discussed in many countries due to differences in opportunity between socioeconomic groups and loss of education. According to UNESCO's April 2020 report, nearly 830 million students do not have access to a computer at home, and 40 % of these students lack an accessible Internet connection (Özer, 2020).

Due to the pandemic, education in formal programs, where up to 4 million students are enrolled at the higher education level in Turkey, has been largely carried out remotely since April 2020, with the exception of some practical courses, especially in health sciences. In this type of education, students are deprived of the learning opportunities and interaction offered by face-to-face education and it is questionable to what extent they are able to acquire or improve the skills and knowledge they require remotely using digital means. It is commonly believed that remote education leads/will lead to a considerable loss in learning and related problems especially for those with limited resources.

In the face of these developments, the main priority of businesses has been to reduce spending budgets and expenses (KPMG, 2020a). The pandemic has forced businesses to prioritize their activity-related spending or to review them in such a way as to achieve maximum efficiency. In this case, any work, task, or practice without any value to the business in the short term has been delayed or canceled (Donthu and Gustafsson, 2020: 284). A study carried out during the pandemic found that businesses have shifted their strategic goal from being profit-oriented to resilience (sustainability) (Supardi and Hadi, 2020: 1265). Entering 2020 aiming to increase investment, sales, and profitability, and growth, most businesses have started to focus on maintaining their current situation and overcome this challenge with minimal loss due to uncertainties brought about by the pandemic. Business policies and practices that have come to the fore during the pandemic are the reduction of spending, proliferation of layoffs and flexible working methods, and benefiting from government employment programs and financial incentives.

2. Impact of the Pandemic on Human Resource Management

The global COVID-19 pandemic has also significantly affected human resource management in businesses and other organizations. These effects can be analyzed under three categories, namely (1) reducing costs, (2) expansion of flexible methods, and (3) improving digitalization.

In particular, the recession and contraction due to containment measures have affected human resource management policies and practices among others. Stagnation and contraction in production and service delivery have led to a severe fall in the labor demand of businesses. As a result, working hours were reduced, flexible working arrangements and layoffs became widespread, major changes were introduced to human resources' budget management, new hiring were minimized, need for labor was mostly met internally through promotion or transfers, many training activities were postponed or canceled, payments were stopped, the variable pay was preferred in organizations with sales personnel, many additional benefits to employees were cut down, salaries of managers were reduced, and state-supported employment programs were preferred (Akbaş Tuna and Çelen, 2020; Eileen Aitken-Fox et al., 2020; KPMG, 2020a). In addition, the COVID-19 crisis has also attached more importance to measure and evaluate the effectiveness/performance of human resources management activities.

Another important and widespread effect of the pandemic has been the shift from regular employment to flexible working arrangements (Spurk and Straub, 2020: 1). Flexible work can be defined as a non-standard working arrangement that can be regulated in a variety of ways by labor law and collective labor agreements in terms of working time and/or space, depending on the nature of the work (Seyyar and Öz, 2007: 20). Flexible work is usually analyzed under three categories, namely (a) arrangement of working hours, (b) arrangement of the workplace, and (c) arrangement of employment relations (Spreitzer, Cameron and Garrett, 2017: 473). Working hours can be made flexible depending on the demand for goods and services offered by businesses and the need for employees. Flexible working hours and condensed working weeks are examples of these programs (Sabuncuoğlu, 2005: 330; Uyargil, 2013: 80). By using information technology tools, employees can perform their work whenever and wherever they like, resuming business activities at different locations. Working from home or remote (tele) working are the main programs that offer flexibility in terms of location (Harris, 2003: 422). Programs that provide flexibility in employment relations include short-term employment contracts instead of full-time permanent employment contracts, temporary work, on-call work or job/duty-sharing. While programs, which offer flexibility in employment relations, give people more unlimited, individualized, and flexible career opportunities by allowing for more job-related autonomy and non-work activities, precarious working arrangements lead to challenging employment conditions (low/interrupted pay, lack of social security, social isolation, over time, less room for development, career insecurity, etc.). This makes the careers of individuals more fragmented and limited (Spurk and Straub, 2020: 2). During the COVID-19 pandemic, interest in flexible programs has increased; the use of these programs, which began to spread before the pandemic, has become more widespread very rapidly during the pandemic. During the pandemic, when the goal is to ensure isolation and minimize the risk of disease, public and private agencies and organizations mainly opted for working from home or remote working, flexible working hours, condensed work days, task sharing, and alternate working.

Another important effect of the global pandemic on human resource management has been to accelerate the transition to digitalization in working methods and practices. The pandemic is thought to have pushed digitalization for businesses well ahead of schedule (Bloomberg, 2020). Studies show that during the pandemic, many businesses have worked from home or remotely by making use of digital methods, employee training, internships, and economic, psychological, and functional services offered by employers have been provided entirely online, recruitment and selection procedures have been conducted online, and performance has been managed remotely using digital tools (Anadolu Ajansı, 2020; Deloitte, 2020d; Ünal, 2020). After the pandemic, it is believed that almost all businesses, not only those who are leaders in technology or operate in certain industries, will push forward investments in communication tools and technology in line with their long-term and strategic goals. Currently, a significant part of operational and repetitive/routine work can be performed using automated systems, while in the future, it is projected that more complex processes can be performed using artificial intelligence. Businesses that have become aware of the importance of flexibility and technology in human resource management are expected to allocate more budget for digitalization and take more interest in artificial intelligence, industry 4.0, etc. (Deloitte, 2020e: 3). In line with these developments, we can assume that practices related to human resource management will be carried out largely through digital platforms, just as in other practices of businesses. Even though these developments regarding digitalization were projected to take place and a vision was put in place for this transformation before the pandemic, it has pushed this transformation forward, making many digital practices in the field of human resources management indispensable for businesses.

In the general sense, the effects of the global COVID-19 pandemic on human resources management are as covered above. Its effects on policies and practices of various functions of human resources management can be put into more detail. The effects of the global COVID-19 pandemic on policies, activities, and practices regarding the five functions of human resources management, namely staffing, training and development, career development, performance management, and pay management will be analyzed in detail below.

2.1. The Effect of the Pandemic on Staffing (HR Planning, Recruiting and Selection)

In businesses and other organizations, HRM activities aimed at identifying and meeting labor needs in terms of quantity and quality are also called "staffing." Staffing includes three phases or functions, namely (1) identification of the need for labor in terms of quality, quantity, time and place (human resource planning), (2) searching and finding the candidates that can satisfy this need (recruiting), and (3) selection and placement of proper employees among the candidates using various methods (personnel selection) (Acar, 2013: 88; Dessler, 2011: 178). This process is under the influence of many factors inside and outside the business, which may be controllable or not. Internal factors such as organizational objectives, strategies, and policies, skills, and performances of employees, production goals, labor turnover, and absenteeism, and external factors such as technology, competitive conditions, market conditions, economic stagnation, and general uncertainty affect the staffing process directly or indirectly (Acar, 2013: 93; Sabuncuoğlu, 2005: 36–37).

The COVID-19 pandemic, together with its impact and uncertainty it causes, is an external and largely uncontrollable factor for the staffing function. The effects of the process on the staffing function are that it reduces the need for labor in many industries, thus reducing employment, increases labor demand and employment in some industries where there is more demand for goods or services, causes challenges in some staffing-related activities, makes remote online methods more preferable, and will increase the need for new labor qualifications, especially after the pandemic. These effects will briefly be covered below.

Impact of COVID-19 on Labor Demand and Recruitment

Many businesses in various industries completed their labor plans for 2020 in line with their analyses and scenarios based on their goals and strategies. However, the sudden emergence of the global COVID-19 pandemic, which has affected many industries directly or indirectly, has forced businesses to cancel, postpone, or review these plans. In China, where the pandemic emerged, many businesses, especially small and medium-sized ones, have had to cancel all of their preplanned hiring and lay off some of their employees to cut down their labor costs (Yin, 2020). In many industries in most countries, except for China, preplanned hiring was canceled due to reduced demand for goods and services as a result of restrictive measures and economic contractions (Barrett, 2020; Haber Global, 2020; İK Magazin, 2020; Lambert, 2020; Maurer, 2020b;

Takahashi, 2020, 2020; TRT Haber, 2020). A survey conducted by Manpower with 1,138 companies from Southeast Europe found that 29 % of companies postponed all new hires, 24 % reduced the number of employees, 21 % cancelled all new hires, 20 % maintained their recruitment process, and 4 % increased their number of employees (Manpower Group, 2020).

In addition, due to the COVID-19 pandemic, the need for labor has risen significantly and suddenly in some industries. There has been a major increase in the demand for new labor in distance education, healthcare, e-gaming, electronic commerce and logistics. E-commerce companies have had to hire more employees than they planned as they were unable to keep up with orders for having to serve millions of customers that stayed home due to isolation. Many e-commerce, retail, cargo and logistics companies, such as Instacart, Walmart, Amazon, CVS, Pizza Hut in the US and Şok and Migros in Turkey, have hired large numbers of people to meet the growing demand for services (Haber Türk, 2020a). The pandemic has also enabled some companies to differentiate their operations and produce goods/ services in new areas. For example, during the early days of the pandemic, Chinese electric vehicle manufacturer BYD established the world's largest surgical mask facility to meet the demand for masks that skyrocketed both in China and around the world (Yin, 2020).

Impact of COVID-19 on Activities Related to Staffing

In addition to forcing businesses to postpone or cancel new hires, the COVID-19 pandemic has also brought about significant challenges for the staffing-related activities of businesses and for the future of the recruitment industry. These challenges, which have been identified by the International Labour Organization in different countries, are as follows (ILO, 2020d);

- Significant delays in human resources planning and recruitment and selection process
- Covering the costs of recruitment and selection process from candidates, some of which are contrary to laws and contracts
- Revision of employment contracts with employees in such a way as to cause loss of rights for employees
- Candidates who are forced to travel for selection, especially for low-quality or blue-collar jobs that require face-to-face interviews, risking being infected with COVID-19
- The fact that intermediary companies that offer services for the recruitment and selection process have faced increased costs, had trouble meeting the

demands of some customers, and had to significantly reduce or completely suspend their activities due to lack of job opportunities
- Challenges faced by already strained governments in terms of oversight and inspection over recruitment and selection procedures despite being obliged to inspect the lawfulness of such procedures

As with other human resource management functions, the challenges in question have led businesses to prefer virtual, electronic, and remote methods for the staffing function and therefore have led to rapid digitalization (Healing, 2020). Given COVID-19 restrictions on gathering indoors and face-to-face contact, electronic systems are widely used for the staffing function and many activities relating to human resource planning and recruitment and selection are carried out remotely using online methods. For example, with regard to human resource planning, which is the first step of the staffing process, meetings that adopt the nominal group technique, where managers, experts, and participants get together face to face to identify the labor required for the next year, are now carried out online using platforms such as MURAL, Retrium, MS Teams, klaxon, miro, Stormz, etc. or using the Delphi technique (Deloitte, 2020b: 7). In addition, in a situation where environmental uncertainties towards country economies and sectors increase due to COVID-19 or similar crises, in order to identify the future labor need more efficiently in terms of quantity, quality, place, and time, simulations or software that make use of advanced artificial intelligence, involve numerous scenarios and variables, and can perform comprehensive analyses will become more widespread.

Along with human resource planning, rapid digitalization is also in place for activities related to the recruitment and selection process. Electronic recruitment and selection, which was expected to be the dominant method in the future before the pandemic, seems to have become an important staffing strategy during the pandemic (Mallik and Ptel, 2020: 83). For the electronic recruitment and selection process, also known as online recruitment and selection, high-technology online software is being used for searching for candidates for available positions, including them in candidate pools, performing relevant selection activities (tests, interviews, etc.), which allow both employers and candidates to be protected from the risk of infection. The main goal of digitalization is to perform related activities more effectively and efficiently by avoiding the negative impact of the pandemic (Ataseven, 2020: 12; Chawla, 2020). For example, electronic/virtual platforms enable employers to reach more people, form a larger pool of candidates, and be more selective when choosing the right candidate. Conducting job interviews with candidates online offers protection from the risk of the pandemic and prevents additional costs. During the pandemic, the number of companies that conduct business interviews online has increased significantly (Hurriyet, 2020; Maurer, 2020a; Stahl, 2020; Unal, 2020). In Turkey during the pandemic, there has been a 300 % increase in online job interviews, this digitalization in recruitment and selection has pushed forward the digital transformation of human resource management, and human resource management has achieved a sudden digital competence, which was expected to take three years (Arslan, 2020). With the said digitalization, the use of online and electronic tools and methods is expected to proliferate as long as the pandemic continues and become permanent after the pandemic.

Another important effect of COVID-19 on the selection process has been on medical examinations, which is an important stage of the process. It is expected that performing a PCR test to make sure that candidates do not have COVID-19 will become mandatory, while medical tests have not been performed until now, except for special cases, in the health examinations carried out to evaluate the physical and mental health of the candidates (Opatha, 2020: 155). In addition, in cases where in-person meeting is necessary during the selection process, checking the body temperature of candidates using thermal cameras or thermometers, making mask-wearing obligatory, maintaining social distance, and paying attention to cleaning and hygiene rules have become ordinary parts of the pandemic, in other words, the new normal.

Competencies That Will Be Sought in Employees after COVID-19

The most important priority for human resource managers after the COVID-19 pandemic is expected to be to find, recruit, retain, and improve new employees who are technically equipped to deal with new jobs and can effectively work under uncertain conditions. The ability to manage stress, tolerate uncertainties, remain productive under changing conditions, be flexible, agile, compatible, and disciplined, work interdisciplinary, have command of all the processes in a business, think analytically, use information and communication technologies, and make utmost use of these technologies will be the qualifications sought the most in employees after the pandemic (Caligiuri et al., 2020: 699; KPMG, 2020a; Quirk, 2020; Thinktech, 2020). Especially given that digitalization will permeate our lives even more with technological advancements, the need for employees that can adapt to this change will increase even more. According to a study carried out by KPMG with 102 companies operating in Turkey, 72 % of the participants think that the shift to digitalization (automation, robotics, artificial intelligence, etc.) will pick up speed during the pandemic and after

(KPMG, 2020a). In this case, it is safe to say that qualifications that can adapt to this change will be sought after and businesses will engage in serious competition to find, attract, and recruit employees with these qualifications. In the process, businesses should design new labor plans, scenarios and models taking into consideration COVID-19's medium and long term impact, review their labor turnover plans, constantly follow their changing needs of talent and skills (Aydın Göktepe, 2020:634), develop long-term strategies that will ensure resilience and agility for possible future crises, and better prepare for future uncertainties. In this regard, it is important to draw the necessary lessons from the COVID-19 pandemic (Mallik and Ptel, 2020: 88).

2.2. Impact of the Pandemic on the Training and Development

Businesses refer to training and development methods both in order to address the shortcomings of new employees they recruit, and in cases where there is a lack of performance of existing employees. As a function of human resource management, training and development is a planned process to positively change employees' attitudes, knowledge, abilities, and/or behaviors in order to ensure an effective performance within a job or workgroup in line with a learning activity (Wilson, 2005: 4). Qualified, productive, and efficient employees are a requirement for businesses to sustain their activities and reach their goals. Thanks to training and development activities, employees having the potential to fully meet the work requirements and exhibit high performance will make a great contribution to give businesses the upper hand in competition.

The COVID-19 pandemic has also directly and indirectly affected activities related to training and development, a function of human resource management in businesses. The main effects of the pandemic on the training and development function are: cancellation of practical training activities in areas directly related to the pandemic (medicine, healthcare, etc.), dissemination of e-training and development using digital and online learning programs, popularization of certain topics of training during and after the pandemic, focusing on these new topics in the future. The effects in question are briefly analyzed below.

Postponement or Cancellation of Training Activities

As businesses around the world postponed or canceled face-to-face meetings due to COVID-19, training and development activities have been among the areas most affected by this process. From March to the end of June 2020, half of the face-to-face programs in North America were canceled, and almost all in some regions in Asia and Europe (Kshirsagar et al., 2020: 2). The cancellation of training activities has put students, interns and employees who have to receive practical training for their professional development, especially in areas such as medicine and health in a difficult position. In a study of 240 medical students in Saudi Arabia, 85 % stated that there had been a decrease in training activities due to COVID-19, while almost all of the participants from the surgical fields noted not having had any practical training (Balhareth et al., 2020: 127). Studies in different countries showed that interns that should begin their surgical training were faced with uncertainties and vastly different training environments and that this situation raised some concerns about their professional development (De Berker et al., 2020: 3; Kaiser Health News, 2020). Aside from medicine and health, postponing or canceling training in other jobs and professions where it is important to receive face-to-face training, puts employees in a difficult position in terms of professional development and performance.

Digitalization of Training and Development Methods and Online Training

Despite the adverse effects of COVID-19 on training activities, businesses, especially those in certain industries, should not risk putting skills and talent development on hold and continue performing activities that create value. In this case, digital and online training programs are usually referred to. There has been a significant increase in the use of electronic training and development programs during COVID-19 that were on the rise before the pandemic, used widely by young employees (Ihlas News Agency, 2020; Para & Stock Exchange, 2020). According to a study of the e-learning company Enocta, the number of digital training courses, which was 1.780 million in March-April 2019, increased by 1041 % in the same period in 2020 to 20.293 million (Milliyet, 2020). In the United States, many businesses have provided online training to their employees who have had to work from home during quarantine, and online executive training programs have also been offered for managers to effectively manage their employees who work remotely (Meister, 2020).

Given that interest in online training will increase as the pandemic goes on, it is important for businesses to go beyond short-term tactical steps to save the day and introduce and implement more comprehensive alternative digital learning strategies. It is debated whether the level of learning with online/remote training and the benefit acquired from such training are as high as in face-to-face training. Research shows that online training, which only uses the instruction method, does not motivate participants as much as face-to-face training does, and is not found to be effective, and that online training that uses a variety of methods such as q&a, discussion, and problem-solving is as effective, and even more effective according to some studies, as face-to-face training (Brady et al., 2018: 433; Coppola and Myre, 2002: 170; Dimeff et al. 2015: 283; Johnson, Aragon, and Shaik, 2000: 29; Neuhauser, 2002: 99). Therefore, remote/online methods that combine instruction with various other methods that improve interaction (case discussion, role-playing, etc.) can increase the effectiveness expected from training activities of hybrid models where both methods are used in conjunction in cases and areas where the risk of disease is reduced. Some of the strategies that can support businesses in this regard are below (Deloitte, 2020a; Kshirsagar et al., 2020):

- Forming a training team that will work on developing plans regarding training activities and will be made up of human resource specialists, trainers, IT experts, etc.
- Providing maximum protection to employees who will participate in face-to-face training programs (applying all the requirements foreseen in relevant guidelines, setting criteria for the implementation, postponement or cancellation of programs, informing employees on these issues)
- Restructuring of face-to-face training (adopting a centrifugal approach to training, reducing global training to a regional or local scale, turning large-scale face-to-face training sessions into video conference sessions for smaller groups)
- Promoting and improving digital learning
- Exploring alternative digital learning strategies (providing collaborative, interactive new social learning experiences with employee groups that make greater use of artificial intelligence, making use of training simulations that benefit from virtual reality, webinars, podcasts, etc.)
- Developing alternative scenarios on training activities for COVID-19 and beyond and devising road maps based on these scenarios, making the most effective decisions according to the realized scenario, and maintaining communication with employees

Many businesses, especially global companies, are trying to maintain the effectiveness and efficiency of training activities by making use of these strategies.

Training Topics That Will Come to the Fore during and after the Pandemic

Another effect of COVID-19 on training activities is that it has highlighted some new training topics during and after the pandemic and will change the content of the training. As people start working more from home, it has become important for employees to improve their digital abilities, and this need will probably gain more significance (Thinktech, 2020). For example, the suddenly growing demand for online teaching in educational institutions due to COVID-19 has forced some teachers who had no prior knowledge of distance education to deal with this issue, but there have been difficulties in using advanced technology effectively in classrooms due to insufficient training in educational technologies (Kimav and Aydın, 2020: 224). Therefore, exploring and learning how communication technologies work, employers organizing training about these technologies, and encouraging participation to training delivered on these technologies by universities and other institutions are important. In order to improve these competencies, employees should see this time as an opportunity and take part in training programs such as podcasts, webinars, digital certificate programs, etc., improve themselves in digital technologies and raise their awareness, regardless of what field they want to pursue a career in or what industry they work in. In addition, given that employees have needed and will need more psychological and emotional support during and after the pandemic, organizing internal coaching and mentoring programs, delivering stress management training, or organizing activities on achieving work-life balance will be quite important (Şener, 2020).

It is believed that improving artificial intelligence will be one of the main topics in training to be delivered after the pandemic. The improvement of artificial intelligence will become an indispensable part of executive training in particular (Deloitte, 2020a). During the COVID-19, businesses from almost every industry have wanted to take advantage of digital applications, increasing their investment in artificial intelligence. According to a 2017 McKinsey report, a third of employees in the U.S. are projected to lose their jobs to artificial intelligence-powered robots by 2030. But recent developments, such as the COVID-19 pandemic, are expected to push this date forward (Thinktech, 2020). Analytics, automation, digitalization, and artificial intelligence disrupt industries and force businesses into digital transformation by changing existing jobs, creating new roles, and creating a talent gap that will require tremendous effort to fill. In order for businesses to maintain their competitiveness and be ready for the future by leveraging the power of artificial intelligence and talented employees, it is critical that today's workforce has the right skills and competencies. In KPMG's Research, 29 % of the participating companies stated that the definition of critical personnel will change in the coming period and that qualities such as maintaining productivity under changing conditions; being flexible, agile, compliant and disciplined; being able to work interdisciplinary and exhibit command of all processes will be particularly sought after in the new critical personnel (KPMG, 2020a). Considering that these qualities will be sought after in the future, it is important to prepare the content and methods of training and development programs in such a way as to offer employees these skills or to allow employees to improve their existing skills in this regard. For this, businesses should conduct training needs analyses to evaluate the gap between existing skills and skills that will be required in the future, develop strategies with regard to their training activities based on these needs, and adopt effective training methods by allocating adequate budget (Deloitte, 2020a).

2.3. Impact of the Pandemic on the Career Development

Activities related to planning and managing the careers of employees in businesses are carried out career development. Career development is aimed at integrating the workforce needs of the business with the needs of individuals, while providing opportunities to improve the skills and careers of individuals and to satisfy their needs in order to obtain the knowledge and talent power that the business needs (Armstrong, 2009: 591). Planning, which is the personal side of career development, involves the selection of professions, businesses, and career paths by an individual while career management, which is the organizational side of career development, refers to harmonizing the career goals of individuals with the goals and needs of businesses, and practices to achieve this harmonization (Dündar, 2013: 276).

The global COVID-19 pandemic has significantly affected career plans of individuals and career management of businesses. These effects can be analyzed under three headings: career shock caused by the pandemic, flexible working, and digitization of career management.

COVID-19 as a Major Career Shock

The global COVID-19 pandemic has been a major career shock for individuals. Career shock can be defined as disruptive and extraordinary events that are caused by factors beyond the control of individuals (Akkermans, Seibert ve Mol, 2018: 2) and that negatively affect their career processes, or when they are confronted with an unexpected situation or environment related to their career (Tunçer, 2012: 227). An extraordinary and devastating event such as the COVID-19 outbreak, the impact of which varies by country and industry, has been a major career shock and ended the careers of thousands of people in an unpredictable way. However, the COVID-19 shock has not affected everyone's career at the same level; a number of factors differentiate the impact of the pandemic on individuals' careers. Some of these factors can be found below (Akkermansa, Richardson and Kraimer, 2020: 2);

- The effects of the pandemic are thought to be directly influenced by individual and contextual factors and the interaction between these factors. For example, people who are developed in terms of knowledge, expertise, and qualification, agile, flexible, can work under uncertain and changing conditions, know themselves (strengths and weaknesses), can follow and be aware of the opportunities and threats brought about by crises, and review their career plans accordingly are more likely to overcome the shock of COVID-19 and turn similar shocks into opportunity. However, significant career problems may arise for individuals lacking these skills. In this process, individual as well as contextual factors are pivotal. For example, given that the jobs and activities performed by humans today will be performed by smart machines or robots in the future, many of the existing work and some professions will disappear due to technological advancements that are thought to speed up after the pandemic. In this case, a workforce will emerge that will be unemployed despite being qualified or skilled, or that will be less likely to be employed long-term. Therefore, due to digitization accelerated by the COVID-19 pandemic, employees are likely to experience significant problems in their careers (job security, low pay, adverse working conditions, etc.).
- Culture is thought to play an important role in assessing stress factors caused by COVID-19 and identifying the methods of dealing with them (Guan, Deng and Zhou, 2020). For example, in individualistic societies, employees tend to have an independent ego and prefer to use their ideal selves to guide their behavior. This cultural tendency focuses the attention of employees during the COVID-19 pandemic on factors closely related to personal career development, such as job insecurity, difficulties working from home, or the emergence of new career opportunities. However, in collectivist societies, employees are more interested in issues related to society in general, beyond career development, such as the business as a whole, working groups, social networks, and the condition of the unemployed and labor unions. This

difference in culture also plays an important role in dealing with stress factors. For example, individualist societies opt for primary control strategies for dealing with problems (such as solving related problems directly); while collectivist cultures opt more for secondary control strategies (addressing problems and reassessing them in a reconciliatory way). Primary control strategies indicate individuals' efforts to change their environment in accordance with their wishes and needs, while secondary control strategies can be defined as individuals changing their goals, expectations, and activities in line with events (Kurt and Uçanok, 2020: 7).

- As with all other career shocks, the impact of the COVID-19 pandemic may vary in the short and long term and depending on what stage individuals are at in their careers. For example, even though the pandemic often leads to negative career outcomes in the short term, such as job loss, low pay, plateau or decline in career, and poor job satisfaction, some employees may be able to shift to a more positive place in their careers by taking on more satisfying jobs with their proactive career behaviors in the long term. The stage of a career is also important for how the pandemic affects them. For example, young people who are at the beginning of their career can more easily overcome the negative effects of the pandemic, as they will probably have less responsibility for providing for home, having children, or paying off credit debt. Individuals who are in the middle of or late in their career will undoubtedly suffer more devastating consequences if they are laid off, lose income, or are deprived of social security due to the pandemic (Kooij, 2020: 233).

- A career shock such as COVID-19 can lead to positive career outcomes by forcing people to engage in new working arrangements and to improve their skills and competencies. Businesses that were reluctant to allow their employees to work from home because the work cannot be done remotely, they are unable to oversee their employees, and teamwork gets disrupted (Alkan Meşhur, 2010: 183) have had to take an interest in new technological methods and tools as they were forced to adopt flexible working arrangements during the pandemic. These developments require employees to improve their skills and competencies, especially in using technology. Some employees, who are reluctant to improve the skills and competencies needed in future and to exhibit some necessary career behavior, can sustain their careers in the short and long term by improving the skills and competencies they must possess for the transformation brought about by the pandemic.

As a result, it is safe to say that the COVID-19 pandemic is a career shock that had significantly affected or has the potential to affect the careers of individuals.

However, these effects vary depending on a number of individual and environmental factors. Individuals who have the necessary competencies, set career goals by correctly reading developments, make career plans and implement these plans are more likely to come out of the COVID-19 pandemic with less damage or even achieve positive career results by turning the crisis into an opportunity.

COVID-19's Impact on Career Approaches and the Flexible (Gig) Economy

During and after the pandemic, it is expected that the number of short-term or temporary jobs will increase, employers will prefer making short-term contracts with the self-employed, and labor markets that are based on flexible employment will become more popular. Such labor markets are defined as flexible (gig) economy or sharing economy. A flexible economy can be defined as an economy that includes short-term and task-based work between individuals or businesses and the payments made in return, through digital platforms that actively facilitate matching between suppliers and customers (Erdoğan and Çiğdem, 2018: 238). As the examples of Uber, Fieverr, Airbnb, and Blalacar show us, the flexible economy is based on temporary and flexible work that allows individuals to exchange products or services by making use of technology, allowing anyone to participate. In this model, where permanent employment contracts are extinct with the exception of a few jobs and staff, and short-term employment contracts are common, intermediary businesses (private employment offices, etc.) are needed and employees who are independent contractors, provided by these enterprises, are paid service fees in exchange for the tasks they perform, rather than regular pay. Therefore, it is safe to say that the flexible economy has destroyed the conventional model where employees are employed full-time, and has built a new order consisting largely of short-term, temporary, and flexible jobs/employees or tasks. The biggest impact of the transition into a flexible economy on the careers of individuals is that it will shift the responsibility and workload for career planning and development from businesses to individuals. With the flexible economy, career management will become an ever-growing individual matter depending on a variety of issues such as shifting from conventional hierarchical organizational structures to non-hierarchical and flexible organizational structures, reduced employment volume of businesses due to technological developments and downsizing strategies, increase in the number of flexible/temporary employees and families with two careers, and the increasing importance of the family-work balance.

The first signs of this change have also begun to be seen and experienced in literature and practice in recent years. In career approaches that have been introduced and spread in recent years in career literature, especially unlimited career, independent career, flexible career and career self-management, the increased responsibility of individuals in their careers plays a pivotal role.

The uncertainty caused by the COVID-19 pandemic has pushed forward the shift towards flexible economy and related career approaches. The COVID-19 pandemic is also a crisis encouraging many activities in a flexible economy that has digital features. With COVID-19, the need for flexibility in many industries and emerging jobs will require employment within a comprehensive flexible economy understanding, with the new normal brought about by COVID-19, businesses no longer have/will have the budget to work their employees five days a week, and they will be interested in the direct or indirect cost savings offered by the flexible economy model (Hasija, 2020; Hunter, 2020). The flexible economy, which is expected to gain speed with the COVID-19 pandemic, can offer major advantages for businesses, while also providing benefits for employees. It can allow employees to remain in control, choose the projects they will enjoy, plan their work lives in accordance with their personal lives, and experience new jobs and career steps. However, one must bear in mind that the flexible economy will bring about, especially for underqualified or under skilled individuals or those with a job that is likely to go extinct due to technological developments despite being qualified and skilled, uncertainties and inconsistencies with regard to job security, continuous work, career continuity, and a stable income, lack of pay and social benefits (insurance premiums, pension pay, etc.) for a considerable amount of time, and the possibility of working under employers that do not have a sense of working hours (Torpey and Hogan, 2020). This will probably bring major career-related problems for those working in certain industries and specialties.

The Way COVID-19 Is Digitalizing Career Development

Another impact of COVID-19 on career development is that it has digitized most activities, as in other human resource management functions, and disseminated the idea of digital career development, which was already being discussed prior to the pandemic. Digital career development can be defined as a more effective and rapid implementation of a number of career development-related activities that are the responsibility of an individual or organization by making use of information and communication technologies (Celep and Fındıklı, 2018: 67). The digitalization of career development can be analyzed under two categories: (1) digitalization of individual career planning activities and (2) digitalization of organizational career management activities.

With the digitalization of career planning, individuals make more use of online career resources and applications to evaluate themselves, follow career opportunities and threats, set career goals, and develop and execute career plans. Given that the responsibility in relation to many career management-related activities will shift from organizations to individuals and that individuals will have more control over managing their careers (career self-management) due to environmental uncertainties caused by crises and the dissemination of flexibility, it is important to offer online career resources and platforms that individuals can assess constantly and rapidly and where they can interact with managers, employers, trainers, etc. and exchange social capital to gain different experiences (Hooley, 2012: 5).

With the digitalization of career management activities, businesses are also exploring how they can effectively use information and communication technologies to provide career support to their employees. Through digital career management, it is important to develop websites or other digital media products (social media accounts, podcasts, etc.) to offer employees detailed information about jobs or career opportunities, offer virtual services tailored for people's needs that aim to get to know them (online career counseling services, online personality tests, online games, case studies, etc.), and enhance communication and interaction between individuals using online tools such as Skype, Zoom, etc. (Bimrose, Kettunen, and Goddard, 2015: 9). Another benefit of digitization for career management is that it provides knowledge for employees to identify the career paths they want to take and what they may encounter in these career paths (Hooley, 2017: 10). Assessments using technology and artificial intelligence will help employees realize their potential and compare their current positions with the roles they want to assume in the future. Thanks to these technology-based assessments, employees will be able to identify any skill gaps and connect with resources and tools they need to close these gaps (Kutam, 2020).

The COVID-19 pandemic has accelerated digitalization of activities related to both career planning and career management. During the pandemic when face-to-face communication has been limited due to social isolation and remote working has become more common, individuals have referred to online resources, applications, and tools on career planning much more, while businesses have taken a lot more interest in programs such as online coaching, mentoring, career counseling, and online methods aiming to sustain career management-related activities and enhance employees' professional experience. In addition, a significant number of businesses consider it necessary to switch to new career models during the pandemic. In new career models, individuals are not limited to a specific field of expertise, job, department, business, or country, the career responsibility shifts to employees to a large extent, gaining knowledge and experience that will open doors to work in other businesses or positions rather than gaining business- or position-specific skills and competencies become more important, and technological facilities are used much more for career management (Dündar, 2013: 291). Digitization has also allowed to overcome the career management restrictions imposed by the pandemic. A study found that assignments targeting employees whose career mobility has been limited due to travel bans and restrictions during the pandemic is now offered virtually (Aydın Göktepe, 2020: 634).

2.4. Impact of the Pandemic on Performance Management

Performance evaluation as a function of human resource management can be defined as a process in which performance differences in businesses are identified using various criteria and methods and employees' success and development are evaluated (Sabuncuoğlu, 2005: 184; Uyergil, 2013: 212). Today, the concept of performance evaluation goes beyond a stable review and is rather considered a dynamic process made up of certain stages and is called performance management. In businesses, first, the criteria and standards to be adopted in a performance evaluation, the person to conduct the review, the time, frequency, and methods of evaluation are identified to put in place a performance management system, then, this system is run by planning, evaluating, and improving performance (Uyergil, 2013: 212).

As with other human resource management functions, the COVID-19 pandemic has directly and indirectly affected performance management-related activities. During the pandemic, most companies have been forced to postpone or cancel performance evaluations (Tank, 2020). It is also believed that many businesses will review/revise their performance goals due to the effects of the pandemic. A Deloitte study of more than 1,000 businesses operating in China found that the pandemic had a serious negative impact on the performance of businesses, and 46 % of respondents expected a significant decrease in performance goals in 2020 (Boichenko and Tymchenko, 2020). So much so that the pandemic has led to negative emotions such as anxiety, frustration, and burnout in the private and working lives of many employees, preventing them from reaching their target performance. To ensure productivity and efficiency, focusing on the emotional state of employees more has become a necessity.

The effects of the global COVID-19 pandemic on performance management activities can be analyzed under three categories: the effect of flexible working on employee performance and performance management, COVID-19-induced changes in goals, criteria, and methods, and the digitalization of performance management.

The Effect of Flexible Working on Employee Performance and Performance Management

Studies have shown that flexible working arrangements, which have become more common with the COVID-19 pandemic, have caused challenges before ensuring employee motivation and performing activities related to performance management. A study of 167 companies in Turkey, 103 global and 64 local, by Mercer Turkey and the Turkish Human Management Association found employee motivation and employee performance management to be the two most challenging issues following the introduction of remote working (Mercer Turkey, 2020). According to KPMG research in Turkey, the most common challenges in working from home have been maintaining work motivation (66 %) and monitoring and feedback on work performance (63 %) (KPMG, 2020a). According to the research report, it is expected that in 2021, performance management systems will be reviewed and approaches that take into account teamwork dynamics will become more common.

Given the results of the research, it is safe to say that flexible working arrangements lower the productivity of employees, especially in certain industries and jobs, and also cause significant difficulties in performance management. The introduction of flexible working arrangements, the effects of which on productivity were widely discussed and were preferred only under certain conditions prior to the pandemic, has become mandatory in many countries and businesses to ensure social isolation; some businesses have asked their employees to not come to work at all, while others asked their employees to come to work once or twice a week. This has made it difficult and challenging for human resource managers and experts to oversee activities related to performance management (Ünal, 2020).

While flexible working has become widespread in the COVID-19 process, it is often discussed how the performance of employees has been affected by it. Given that most businesses have adopted flexible programs such as remote working for the first time, it is safe to say that it is not yet known exactly how flexible working impacts performance and productivity (Aitken-Fox et al., 2020). Flexible working arrangements offer employees benefits such as flexibility, autonomy, individual working space, and cost reduction, but they may also lower individual performance by reducing motivation, increasing workload, making teamwork more difficult, causing concerns over demotion or lack of promotion, weakening relations with seniors, and causing psychological problems and social isolation (Alkan Meşhur, 2020: 7). A study conducted with ten thousand people from European countries found that performance decreases, especially when working remotely for more than eight hours a week, and remote working makes it challenging to oversee and monitor employees' activities (Gigauri, 2020: 15).

In order for flexible working to offer the desired performance, the situation and conditions should be identified and the appropriate programs should be well planned and managed. For this purpose, it is necessary to support, motivate and empower employees who will take part in flexible programs during the pandemic and provide them with the necessary training (Akca and Tepe Küçükoğlu, 2020: 75). In this process, important responsibilities fall to senior personnel. In addition to maintaining their own motivation during the pandemic, seniors have to pay more attention to their subordinates and effectively manage them from outside the workplace in order to get more information about how they perform their work. As it is important to oversee whether employees fulfill their tasks effectively and remain in good physical and mental shape, seniors have to exhibit their leadership skills (inspiring, encouragement, emotional communication, stress management, etc.) more than ever. To ensure employee motivation and commitment, it is important to identify and share with employees rules, instructions, work plans, technological methods, and communication tools to be used in flexible working and to also organize a variety of activities (chat over tea or coffee, virtual luncheons, etc.), other than tasks, online (Leons, 2020).

Performance Targets, Criteria and Methods Changing with COVID-19

The greatest impact of flexible working arrangements on performance management is the change in performance evaluation goals, criteria, methods, time, and frequency. Most businesses set their performance goals for 2020 in line with their strategies and policies and planned their employee performance evaluations. However, COVID-19 and flexible working arrangements brought because of it have forced businesses to cancel or review their goals and plans. The study conducted by Mercer Turkey and PERYÖN found that 74.3 % of participants were considering reviewing their business and year-end employee performance goals (Mercer Turkey, 2020). Another study found flexible working arrangements to be the reason why businesses have reviewed their performance plans during the pandemic (Aydın Göktepe, 2020: 635). In addition, there are businesses that have completely abandoned performance evaluation due to communication difficulties experienced during the pandemic. Considering that it would not be appropriate to review all employees based on the same standards during the pandemic, these businesses have temporarily suspended performance evaluations, stating their belief that employees would fulfill their responsibilities during this extraordinary time (O'Connell, 2020).

In addition to new performance goals, flexible working has also brought about new success factors, performance criteria, and reviewing tools. The changes experienced or likely to be experienced by performance evaluation due to the effects of COVID-19, particularly the dissemination of flexible working, as noted in literature are discussed below (Adler, 2020; Alkan Meşhur, 2020: 7; Demirci and Kocavelioğlu, 2020; Hancock ve Bill Schaninger, 2020; Mercer Turkey, 2020; O'Connell, 2020; Tank, 2020; Thinktech, 2020):

- Due to the uncertainties caused by the COVID-19 pandemic and the dissemination of flexible working, businesses now evaluate individual performance based on easy-to-understand output-based performance criteria or business results, rather than behavior. Reducing the process to its most fundamental elements by identifying critical issues/goals for the overall performance of the business and evaluating the contributions of employees to these critical points have facilitated evaluations during the pandemic. Regulating performance evaluations in a way that is more flexible and simple, directly related to the work being done, and providing greater clarity for what is expected of employees has been an effective solution for both seniors and employees. In cases where measuring work/production/service delivery is difficult, costly or impossible, and clear measurable criteria cannot be set, managers have had to conduct more regular interviews with their employees in order to associate employee goals to overall business goals in a clear and understandable fashion. In addition, it has become important to identify and solve communication failures in remote working programs, problems in cloud systems, and failures in remote access. Performance criteria for managing such processes and successfully conducting activities related to these issues have become important in evaluations.
- During the pandemic, businesses have started to conduct performance evaluations on a more frequent basis. Companies such as Deloitte, Accenture, Microsoft, IBM and PwC have abandoned annual performance evaluations,

opting for more regular and daily evaluations. This offers managers much more opportunity to set short-term expectations, receive instant feedback, and review priorities. This also allows instant feedback on performance to be provided to employees, wishing to know what they have done right and where there is room for improvement.
- In line with the challenges caused by the pandemic, it is recommended to use simpler systems by reducing the scale of performance in businesses. In line with the budget which is shaped by the financial crisis caused by the pandemic, the best-performing employees have been offered financial incentives while moderately-performing employees have been offered with non-financial incentives (participation in decision-making, transfer of authority, autonomy, responsibility, etc.).
- The COVID-19 pandemic has also revealed hidden leadership skills or deficiencies. The performance of some managers/ candidate managers, who were considered to have great potential in terms of their abilities in prepandemic reviews, has failed to meet expectations under the pressure, stress and uncertainty caused by the pandemic. However, some managers who were considered mediocre in prepandemic evaluations have been quite bold and agile during the pandemic, leading their teams by encouraging them and boosting their morale by maintaining frequent, deep, and emotional contact with them. The said behaviors and competencies are the most important leadership characteristics that should be possessed by senior employees after the pandemic. Businesses are believed to take these competencies more into account when dealing with talent management.

In summary, it is safe to say that today, when the pandemic is tightening its grip, the performance goals or criteria set by businesses before the pandemic have lost their significance, while new goals, criteria, or professional behaviors have gained importance. Today, the core competencies and professional behaviors businesses look for in their employees are the ability to remain agile and productive in crises, focus on the job by staying focused under pressure and stress, establish deep and long-term relations with customers and relevant partners, be brave under extraordinary risk, and consider the pandemic a time to improve skills and competencies for the future. In addition, as mentioned in sections covering staffing and training and development, the digitalization accelerated by the pandemic and uncertainties brought by it have highlighted certain competencies. The most important ones are the ability to make use of artificial intelligence, think analytically, use information and communication technology tools, maintain productivity under changing conditions, remain flexible, harmonious, and disciplines, work between disciplines, tolerate uncertainty, and have command of all procedures in a business. It is believed that all these competencies and professional behaviors will be the foundation of performance evaluations during and after the pandemic.

Digitalization of Performance Management Activities

With the latest developments, human resource management technologies have played an important part in performance management, the related activities of which have become increasingly online (Ataseven, 2020: 12; Ünal, 2020). Digital tools and methods were being used in performance management activities prior to the pandemic however, the transformation brought by the pandemic has increased the use of the digital workplace, and digital tools and data collected online have helped control and improve performance online using descriptive, predictive, and guiding analyses. During the pandemic, more and more businesses have started making use of virtual online performance management tools. Performance evaluations are conducted via cloud software, especially in IT, finance, insurance, etc. A study conducted with 137 IT managers working at the software company OpsRamp, found that both online monitoring of performance in the IT industry and the development of software to facilitate performance management had been the top priorities during the pandemic (McKendrick, 2020). For programmers, it will be critical to monitor the efficiency of available software tracking and evaluating performance online and to develop new software making more use of artificial intelligence so as to meet the future demands of businesses (Deloitte, 2020c: 12).

During the pandemic when there is less in-person communication between employees and employers, businesses have faced the need to develop new strategies to manage performance in a virtual world. Based on the research performed on the topic, the recommended strategies for managing performance in an online and virtual environment are listed below (Moses, McLean ve Bumstead, 2020):

- Defining clear, clear and achievable individual goals by communicating business priorities to employees
- Communicating with employees about both their performance and their overall physical and mental health
- Performing regular checks on work performed at home using various software, such as Trello, Slack, Groove or Zoom

- Monitoring the outcomes obtained by employees using software such as Todoist, Twist, etc. and evaluating the impact of these outcomes on results (business performance)
- Supporting activities related to employee development (encouraging new ideas, recommending participation in training programs, informing employees about other areas of work, etc.)
- Making use of 360-degree feedback via software such as Mercer360 or Mettl
- Organizing online activities to encourage positive behavior, which is an important aspect of performance, and preserve organizational culture (non-work-related meetings, online parties celebrating birthdays, tea-coffee hours, book-reading, e-gaming events, etc.)

It has often been discussed how effectively performance management activities were carried out before the pandemic and how much the related processes contributed to the achievement of the goals of businesses. Even though performance management-related activities have become increasingly challenging due to the pandemic and remote work, making more use of digital tools and methods can offer major opportunities in achieving goals, conducting performance management more effectively, and creating more value. Therefore, it is safe to say that this challenging time brings with it a number of opportunities for businesses to renew and make more effective use of their performance management processes using digital and online methods and applications.

2.5. Impact of the Pandemic on Pay Management

Pay management (compensation), which is an important function of human resource management, can be defined as a process consisting of pay policies, structures and systems in relation to the identification of employees' pay. Businesses decide on certain issues related to compensation, especially the level of pay according to the market and the elements that make up the total pay. The main components of the total pay are basic/root pay, variable pay, and fringe and social benefits (Acar, 2013: 353). Basic pay usually refers to a guaranteed and fixed amount determined by the value of the work performed by employees or their skills and competencies. As it reflects the basis value of the work or relevant skills, basic pay is usually the basis of pay structures. Variable pay varies according to the performance and contribution of employees, aiming to encourage (incentivize) employees on certain issues (increase in production or quality). Fringe and social benefits are offered in addition to basic pay and variable pay and include any additional benefits provided to employees for being a member of the business (bonuses, meal subsidization, commuter benefits, health insurance, etc.). By using pay systems, businesses determine which of these elements will be included in the total pay and their proportion, make calculations, and then make individual payments (Acar, 2007: 49).

One of the human resource management functions affected by the global COVID-19 pandemic has been pay management. During the pandemic, most businesses around the world suspended pay increases, pay cut, canceled some fringe benefits, or resorted to protective programs provided by governments. The impact of the COVID-19 pandemic on pay management can be analyzed under four categories: the impact of the pandemic on pay levels, the impact of the pandemic on performance- pay relations and fringe benefits, pay practices highlighted during the pandemic, and flexibility and digitalization caused by the pandemic.

Impact of the Pandemic on Pay Levels

Until the COVID-19 pandemic, most businesses, especially those with robust financial infrastructure, worked on growing, expanding their market share, and increasing profits, while after the pandemic, they have been focused on focused on maintaining cash flow, reducing costs, and maintaining efficiency. As they were shut down for a long time due to social isolation and could not sustain daily activities, many businesses have had difficulty paying their employees regularly during the pandemic. As in other areas, pay experts discuss what to do about pay in line with new developments and the outcomes when crises that cause major impacts around the world, such as the COVID-19 outbreak, disrupt the workflow. Such crises bring about many changes in the business world, however, it is important to predict and identify the level, scope, industries, and jobs that will be affected. For example, some businesses have tried to overcome the challenges brought the pandemic by laying off, while some have had to make pay cuts. Many studies that analyze the impacts of the pandemic on pay levels found that there are a large number of businesses that resorted to pay freezes or pay cuts and that salaries of senior employees were cut significantly to be able to pay lower-level workers. Below are the results of some of these studies conducted in different countries.

A report by the Economic Research Institute (ERI) predicted that with the pandemic, pay growth in the United States will slow down, and pay cuts will be avoided as much as possible, as in many cases it is considered to be the last resort. The situation also reveals the influence of culture over practices. In some cultures, job-sharing programs or pay cuts instead of layoffs are considered to be more favorable to overcome the crisis, while in some cultures layoffs are preferred as pay cuts are frowned upon. In American culture, reducing pay is also considered to be demoralizing for employees, so it is more favorable to save costs by reducing the number of employees with layoffs. Pay is expected to fall overall with lower increases, at least for next year, as more people will compete to get fewer jobs available due to rising unemployment. According to growth forecasts for different countries, it is estimated that most G20 countries will fall into recession in 2020, which will result in a 2.2 % decline in the global economy. Given that the decline in pay due to the economic crisis in 2008 lasted for three years afterward, the same possibility can also be applied to the crisis caused by the pandemic, and pay increases are expected to remain on the lower side for the upcoming one to three years (Johnson, 2020).

While the overall trend towards pay increases is expected to remain stable due to the pandemic, the differences between industries are notable. Certain industries have been hit more by the pandemic in terms of pay levels: Travel, energy, and durable goods. Large businesses in these industries will probably survive, although they have suffered and made layoffs as a result of suspending or limiting their activities. The main concern here is the challenges that smaller businesses that support these industries will face. For example, most small and medium-sized businesses that support large businesses in these industries have temporarily cut their employees' pay by 10 to 30 %. Aside from pay levels, such businesses are expected to undergo major changes in terms of pay practices. During the pandemic, many companies, especially in aviation, energy, and durable goods manufacturing and sales industries, have tried to allocate resources to pay their lower-level employees by cutting the pay of higher-level employees, deferring salaries, or cutting fringe benefits (Johnson, 2020).

As for pay levels, there are positive developments in some industries. Transportation and logistics, healthcare, nondurable consumables, and grocery shopping are examples of these industries. Large and small businesses in these industries have achieved a significant growth rate during the pandemic and have increased the number of their employees accordingly. There also reports of pay increases, possibly temporary, in these industries. Some business examples are: Costco, a supermarket chain, has offered an additional $2 pay an hour to its employees in the US due to an increase in customer volume, J. B. Hunt, a transportation and logistics company, has paid $500 one-time bonus to its drivers, field operators, and customer service personnel, Target, a supermarket chain, has offered an additional $2 pay an hour to its employees due to soaring retail sales and paid up to $1500 bonuses to thousands of its employees, Safeway, Vons, Albertsons, and Pavilions, online supermarket chains, have offered an additional $2 pay an hour to their employees working at their supermarkets, J. M.

Smucker, a food producer, has made a $1500 hazard pay to its employees over Coronavirus concerns, and Walmart, a chain of retail stores, has announced $300 bonus to its full-time employees employed before March 1, 2020, and $150 bonus to its part-time employees (Johnson, 2020). In addition, travel nurses, who are contracted personnel, have been offered high hazard pays across the US due to the pandemic.

A June and July 2020 survey conducted by the Economic Research Institute (ERI) of 455 companies in the United States found that 1.5 % of businesses have increased pay and 21 % acted as previously planned. Another study conducted by the same organization in April 2020 found that 6.6 % of respondents have increased pay and 50 % have maintained their pay policy, clearly showing the increased negative effect of the pandemic on pay from April to June. 15.4 % of respondents said they would cut pay, 9 % said they would freeze pay and 5.5 % said they would increase pay at a lower rate. 45.5 % of respondents were still undecided about what to do about pay. According to the research conducted in April, the proportion of companies that were undecided about pay was 33.3 %, indicating that uncertainty about the long-term effects of the pandemic has significantly heightened. Other results of the research showed that 37.6 % of respondents have cut the salaries of seniors, and 19.2 % have made hazard payments for at least one employee group. The pay cuts were 28.5 % for board members; 16 % for senior managers; 15 % for out-of-scope staff, 10 % for in-scope staff and 8.5 % for staff in direct contact with customers. Mobile healthcare and home care services, retail and banking industries have increased pay, transportation, air defense, and durable consumer goods industries have made pay cuts, energy, durable consumer goods, and service industries have frozen pay, and accommodation, entertainment, and e-game industries have increased pay at a lower rate. As for how long the changes in pay will last during the pandemic, 20 % of respondents said between four and six months and 13 % said between seven and twelve months. 4.3 % of the respondents stated that the changes in pay would be permanent, while 48 % stated that they could not predict how long the changes would last (Economic Research Institute, 2020).

In a business in Sri Lanka, all senior managers have been asked to voluntarily defer their salaries starting from April 2020, and they have been given options to cut their salaries based on the basis value at varying rates such as 20 %, 40 % and 50 % (Opatha, 2020: 155). With these reductions, the goal has been to allocate enough resources to keep on paying lower-level employees. A study conducted by Compensation Advisory Partners (CAP) of 64 private companies operating in the United States found that 40 % of respondents froze salaries for their employees and managers, with pay cuts of 20 % for white-collar employees and 8 % for blue-collar employees (Milford, 2020). A study conducted by Mercer of 522 companies operating in Arab Cooperation Council countries found that 27 % of companies have made cuts on basic pay and 15 % on total pay, 22 % have made or was planning to make changes to short-term incentive pay, and 20 % was reviewing their pay increase plans for 2020 (73 % of this 20 % suspending pay increases). Most companies have created resources by cutting the basic pay of high-level employees with high salaries, trying to maintain the income level of lower-level employees. The median of the deduction from the basic pay of senior executives has been 20 % (Mercer, 2020). A study conducted in Nigeria also found that in order to reduce the economic impact of the pandemic, cuts of up to 15 % have been made from the salaries of senior managers (KPMG, 2020b).

Studies conducted on pay in Turkey demonstrate the limited impact of the pandemic on pay levels compared to other countries. According to the results of KPMG's research in Turkey, 8 % of the participating companies paid a portion of pay and 5 % postponed the annual increase in pay. In addition, 28 % of the companies participating in the study stated that they would differentiate pay among employees, taking into account the working arrangement and business dynamics after the pandemic, while increasing pay at the end of the year. It has been stated that employee qualities that will ensure positive differentiation in pay increases are the ability to maintain productivity under changing conditions, flexibility, agility, compatibility, and discipline, the ability to work interdisciplinary, and have command of all processes (KPMG, 2020a). The study conducted by Mercer Turkey and PERYÖN showed that 9 % of companies have postponed or suspended pay increases (Mercer Turkey, 2020).

Impact of the Pandemic on Variable Pay and Fringe Benefits

Crises such as the COVID-19 pandemic can financially put businesses in a difficult position, affecting variable pay given based on performance and fringe benefits. Employees who have to provide for themselves and their families may have concerns over the lack of fringe benefits. To manage the stress and support the well-being of employees, it is important for businesses to clearly indicate how they support employees and their families under difficult conditions, contemplate how they can bend or change pay programs, and make short-term choices by thinking about their long-term effects (Deloitte, 2020d). During the pandemic, most companies have had to review variable pay elements (premiums, short or long-term incentives, bonuses, etc.) that are based on performance- pay relationship and cut many additional benefits. However, some new additional benefits have been offered to employees to curb the financial difficulties caused by the pandemic.

In the study conducted by the Incentive Research Foundation (IRF) of 177 people consisting of pay experts, senior executives, and human resources directors, 34 % of the participants stated that the incentive programs continued without any changes, 27 % said they were suspended, 19 % said that they were restructured, and 19 % said they were canceled. Of those who stated that their program had been suspended or canceled, 31 % cited senior management concerns over economic conditions, 15 % cited budget shortages and 8 % cited insufficient personnel to manage the program to be the reasons. Other results of the study show that 24 % of participants reduced travels (which was a fringe benefit), while 11 % canceled them completely. Among fringe benefits, the use of prepaid cards/gift cars has increased the most by 6 % (Incentive Research Foundation, 2020).

A study of 764 employees from the UK technology industry found that 49 % of respondents agreed that pay and fringe benefits should be determined by merit, regardless of where they work. In case working from home becomes more widespread, fringe benefits that employees will value the most are retirement plans by 41 %, home work allowance by 39 %, and healthcare services by 36 %. Employees have indicated that they are ready to accept a 10 % reduction in their pay if they are given the chance work remotely from anywhere in the world (Van Der Voort, 2020).

In terms of fringe benefits offered during the pandemic, the study of the Economic Research Institute found that 95 % of participating companies offered their employees the option to work from home, 54 % adopted flexible working arrangements, 37 % allowed paid leave, 15 % offered additional health and care benefits, and 13 % offered back pay to employees so that they can cover additional costs (Economic Research Institute, 2020).

A study conducted in Nigeria found the most common pay practices to be as follows: establishing the relationship between performance and pay based not on absolute goals but on relative ones, making long-term payments instead of monthly payments by reviewing the pay systems, and offering incentives or other rewards to employees who are performing jobs that increase the risk of infection or cannot be performed remotely. The study also found that many companies entirely eliminated fringe benefits such as gym/club memberships, company car allocation, and overseas vacation (KPMG, 2020b).

Studies conducted in Turkey show the impact of the pandemic on pay and fringe benefits. According to the results of KPMG's study in Turkey, 9 % of companies postponed performance-based bonuses during the pandemic, 6 % offered job-attendance incentives, and about 3 % reduced, postponed or deferred long-term incentives while canceling performance-based bonuses (KPMG, 2020a). The study conducted by Mercer Turkey and PERYÖN found that 39.5 % of companies plan to temporarily suspend fringe benefits. The benefits in question are related to transportation (24 %), shuttle (19.8 %), and food (15.6 %) services.

In addition, some companies have offered new fringe benefits to their employees to mitigate the negative effects of the pandemic. These benefits are allowance offered to employees, who are quarantined or had to remain in-country due to travel restrictions, bonuses or incentives for those doing jobs open to the risk of infection, programs to support employees to maintain their mental health as they fight pandemic-related fears and concerns, healthcare and welfare programs, and care programs for children and dependents (Deloitte, 2020d).

Pay Practices Highlighted during the Pandemic

Short-time working allowance has been the most preferred pay practice during the pandemic in Turkey and the rest of the world. Pursuant to Unemployment Insurance Law No. 4447, short-time work defined as the type of work introduced in workplaces for a period of no longer than three months in cases where weekly working hours are significantly reduced or activities are entirely or partially suspended due to a general economic, industrial, or regional crisis, or a force majeure (Official Gazette, 1999). The employer that will employ workers under short work informs the Turkish Employment Agency and the relevant trade union, if any, along with justifications for the request. The short-time working allowance is paid from the Unemployment Insurance Fund in case of short-time work. Daily short-time working allowance is 60 % of the average daily gross gain based on the insured's earnings based on the insurance premium for the last 12 months. The amount of short-time working allowance cannot exceed 150 % of the gross monthly minimum wage. The president has the authority to extend short-time working allowance until the end of 2020 for certain industries or countrywide. Policies adopted in Turkey to mitigate the impact of the pandemic on the labor market have made it easier for businesses to benefit from short-time working allowances to pay their employees' pay. As of August 31, 2020, 4 million people have benefited from short-time working allowance. While some of these people received allowance only for the first few months, some have been receiving it since April. The number of short-time working allowance beneficiaries fell to 1.2 million in August, from 3.2 million in April, 3.3 million in May, 2.5 million in June and 1.8 million in July. The total amount of short-time working allowance granted to employees in workplaces affected by the pandemic exceeded TRY 19 billion as of the end of August (Haber Türk, 2020b).

Another method that employers have adopted during the pandemic is paid leave. If, due to the pandemic, employees want to take annual leave as a precautionary, businesses can allow their employees to take annual paid leave. In addition, even if the request to take annual leave is not made by employees, businesses can resort to paid leave for all or a part of their employees according to the Annual Paid Leave Regulation. If businesses resort to collective paid leave, employees who have not yet earned the right to annual paid leave can also benefit from it. According to the Labor Law, 15 days of the time that a person has not worked as a result of more than one consecutive week of shutdown due to compelling reasons in the workplace shall be considered to have been worked when calculating his/her annual right to paid leave (on condition that he/she starts to work again). Therefore, in case of a shutdown of more than one consecutive week due the pandemic, 15 days of the time that a person has not worked is considered to have been worked when calculating annual right to paid leave (on the condition that work is started again) (Yürekli, 2020:50).

Another method adopted during the pandemic has been unpaid leave. Normally, according to Labor Law No. 4857, employers do not have the right to put employees on unpaid leave without their written consent. However, specific to the pandemic, employers can take this course due to a ban on layoffs. In May 2020, 1.3 million people were put on unpaid leave and received cash support of TRY 1,177, while in August this number reached 1.9 million (Karar, 2020). Payment made to employees on unpaid leave totaled TRY 4.4 billion (Haber Türk, 2020b).

Same as in the rest of the world, employers in Turkey have also widely opted for short-time working allowance, paid and unpaid leave during the pandemic as shown by research. A KPMG study conducted in Turkey found that 52 % of companies have tried to establish a sustainable working order with unpaid leave, and short-time working and working in shifts have been the two methods preferred the most during the pandemic. The most preferred methods have been paid leave (52 %), new incentives (short-time working) (32 %), shift working (19 %), and unpaid leave (9 %) respectively. 31 % of the companies have not adopted any new methods during the pandemic (KPMG, 2020a). In Mercer Turkey and PERYÖN's study, 33.3 % of the companies stated that they would apply for short-time working allowance and 23.1 % would put their employees on unpaid leave. 42 % of companies expect to make financial payments to employees that get infected. The rate of companies with employees who benefit from SSI's incapacity benefit is 12 % (Mercer Turkey, 2020).

Flexibility and Digitalization in Pay Management

Human resource management experts note that pay strategies must be dynamic to combat crises and challenges arising from economic conditions. Processes determining the pay of geographically-dispersed workforce have required to be more dynamic and flexible. A study conducted found that pay plans had to be reviewed due to the pandemic, largely as a result of switching to working from home (Aydın Göktepe, 2020: 635). Traditionally, companies determine pay based on living costs in regions. However, working from home during the pandemic has made it necessary to reconsider pay strategies on how to remunerate employees that change regions. The change in the way employees work also brought on a change in pay strategies. Conventional payment plans (fixed, variable, and full-time employees) have given way to on-demand, project-based, flexible, etc. plans. Because of the pandemic, businesses have had to change their payment procedures rapidly and on a wide scale, resorting emergency payments (hardship pay), one-time bonuses, and pay cuts. Pay equality and justice have become important issues in today's economic uncertainty caused by the pandemic. In addition, although the COVID-19 pandemic negatively affects pay-related issues, we can say that these effects will be temporary given that consumer spending will increase as conditions get better. For this reason, employers can reduce costs without layoffs and increase employee sensitivity by opting for temporary pay cuts instead of laying off their employees, taking into account the country and organizational culture. As a fundamental pay strategy for the pandemic, pay can be reviewed taking into consideration which jobs or titles are considered essential for income or production or by focusing on jobs that have become less competitive due to widespread layoffs or that have received high demand (Starner, 2020b).

Using the right technology can also benefit human resources experts and managers who are trying to effectively carry out pay-related activities. Unilever has developed uFlexReward, a human resources data analysis platform, to manage complex remuneration procedures. The system brings together all employee-related pay elements (basic pay, variable pay, fringe benefits, etc.) and costs resulting from these elements in a single platform in real time. It conducts analyses to identify and solve organizational issues such as pay inequality and produced individualized and detailed reports on pay and rewards. In addition, like many global companies, Unilever has been able to make use of the system to test various scenarios to manage the ongoing economic impact of the pandemic and had instant and real-time access to all pay and reward data for all its employees in different countries (Starner, 2020a). The system brings together numerous pay-related elements such as personnel salaries, pensions, bonuses, etc. and helps businesses explore various ways to reduce their costs by sharing these elements in real-time on a cost basis (TRT World, 2020). Taking decisions about pay management via digital software that makes use of artificial intelligence and performing pay management-related activities through such software will bring on many benefits. Some of these benefits are being able to take the most effective decisions on pay taking into account various scenarios based on internal and external factors, being able to perform pay management-related activities more effectively and faster, and the ability to monitor data in real-time. In a time when new working arrangements are introduced and businesses are caught off guard, making use of digital payroll management software that is developed in line with the impact of the pandemic and legal framework is of critical importance for the efficient and timely implementation of pay management-related activities (Logo Blog, 2020).

CONCLUSION

The Coronavirus pandemic, which emerged in late 2019 in China and spread all over the world rapidly, has morphed into a global crisis, affecting social and economic life, and naturally businesses and organizations.

Due to the Coronavirus pandemic, many people have been infected and lost their lives and restrictive measures have reduced mobility in all aspects of life and led to macro and micro level stagnation and contraction in many industries and in the overall economy. As a result of these impacts, employment has contracted, unemployment has increased, and significant losses have been suffered in terms of labor income.

The effects of COVID-19 on the global economy and national economies at the macro level have manifested themselves as recession and contraction. In this context, there have been significant declines in growth and employment rates at the global level, major increases in underemployment and unemployment, and losses in household and operating income. It is a generally accepted view that the negative effects of the crisis on economic life will continue even after the pandemic, during the so-called "new normal."

As expected, the Coronavirus crisis has also negatively affected businesses and public and private organizations operating in most industries, with the exception of some lines of work. At the micro level, businesses and other organizations suffered a major decline in business and employment volumes and income. In this context, there have also been declines and losses in the working conditions and income of the self-employed and paid workers. In addition, new working arrangements, especially the dissemination of remote and flexible work, have been quite influential. The attempt to continue education by means of "distance learning" has been one of the most important outcomes of the crisis.

In the dissemination of remote/flexible working arrangements, smart communication and information technologies have been decisive and the effects of COVID-19 have been accelerating and deepening. As a result, there has been a significant rise in the use of electronic(e-) or digital forms of business and work.

The impact of the COVID-19 crisis on workforce, employment, job opportunities, and income and policies and practices about human resource management has been quite important for being relevant for many people. In terms of HRM policies and practices, the crisis has impacted staffing, career management, training and development, performance, and pay management aspects the most.

The contraction in the business and employment volume of businesses has also led to significant changes in human resource management policies and practices. In this context, businesses and many organizations have experienced stagnation and contraction in labor demand and personnel recruitment and selection, and the surplus workforce has tried to be eliminated via government-supported policies without having to resort to layoffs. To this end, businesses have reduced working time, gave paid-unpaid leave, and introduced flexible working arrangements.

Many prepandemic HRM plans, systems, and activities have been reviewed or canceled, and new plans, systems, and activities have been introduced. In these new HRM policies and practices, "flexibility/remote work" and "use of intelligent technologies" have played a decisive role. In this context, changes in policies, systems, and methods on issues such as employee recruitment and selection, training and development, career development, performance, and pay management have occupied an important place on the agenda, and the use of intelligent technologies has rapidly disseminated.

What came to the fore in the field of HRM in businesses has been: organizational downsizing, change in business and organizational structures and needed qualifications, proliferation of flexible/remote/temporary working methods, contraction of payroll employment with relatively good conditions, individuals having more responsibility over career planning and development, increased importance of goal- or result-based performance evaluation criteria and methods, increased importance of performance- and result-based pay elements, reduction in fringe benefits, and more use of smart technologies across all functions.

To conclude, as in other areas, the COVID-19 crisis is expected to trigger significant change in human resource management and relevant functions, personnel qualifications, labor demand, business and organizational structures, working methods, and used technologies and increases the responsibility of individuals over career management.

REFERENCES

Ahmet Cevat Acar (2007). İşletmelerde Ücret Yapısının Oluşturulması ve Bir Uygulama, Literatür Yayınları, İstanbul.

Ahmet Cevat Acar (2013). Ücret Yönetimi, Ömer Sadullah vd., İnsan Kaynakları Yönetimi, Beta Yayınları, İstanbul, ss. 351–449.Ahmet Cevat Acar (2020). Effects of COVID-19 Crisis on Employment and Working Arrangements, Reflections on the Pandemics, Editors: Muzaffer Şeker, Ali Özer, Cem Korkut, Türkiye Bilimler Akademisi, Ankara, ss. 463–488.

Ali Seyyar and Cihan Selek Öz (2007), İnsan Kaynakları Terimleri Ansiklopedik Sözlük, Değişim Yayınları, İstanbul.

Ali Ulus Kımav and Belgin Aydın (2020). A Blueprint for In-Service Teacher Training Program in Technology Integration, Journal of Educational Technology & Online Learning, 3(3), 224–244.

Alok Kshirsagar, Tarek Mansour, Liz McNally and Marc Metakis (2020). Adapting Workplace Learning in the Time of Coronavirus, McKinsey & Company. Retrieved July 9, 2020, from https://www.mckinsey.com/~/media/McKinsey/Business%20Functions/McKinsey%20Accelerate/Our%20Insights/Adapting%20workplace%20learning%20in%20the%20time%20of%20coronavirus/Adapting-workplace-learning-in-the-time-of-coronavirus-vF.pdf

Ameera Balharetha, Mohammed Abdulrazzaq AlDuhileba, Fozan A Aldulaijana, and Mohammed Yousef Aldossary (2020). Impact of COVID-19 Pandemic on Residency and Fellowship Training Programs in Saudi Arabia: A Nationwide Cross-Sectional Study, Annals of Medicine and Surgery, 57, 127–132.

Anadolu Ajansı (2020, August 11). Pandemiyle birlikte İnsan Kaynakları'nda Dijitalleşme Dönemi Başladı. Retrieved September 27, 2020, from https://www.aa.com.tr/tr/sirkethaberleri/hizmet/pandemiyle-birlikte-insan-kaynaklarinda-dijitallesme-donemi-basladi/658778

Andrew M. Campbell (2020). An Increasing Risk of Family Violence during the COVID-19 Pandemic: Strengthening Community Collaborations to Save Lives, Forensic Science International: Reports, 2. Retrieved July 9, 2020, from https://reader.elsevier.com/reader/sd/pii/S2665910720300384?token= D26CDF3EE2310AD80FD26E4FD33CCA4991AACA9FEB9AB7942EA023 BB01CC534974BA2A968E6E3ED518BE09CECA478236

Ashley Stahl (2020, June 4). Virtual Interview Tips to Land You the Job during the COVID-19 Pandemic, Forbes. Retrieved July 10, 2020, from https://www.forbes.com/sites/ashleystahl/2020/06/04/virtual-interview-tips-to-land-you-thejob-during-the-COVID-19-pandemic/#1b1061341bdc

Ayşen Akbaş Tuna and Onur Çelen (2020). İşletmelerin İnsan Kaynakları Yönetimi Uygulamaları Üzerinde COVID-19 Pandemisinin Etkileri, OPUS Uluslararası Toplum Araştırmaları Dergisi, 16(30), 2710–2759.

Aytekin Tank (2020). Performance Reviews in the Time of Coronavirus, Jotform.com. Retrieved July 11, 2020, from https://www.jotform.com/blog/coronavirus-performance-reviews/

Bloomberg (2020, August 5). Pandemi Sonrası İnsan Kaynakları Açısından Yeni Fırsatlar ve Riskler Neler? Retrieved September 25, 2020, from https://www.bloomberght.com/pandemi-sonrasi-insan-kaynaklari-acisindan-yeni-firsatlar-ve-riskler-neler-2261566

Brian O'Connell (2020, April 28). How Managers Are Handling Performance Reviews during COVID-19, Society for Human Resource Management (SHRM). Retrieved July 9, 2020, from https://www.shrm.org/resourcesandtools/hr-topics/people-managers/pages/performance-reviews-during-coronavirus-.aspx

Bryan Hancock and Bill Schaninger (2020). HR Says Talent is Crucial for Performance – and the Pandemic Proves It, McKinsey & Company. Retrieved July 9, 2020, from https://www.mckinsey.com/~/media/McKinsey/Business%20Functions/Organization/Our%20Insights/HR%20says%20talent%20is%20crucial%20for%20performance%20and%20the%20pandemic%20proves%20it/HR-says-talent-is-crucial-for-performance-and-the-pandemic-proves-it-v3.pdf

Cavide Uyargil (2013). "İş Analizi ve İş Dizaynı," Cavide Uyargil ve diğ, Editors: İnsan Kaynakları Yönetimi, Beta Yayınları, İstanbul, pp. 55–95.

Charlotte Neuhauser (2002). Learning Style and Effectiveness of Online and Face-to-Face Instruction, The American Journal of Distance Education, 16(2), 99–113.

D.M. Arvind Mallik and Arpita Ptel (2020). Social Posting in COVID-19 Recruiting Era- Milestone HR Strategy Augmenting Social Media Recruitment, Dogo Rangsang Research Journal, 10(2), 82–89.

Dan Healing (2020, August 3). More Corporate Meetings to Go Virtual after Success during Pandemic, CTV News. Retrieved September 25, 2020, from https://www.ctvnews.ca/business/more-corporate-meetings-to-go-virtual-after-success-during-pandemic-1.5049622

Daniel Spurk and Caroline Straub (2020). Flexible Employment Relationships and Careers in Times of the COVID-19 Pandemic, Journal of Vocational Behavior, 119, 1–4. Retrieved July 9, 2020, from https://www.sciencedirect.com/science/article/pii/S0001879120300609?via%3Dihub

Dean Takahashi (2020, March 28). Candor: 267 Companies Have Frozen Hiring, 44 Had Layoffs, 36 Rescinded Offers, 111 Are Hiring, VentureBeat. Retrieved July 9, 2020, from https://venturebeat.com/2020/03/28/candor-267-companies-have-frozen-hiring-44-had-layoffs-36-rescinded-offers-111-are-hiring/

Deloitte (2020a). COVID-19: The Upskilling Imperative Building a Future-Ready Workforce for the AI Age. Retrieved September 25, 2020, from https://www2.deloitte.com/content/dam/Deloitte/ca/Documents/deloitte-analytics/ca-covid19-upskilling-EN-AODA.pdf

Deloitte (2020b, March). Remote Collaboration Facing the Challenges of COVID-19. Retrieved July 25, 2020, from https://www2.deloitte.com/content/dam/Deloitte/de/Documents/human-capital/Remote-Collaboration-COVID-19.pdf

Deloitte (2020c, March). COVID-19 Workforce Strategies for a Post-COVID-19 Recovery Workbook. Retrieved July 25, 2020, from https://www2.deloitte.com/content/dam/Deloitte/global/Documents/About-Deloitte/COVID-19/ca-workbook-covid-aodo-en.pdf

Deloitte (2020d). Accelerating Digital HR during- and Post COVID-19: The Future of HR in the Face of COVID-19. Retrieved September 25, 2020, from https://www2.deloitte.com/nl/nl/pages/human-capital/articles/accelerating-digital-hr-during-and-post-COVID-19.html

Deloitte (2020e). Addressing the Impact of COVID-19 Reward and Well-Being Program Impacts. Retrieved September 25, 2020, from https://www2.deloitte.com/content/dam/Deloitte/global/Documents/About-Deloitte/gx-respond-tal-strat-optimize-corporate-hr-policy.pdf

Deniz Kurt and Zehra Uçanok (2020). Yaşam Boyu Gelişimde Motivasyon Kuramı Çerçevesinde Kontrol Stratejilerinin İncelenmesi, Psikoloji Çalışmaları, 1–31. Retrieved September 25, 2020, from https://dergipark.org.tr/tr/download/article-file/1046571

Deutsche Welle (2020, October 25). Karantina Psikolojik Sorunları Artırdı. Retrieved November 2, 2020, from https://www.dw.com/tr/karantina-psikolojik-sorunlar%C4%B1-art%C4%B1rd%C4%B1/a-55390198

Dorien T A M Kooij (2020). The Impact of the COVID-19 Pandemic on Older Workers: The Role of Self-Regulation and Organizations, Work, Aging and Retirement, 6(4), 233–237.

Ebere Chika John-Eke and John Kalu Eke (2020). Strategic Planning and Crisis Management Styles in Organizations: A Review of Related Literature, Journal of Strategic Management, 5(1), 36–46.

Economic Research Enstitute (2020). Coronavirus Compensation Survey Results. Retrieved September 25, 2020, from http://downloads.erieri.com/pdf/Coronavirus_Compensation_Survey_Results_Summer.pdf?hsCtaTracking=2286fcef-ce78-40d4-9e4a-46943d3af211%7Cde9e9413-69d9-4501-bd66-e273c259b846

Eileen Aitken-Fox, Jane Coffey, Kantha Dayaram, Scott Fitzgerald, Chahat Gupta, Steve McKenna and Amy Wei Tian (2020). The Impact of COVID-19 on Human Resource Management: Avoiding Generalisations, The London School of Economics and Political Science. Retrieved September 25, 2020, from https://blogs.lse.ac.uk/businessreview/2020/05/22/the-impact-of-COVID-19-on-human-resource-management-avoiding-generalisations/

Ekrem Erdoğan and Serpil Çiğdem (2018). "GİG Ekonomisi ve Freelance İşgücünün Yükselişi: Freelancer.com," Üzerinden Bir Değerlendirme, Editör: Ekrem Erdoğan, Seçme Yazılar-II, Sakarya Yayıncılık, Sakarya, 229–261.

Elka Torpey and Andrew Hogan (2020). Working in a Gig Economy, U.S. Bureau of Labor Statistics. Retrieved November 2, 2020, from https://www.bls.gov/careeroutlook/2016/article/what-is-the-gig-economy.htm

Ellen Yin (2020, June 15). Recruiting in China after COVID-19: HR Planning and Talent Acquisition for SMEs, China Briefing. Retrieved July 12, 2020, from https://www.china-briefing.com/news/recruiting-china-COVID-19-hr-planning-talent-acquisition-smes/

Ergi Şener (2020, September 27). Dr. Umut Köksal ile İK'nın Yeni Normali Üzerine, Hürriyet. Retrieved November 2, 2020, from https://www.hurriyet.com.tr/yazarlar/ergi-sener/dr-umut-koksal-ile-iknin-yeni-normali-uzerine-41621215

Esra Aydın Göktepe (2020). Kriz Döneminde İş Sürdürülebilirliğine Yönelik Yönetim Uygulamaları; COVID-19 Pandemi Araştırması, International Journal of Social, Humanities and Administrative Sciences, 6(26), 630–638.

Eunice Leons (2020, April 21). Performance Management during the COVID-19 Era, Arthan Careers. Retrieved July 2, 2020, from https://arthancareers.com/blog/performance-management-during-the-COVID-19-era/

Eylem Arslan (2020, May 5). Salgın Sürecinde Online İşe Giriş Görüşmeleri Yüzde 300 Arttı, Marketing Türkiye. Retrieved July 12, 2020, from https://www.marketingturkiye.com.tr/haberler/salgin-surecinde-online-ise-giris-gorusmeleri-yuzde-300-artti/

Garry Dessler (2011). Human Resource Management, 12th Edition, Pearson Education, New Jersey.

Gönen Dündar (2013). "Kariyer Geliştirme", Cavide Uyargil ve diğ, Editors: İnsan Kaynakları Yönetimi, Beta Yayınları, İstanbul, pp. 268–300.

Gretchen M. Spreitzer, Lindsey Cameron and Lyndon Garrett (2017). Alternative Work Arrangements: Two Images of the New World of Work, Annual Review of Organizational Psychology and Organizational Behavior, 4, 473–499.

H. Filiz Alkan Meşhur (2020). Organizasyonların Tele Çalışmaya İlişkin Tutumlarına Yönelik Bir Araştırma, Dokuz Eylül Üniversitesi İktisadi ve İdari Bilimler Fakültesi Dergisi, 25(1), 1–24.

H.H.D.P.J. Opatha (2020). COVID-19 in Sri Lanka and Seven HRM Related Recommendations against COVID-19, Asian Journal of Social Sciences and Management Studies, 7(2), 152–157.

Haber Global (2020, April 16). Koronavirüs Silikon Vadisini Vurdu: İşe Alımlar Durdu! Retrieved July 2, 2020, from https://haberglobal.com.tr/ekonomi/koronavirus-silikon-vadisini-vurdu-ise-alimlar-durdu-40496

Haber Türk (2020a, March 3). Koronavirüs Yoğunluğu Artırdı, İşe Alım Yarışı Başladı. Retrieved July 2, 2020, from https://www.haberturk.com/koronavirus-yogunlugu-artirdi-ise-alim-yarisi-basladi-2629300-ekonomi

Haber Türk (2020b, September 14). Kısa Çalışma Ödeneği Alan İşçi Sayısı 1.2 Milyon Kişiye Geriledi. Retrieved October 2, 2020, from https://www.haberturk.com/koronavirus-yogunlugu-artirdi-ise-alim-yarisi-basladi-2629300-ekonomi

Hakkı Demirci and Murat Kocavelioğlu (2020, May 12). Pandemi Sürecinde Şirketlerin İK Yönetimi Nasıl Olmalı, Finans Gündem. Retrieved July 2, 2020, from https://www.finansgundem.com/haber/pandemi-surecinde-sirketlerin-ik-yonetimi-nasil-olmali/1490584

Hank Tucker (2020). Coronavirus Bankruptcy Tracker: These Major Companies Are Failing Amid the Shutdown, Forbes. Retrieved July 12, 2020, from https://www.forbes.com/sites/hanktucker/2020/05/03/coronavirus-bankruptcy-tracker-these-major-companies-are-failing-amid-the-shutdown/?sh=77e458b43425

Henry T de Berker, Morgan J Bressington, Isaac M Mayo, Anna Rose and Calum Honeyman (2020). Surgical Training During the COVID-19 Pandemic: Challenges and Opportunities for Junior Trainees, Journal of

Plastic, Reconstructive & Aesthetic Surgery. Retrieved October 2, 2020, from https://www.sciencedirect.com/science/article/pii/S1748681520303430

Hiram Ting, Jeffrey Ling and Cheah Jun Hwa (2020). Editorial: It Will Go Away!? Pandemic Crisis and Business in Asia, Asian Journal of Business Research, 10(1), 1–7.

Hürriyet (2020, June 1). Turkcell'de İşe Alım Süreci Online Olarak Gerçekleştiriliyor. Retrieved July 2, 2020, from https://www.hurriyet.com.tr/teknoloji/turkcellde-ise-alim-sureci-online-olarak-gerceklestiriliyor-41530601

Ian Hunter (2020, May 7). COVID 19 – Accelerating the Gig Economy, Uctoday. Retrieved July 2, 2020, from https://www.uctoday.com/contact-centre/ccaas/COVID-19-accelerating-the-gig-economy/

ILO (2020a, September 23). ILO Monitor: COVID-19 and the World of Work, 6th Edition. Retrieved October 12, 2020, from https://www.ilo.org/wcmsp5/groups/public/---dgreports/---dcomm/documents/briefingnote/wcms_755910.pdf

ILO (2020b, August 19). The Impact of the COVID-19 Pandemic on Jobs and Incomes in G20 Economies. Retrieved October 12, 2020, from https://www.ilo.org/wcmsp5/groups/public/---dgreports/---cabinet/documents/presentation/wcms_753607.pdf

ILO (2020c, March 18). COVID-19 ve Çalışma Yaşamı: Etkiler ve Yanıtlar. Retrieved July 2, 2020, from https://www.ilo.org/wcmsp5/groups/public/---europe/---ro-geneva/---ilo-ankara/documents/briefingnote/wcms_740193.pdf

ILO (2020d). Ensuring Fair Recruitment during the COVID-19 Pandemic, ILO Brief. Retrieved October 12, 2020, from https://www.ilo.org/wcmsp5/groups/public/---ed_protect/---protrav/---migrant/documents/publication/wcms_748839.pdf

Incentive Research Foundation (2020). COVID-19's Impact on Rewards & Recognition. The IRF Pulse Survey. Retrieved November 2, 2020, from https://theirf.org/research/irf-pulse-survey-COVID-19s-impact-on-rewards-recognition/2812/

Iza Gigauri (2020). Influence of COVID-19 Crisis on Human Resource Management and Companies' Response: The Expert Study, International Journal of Management Science and Business Administration, 6(6), 15–24.

İhlas Haber Ajansı (2020, October 20). Şirketler Salgın Döneminde Eğitime Yöneldi. Retrieved November 2, 2020, from https://www.iha.com.tr/istanbul-haberleri/sirketler-salgin-doneminde-egitime-yoneldi-istanbul-2725619/

İK Magazin (2020). HSBC İşe Alımları Durdurdu. Retrieved November 2, 2020, from https://ikmagazin.com/insan-kaynaklari/hsbc-ise-alimlari-durdurdu/

İsmail Ünal (2020, October 6). Pandemi Döneminde İnsan Kaynakları Yönetimi, Amfiweb.net. Retrieved October 25, 2020, from https://www.amfiweb.net/pandemi-doneminde-insan-kaynaklari-yonetimi/

Jeanne Meister (2020, March 31). The Impact of the Coronavirus on HR and the New Normal of Work, Forbes. Retrieved July 2, 2020, from https://www.forbes.com/sites/jeannemeister/2020/03/31/the-impact-of-the-coronavirus-on-hr-and-the-new-normal-of-work/#b9acb522b602

Jenny Bimrose, Jaana Kettunen and Tannis Goddard (2015). ICT the New Frontier? Pushing the Boundaries of Careers Practice. British Journal of Guidance and Counselling, 43 (1), 8- 23.

Job Van Der Voort (2020, August). What Impact Has COVID-19 Had on the Employee Pay and Benefits? Retrieved September 25, 2020, from https://www.thehrdirector.com/business-news/hr_in_business/brand-new-study-reveals-the-impact-of-COVID-19-on-the-future-of-work-employee-pay-and-benefits/

Joe McKendrick (2020). COVID-19 Crisis Pushing Organizations Deeper into Digital Transformation, ZD Net. Retrieved October 2, 2020, from https://www.zdnet.com/article/COVID-19-crisis-pushing-organizations-into-digital-transformation/

John P. Wilson (2005). Human Resource Development: Learning and Training for Individuals and Organizations, 2nd Edition, Kogan Page, London.

Jonas Johnson (2020). What Are the Effects of the Coronavirus on Compensation? Economic Research Enstitute. Retrieved November 2, 2020, from https://www.erieri.com/blog/post/what-are-the-effects-of-the-coronavirus-on-compensation

Jos Akkermansa, Julia Richardson and Maria L. Kraimer (2020). The COVID-19 Crisis as a Career Shock: Implications for Careers and Vocational Behavior, Journal of Vocational Behavior, 119, 1–5.

Jos Akkermans, Scott E. Seibert and Stefan T. Mol (2018). Tales of the Unexpected: Integrating Career Shocks in the Contemporary Careers Literature. SA Journal of Industrial Psychology, 44(1), 1–10. Retrieved July 2, 2020, from https://pdfs.semanticscholar.org/fd2d/3c5ec330ea10024f9e98ceb96cc7f2673e6b.pdf?_ga=2.137113136.1027138165.1603663869-940450107.1601555134

Kaiser Health News (2020, March 17). In Face of Coronavirus, Many Hospitals Cancel On-Site Training for Nursing and Med Students. Retrieved July 2,

2020, from https://khn.org/news/in-face-of-coronavirus-many-hospitals-cancel-on-site-training-for-nursing-and-med-students/

Karar (2020, September 16). Ücretsiz İzne Çıkartılanların Sayısı 2 Milyona Dayandı. Retrieved November 2, 2020, from https://www.karar.com/ucretsiz-izne-cikartilanlarin-sayisi-2-milyona-dayandi-1585690

KPMG (2020a, April). COVID-19 ile Çalışma Hayatındaki Yeni Uygulamalar Anket Raporu. Retrieved July 2, 2020, from https://assets.kpmg/content/dam/kpmg/tr/pdf/2020/04/covid19-calisma-hayatindaki-yeni-uygulamalar.pdf

KPMG (2020b, April). COVID-19 and Employee Rewards. Retrieved July 2, 2020, from https://assets.kpmg/content/dam/kpmg/ng/pdf/advisory/COVID-19-and-employee-rewards.pdf

Lance Lambert (2020, June 30). 59 % of CEOs Implemented Hiring Freezes during the Pandemic: Fortune Survey, Fortune. Retrieved September 25, 2020, from https://fortune.com/2020/06/29/59-of-ceos-implemented-hiring-freezes-during-the-pandemic-fortune-survey/

Leah Asmelash and Aaron Cooper (2020). Nearly 80 % of Hotel Rooms in the US are Empty, According to New Data, CNN. Retrieved July 2, 2020, from https://edition.cnn.com/2020/04/08/us/hotel-rooms-industry-coronavirus-trnd/index.html

Linda A. Dimeff, Melanie S. Harned, Eric A. Woodcock, Julie M. Skutch, Kelly Koerner and Marsha M. Linehan (2015). Investigating Bang for Your Training Buck: A Randomized Controlled Trial Comparing Three Methods of Training Clinicians in Two Core Strategies of Dialectical Behavior Therapy, Behavior Therapy, 46(3), 283–295.

Logo Blog (2020, September 7). Pandemi Süreci Bordro ve İnsan Kaynakları Uygulamalarını Nasıl Etkiledi? Retrieved October 12, 2020, from https://blog.logo.com.tr/pandemi-sureci-bordro-ve-insan-kaynaklari-uygulamalarini-nasil-etkiledi/

Lynette Harris (2003). Home-Based Teleworking and the Employment Relationship Managerial Challenges and Dilemmas. Personnel Review, 32(4), 422–437.

Madeleine Petzer (2020). Coronavirus and the Workforce: How Can We Limit Redundancies? CIPD. Retrieved November 25, 2020, from https://www.cipd.co.uk/news-views/changing-work-views/future-work/thought-pieces/coronavirus-workforce-redundancies

Mahmut Özer (2020, May 18). Covid 19 Salgını Sonrası Dünyada Eğitim, TC Milli Eğitim Bakanlığı. Retrieved July 2, 2020, from https://www.meb.gov.tr/covid-19-salgini-sonrasi-dunyada-egitim/haber/20936/tr

Manpower Grup (2020). COVID-19 Business Impact Survey. Retrieved September 25, 2020, from https://www.manpower.com.tr/mp-include/uploads/2020/08/COVID-19-business-impact-survey.pdf

Maureen Milford (2020). The Compensation Impact of COVID-19. Retrieved September 25, 2020, from https://www.privatecompanydirector.com/news/compensation-impact-COVID-19

Mehmet Karakaş (2020). COVID-19 Salgınının Çok Boyutlu Sosyolojisi ve Yeni Normal Meselesi, İstanbul Üniversitesi Sosyoloji Dergisi, 40(1), 541–573.

Meltem Akca and Mübeyyen Tepe Küçükoğlu (2020). COVID-19 ve İş Yaşamına Etkileri: Evden Çalışma, Journal of International Management, Educational and Economics Perspectives, 8(1), 71–81.

Mercer (2020, May). Compensation and Benefits Impacts of COVID-19. Retrieved July 2, 2020, from https://www.me.mercer.com/content/dam/mercer/attachments/private/me/me-2020-Mercer-GCC-COVID-19-C&B-Response-Survey.pdf

Mercer Türkiye (2020). Mercer Türkiye ve PERYÖN İşbirliğinde Gerçekleştirilen Koronavirüs Salgının İş Hayatına Etkisi Anketi'nin Sonuçları Açıklandı. Retrieved July 2, 2020, from https://www.mercer.com.tr/basin-odasi-haberler/peryon-nisan-2020-koronavirus-turkiye-arastirmasi-basin-bulteni.html

Michael Armstrong (2009). Armstrong's Handbook of Human Resource Management Practice, 11th Edition, Kogan Page, London.

Michael Moses, Louise McLean and Christopher Bumstead (2020). Managing Performance in a Virtual World, Marsh & McLennan Companies. Retrieved September 25, 2020, from https://www.mmc.com/insights/publications/2020/july/managing-performance-in-a-virtual-world.html

Milliyet (2020, May 10). Kovid-19 ile Uzaktan Eğitime Talep Arttı. Retrieved July 2, 2020, from https://www.milliyet.com.tr/ekonomi/kovid-19-ile-uzaktan-egitime-talep-artti-6209027

Mine M. Afacan Fındıklı and Murat Celep (2018). The Effects of Electronic Human Resources Practices on Organizational Outcomes: A Study on Foreign Enterprise Insurance Companies in Turkey, Bilgi Ekonomisi ve Yönetimi Dergisi, 13(1), 63–77.

Nancy W. Coppola and Robert Myre (2002). Corporate Software Training: Is Web-Based Training as Effective as Instructor-Led Training? IEEE Transactions on Professional Communication, 45(3), 170–186.

Naveen Donthu and Anders Gustafsson (2020). Effects of COVID-19 on Business and Research, Journal of Business Research 117, 284–289.

OECD (2021a). GDP Projections. Retrieved February 20, 2021, from https://www.oecd.org/economic-outlook/

OECD (2021b). Unemployment Rate. Retrieved February 20, 2021, from https://data.oecd.org/unemp/unemployment-rate.htm

OECD (2021c). Unemployment Rate. Retrieved February 20, 2021, from https://data.oecd.org/unemp/unemployment-rate.htm

Official Gazette (1999). 4447 sayılı İşsizlik Sigortası Kanunu, Sayı: 23810. Retrieved September 25, 2020, from https://www.mevzuat.gov.tr/MevzuatMetin/1.5.4447.pdf

Olena Boichenko and Natalia Tymchenko (2020). How to Reduce the Pandemic Impact on Employees: A Guide for Company Leaders, Deloitte. Retrieved September 20, 2020, from https://www2.deloitte.com/ua/en/pages/human-capital/articles/impact-of-COVID-19.html

Olgar Ataseven (2020). COVID 19: İK'nın Teknolojiyle Sınavı, PERYÖN Popüler Yönetim Dergisi, Nisan Özel Sayısı (86), 12.

Para & Borsa (2020, May 11). Çalışanlar Eve Kapanınca Şirketler Uzaktan Eğitime Sarıldı. Retrieved July 2, 2020, from https://www.paraborsa.net/i/calisanlar-eve-kapaninca-sirketler-uzaktan-egitime-sarildi/

Paula Caligiuri, Helen De Cieri, Dana Minbaeva, Alain Verbeke and Angelika Zimmermann (2020). International HRM Insights for Navigating the COVID-19 Pandemic: Implications for Future Research and Practice, Journal of International Business Studies, 51, 697–713.

Polat Tunçer (2012). Değişen İnsan Kaynakları Yönetimi Anlayışında Kariyer Yönetimi, Ondokuz Mayıs Üniversitesi Eğitim Fakültesi Dergisi, 31(1), 203–233.

Roy Maurer (2020a, May 17). Job Interviews Go Virtual in Response to COVID-19, Society for Human Resource Management (SHRM). Retrieved July 2, 2020, from https://www.shrm.org/resourcesandtools/hr-topics/talent-acquisition/pages/job-interviews-go-virtual-response-COVID-19-coronavirus.aspx

Roy Maurer (2020b, April 2). Companies Look to Cut Costs with Hiring Freezes, Society for Human Resource Management (SHRM). Retrieved July 2, 2020, from https://www.shrm.org/resourcesandtools/hr-topics/talent-acquisition/pages/companies-cut-costs-with-hiring-freezes.aspx

Sabahattin Yürekli (2020). Çalışma Hayatında Koronavirüs (COVID-19) Salgınının Etkileri, İstanbul Ticaret Üniversitesi Sosyal Bilimler Dergisi COVID-19 Hukuk Özel Sayısı, 19(38), 34–61.

Sameer Hasija (2020, June 1). Will the Pandemic Push Knowledge Work into the Gig Economy? Harward Business Review. Retrieved July 2, 2020, from https://hbr.org/2020/06/will-the-pandemic-push-knowledge-work-into-the-gig-economy

Scott D. Johnson, Steven R. Aragon and Najmuddin Shaik (2000). Comparative Analysis of Learner Satisfaction and Learning Outcomes in Online and Face-to-Face Learning Environments, *Journal of Interactive Learning Research*, 11(1), 29–49.

Seymour Adler (2020). Performance Management in the Year of COVID-19: Carpe Diem, Kincentrick. Retrieved October 12, 2020, from https://www.kincentric.com/insights/performance-management-in-the-year-of-covid19-carpe-diem

Sreeni Kutam (2020). How HR Can Use Technology to Impact Career Development, The Spark Newsletter. Retrieved July 2, 2020, from https://www.adp.com/spark/articles/2020/02/how-hr-can-use-technology-to-impact-career-development.aspx

Statista (2020). Unemployment Rates. Retrieved November 25, 2020, from https://www.statista.com/search/?q=unemployment%20rate

Sully Barrett (2020, March 30). Coronavirus Jobs Survey: 49 % of Companies Considering Layoffs, More than One-Third Freezing New Hires, CNBC. Retrieved July 2, 2020, from https://www.cnbc.com/2020/03/30/coronavirus-jobs-survey-49percent-of-companies-considering-layoffs.html

Sunny Chawla (2020, July 24). 8 Tips How COVID-19 Effect on Recruitment, Human Engineers. Retrieved September 25, 2020, from https://humanengineers.com/8-tips-how-COVID-19-effect-on-recruitment/

Supardi Supardi and Syamsul Hadi (2020). New Perspective on the Resilience of SMEsProactive, Adaptive, Reactive from Business Turbulence: A Systematic Review, Journal of Xi'an University of Architecture & Technology, 12(5), 1265–1275.

Susan L. Brady, Noel Rao, Patricia J. Gibbons, Letha Williams, Mark Hakel and Theresa Pape (2018). Face-to-Face Versus Online Training for the Interpretation of Findings in the Fiberoptic Endoscopic Exam of the Swallow Procedure, Advances in Medical Education and Practice, 9, 433–441.

Susie Quirk (2020, July 2). COVID-19: HR Transformation, KMPG Insights. Retrieved September 25, 2020, from https://home.kpmg/au/en/home/insights/2020/07/coronavirus-COVID-19-hr-transformation.html

Thinktech (2020). COVID-19 Sonrası Çalışma Hayatının Geleceği. Retrieved July 2, 2020, from https://thinktech.stm.com.tr/uploads/raporlar/pdf/296202010257354_stm_blog_covid_19_sonrasi_calisma_hayatinin.pdf

Tom Starner (2020a, July). How HR Tech Can Help Manage COVID Compensation Changes, Human Resource Executive. Retrieved September 25, 2020, from https://hrexecutive.com/how-hr-tech-can-help-manage-covid-compensation-changes/

Tom Starner (2020b, August). What COVID means to compensation, Human Resource Executive. Retrieved September 25, 2020, from https://hrexecutive.com/what-covid-means-to-compensation/

Tristram Hooley (2012). How the Internet Changed Career: Framing the Relationship Between Career Development and Online Technologies, Journal of the National Institute for Career Education and Counselling (NICEC), Issue 29, 3–12.

Tristram Hooley (2017). Developing Your Career: Harnessing the Power of the Internet for "Digital Career Management", Development and Learning in Organizations: An International Journal, 31(1), 9–11.

TRT Haber (2020, February 26). Koronavirüs Lufthansa'yı vurdu: İşe alımlar durduruldu. Retrieved July 2, 2020, from https://www.trthaber.com/haber/dunya/koronavirus-lufthansayi-vurdu-ise-alimlar-durduruldu-463293.html

TRT World (2020, November). Beyond the Axe? A COVID-19 "War Game" that Wants to Save Jobs. Retrieved November 22, 2020, from https://www.trtworld.com/magazine/beyond-the-axe-a-COVID-19-wargame-that-wants-to-save-jobs-41404

Turkstat (2021). Employment, Unemployment and Wages. Retrieved March 10, 2021, from, https://data.tuik.gov.tr/Kategori/GetKategori?p=istihdam-issizlik-ve-ucret-108&dil=2

Worldometers (2021). COVID-19 Coronavirus Pandemic. Retrieved March 10, 2021 https://www.worldometers.info/coronavirus/?

Yanjun Guan, Hong Deng and Xinyi Zhou (2020). Understanding the Impact of the COVID-19 Pandemic on Career Development: Insights from Cultural Psychology, Journal of Vocational Behavior, 119. Retrieved November 22, 2020, from https://www.ncbi.nlm.nih.gov/pmc/articles/PMC7204647/

Yusuf Balcı and Güldenur Çetin (2020). COVID-19 Pandemi Sürecinin Türkiye'de İstihdama Etkileri ve Kamu Açısından Alınması Gereken Tedbirler, İstanbul Ticaret Üniversitesi Sosyal Bilimler Dergisi COVID-19 Sosyal Bilimler Özel Sayısı, 19(37), 40–58.

Zeyyat Sabuncuoğlu (2005). İnsan Kaynakları Yönetimi, Alfa Yayınları, Bursa.

Fatih Sarıoğlu[*]
Gözde Nalbant Efe[**]

Effects of COVID-19 on Turkish Higher Education

Abstract In this study, we aim to examine how global pandemic and distance learning practices affect students' achievement levels in Turkish Higher Education. Using the results of a survey conducted with 570 students from Istanbul Medeniyet University Faculty of Political Sciences, we study the effects of the changing learning environment on success grades of students. Firstly, we compare the GPAs of students between the periods of 2019–2020 Fall and Spring Semester, which in the latter we have confronted with COVID-19 pandemic and applied online teaching methods with the closure of schools. We document the positive effect of pandemic on students' achievement levels between the two semesters. Then we compare the GPAs amongst students in the spring semester to analyze if their opportunities for reaching online education have affected their success. We document the negative effect of pandemic on students' achievement levels that have fewer opportunities to use technological devices and for connection to internet than the others do in the period of the spring semester. Connection method of students to the courses did not cause a difference in terms of achievement levels among students because most of the students in our sample are able to connect to lessons somehow. Finally we found no significant effect of students' gender or spatial opportunities on their achievement levels.

Keywords: educational technology, opportunity equality, distance learning

INTRODUCTION

The outbreak of Coronavirus (COVID-19) that began in China on December 1, 2019, has expanded throughout the world in a couple of months. The World Health Organization declared it "a global pandemic" on March 11, 2020 (WHO, 2020). The number of infections and deaths has increased rapidly around the world. This situation has forced governments to implement various restrictions

---

[*] Prof., Istanbul Medeniyet University, Faculty of Political Sciences, Department of Public Finance, fatih.sarioglu@medeniyet.edu.tr
[**] Res. Asst., Istanbul Medeniyet University, Faculty of Political Sciences, Department of Public Finance, gozde.nalbant@medeniyet.edu.tr

such as foreign travel controls, limitations on internal movement, social distance measures, etc. to prevent the spread in the country. The COVID-19 pandemic has also affected educational systems, leading to the closure of schools of almost all levels worldwide.

In response to school closures because of the outbreak and measures to implement social distancing, UNESCO and many governments have recommended the use of distance learning, open educational applications, and online teaching to reduce disruption to education (UNESCO, 2020b). In Turkey, as a precautionary measure to prevent the outbreak of the pandemic similar to other countries, most education institutions including higher education have started to distance education on March 23.

This study is organized as follows. In the first part the concept of equal opportunities in education is discussed, and the opportunities and inequalities created by distance education with the COVID-19 period are evaluated. Second and third parts of the study, developments in higher education in the world and Turkey with the spread of the pandemic are briefly discussed. In the fourth part, the effects of the transition to distance education on students' achievement levels were examined by using various statistical methods. The sample of the analysis consists of students from Istanbul Medeniyet University, Faculty of Political Sciences. Firstly, their success grades between the periods of 2019–2020 Fall and Spring Semester are compared, which in the latter the world has confronted with COVID-19 pandemic. Then their success grades amongst themselves in the Spring Semester are compared to analyze if their opportunities for reaching the online education have affected their success. The last part of the study concludes and points out directions for further research.

1. COVID-19 and Opportunity Equality in Education

From the perspective of public economics, education is a rival and excludable good. At the same time, some positive externalities to education justify the inclusion of government in its provision. When the education level increases in a society, the productivity of workers increases, the quality of democratic processes improves and a higher standard of living can be reached. On the other hand, when government intervenes in education, low-income people have a chance to raise their incomes, so the government makes sure income mobility is promoted (Gruber, 2013: 293–296). Society benefits from all these positive externalities when the education level increases. To make sure the maximization of social welfare, governments must intervene in the provision of education services. The efficiency rationale of public provision is externalities both civic and economic. The equity rationale is equality of opportunity rather than equality of results (Ulbrich, 2003: 344).

In the public economics literature, it is stated that higher education is different from primary and secondary education. More of the benefits accrue to the student and less to society as a whole in the form of higher lifetime earnings (Ulbrich, 2003: 362). According to empirical researches, the economic returns for higher education graduates are the highest in the entire educational system. After completing higher education, it is estimated a 15 % increase in earnings as compared with 11 % for primary and 7 % for secondary education (Montenegro and Patrinos, 2014: 12). Private institutions play a much greater role in higher education than in primary and secondary education. Nevertheless, the public share in the provision is still quite large in most of the countries just as in Turkey.

The first argument for publicly supported higher education is equity. Equality of opportunity requires access to higher education. The second argument is the benefits of society from research and development, which comes from a publicly funded objective source. Besides, the other arguments can be sorted like market failures for private financing, benefits for economic development, etc. (Ulbrich, 2003: 363).

Equality of opportunity means to promote equal chances of access to education for all students, education institutes must be open to all students regardless of their income, ethnic or cultural origin, gender, color, or any disability may have. In other words, factors specific to one's personal conditions should not interfere with the potential of academic success (OECD, 2008: 2). After the COVID-19 pandemic, the conditions determining the availability and affordability of education have changed. According to Pedro (2020) who is the Director of UNESCO International Institute for Higher Education in Latin America and the Caribbean (UNESCO-IESALC), the COVID-19 crisis affects differently on different student profiles, but it is undeniable that it deepens existing inequalities and generates new ones. According to Onyema et al. (2020: 114), the realities of receiving distance education from home could be very challenging to many students especially those in developing countries where the accessibility, availability, and use of technology in education are not widespread.

Attending online classes requires long hours of internet connection, peaceful space to focus on the lessons and one device or phone dedicated to each student in a family and these might not be affordable for everyone (Bania and Banerjee, 2020: 6). Affordability is another important factor to limit access to distance education, such that students from economically weaker sections of the society are facing a greater burden. The impact of accessibility and affordability can have serious implications on students in the higher education system. Thus, governments should adopt student-friendly policies and make sure that every student can access and afford an internet connection (Rashid and Yadav, 2020: 342).

The challenges students can encounter with the transition to distance education can be collected under three headings according to IAU (2020: 24):

1. Technical infrastructure and accessibility,
2. Distance learning competencies and pedagogies,
3. The field of study.

Infrastructure and internet access are a prerequisite for distance learning. If students do not have an adequate internet connection, a technical device and a peaceful space, learning is fully disrupted and they will not complete the academic year. There will also be a divide between students who have access and the device, and those who do not (Di Pietro et al. 2020:4). The other important factor for successful distance education is that a different pedagogy is required for distance teaching and learning. The field of study determines the efficiency of distance learning experience. If students need access to laboratories as in clinical medicine, veterinary studies, etc. or if they need to perform or practice face to face as in arts, music, and design disciplines, etc. it has potential to affect the educational services adversely.

On the other hand, distance education may offer additional advantages and opportunities for students, which they do not have in formal education. Students spend less time to reach the learning content, just sitting in front of the computer, tablet or mobile phone and not leaving home. Individuals who are unable to attend a traditional full-time face-to-face university due to personal or financial circumstances are now having access to education more easily. Besides, the flexibility of asynchronous distance learning may provide wider access. If a student miss the class, she can watch the video recording whenever and wherever she is convenient. Moreover, even within traditional higher education institutions, hybrid or blended forms may improve the quality of face-to-face teaching by moving the course content delivery to online platforms (Bowen, 2012). It is therefore possible that this experience can open a new horizon of opportunities for teaching and learning. In the period after COVID-19, flexible and digital learning can become more accepted and integrated with study plans. In addition, the assessment and examination methods can be reviewed after this experience and methods that are more flexible can be applied with the inclusion of successful online experiences (IAU, 2020: 26).

2. The Effects of COVID-19 on Higher Education around the World

According to the estimates of the Institute for Statistics (UNESCO), there are 227.5 million students in higher education all over the world in 2019 (UIS, 2020). The COVID-19 pandemic caused the closure of universities around the world with government instructions to keep people social distancing, which could reduce the pace of the outbreak. China became the first to close all universities and schools around the country on 26, January (China Daily, 2020). Then with the quick spread of the virus, many countries enacted preventive measures including the temporary or permanent closure of schools and universities. As of mid-March, over 70 % of the students in the world were affected by school closures (UNESCO, 2020a). By mid-April, 192 countries have implemented nationwide closures, about 1.725 billion students which correspond to 99 % of the world's total student population had been affected by the closure of schools and universities (Reddy, Soudien and Winaar, 2020).

Due to the crisis caused by the coronavirus pandemic, innovations in academia and higher education, which would normally take several years due to various administrative regulations, were implemented within a few weeks (Strielkowski, 2020:1). According to the survey of IAU (International Association of Universities) (2020: 23) between March 25 and April 17, two-thirds of higher education institutions were able to move to teach online while one-third was not. As of May, the majority of them were working on developing solutions to begin to teach online.

The results of the regional analysis of COVID-19 impact on higher education are reported in Table 1:

Table 1: Impact of COVID-19 on Higher Education Teaching and Learning by Region

	Not affected	Classroom teaching replaced by distance teaching and learning	Teaching suspended but the institutions are developing solutions	Teaching canceled
Africa	3 %	29 %	43 %	24 %
Americas	3 %	72 %	22 %	3 %
Asia & Pacific	1 %	60 %	36 %	3 %
Europe	Almost zero	85 %	12 %	3 %

Source: IAU, 2020: 24.

The table shows that the percentage of teaching canceled is very low except in Africa. Only 29 % of African universities were able to move quickly teaching online compared to 85 % of universities in Europe. It can be said that a vast "digital inequality" exists in societies around the world (Rashid and Yadav, 2020: 342). This situation shows that there is no equality of opportunities in education provision during the pandemic, especially for underdeveloped and developing countries.

The use of educational technologies facilitated online education, student-teacher interactions, and connections. There are broad ranges of platforms that facilitate online education particularly in times of outbreaks like the Coronavirus pandemic. Some of these technology platforms are Zoom, Edmodo, Google Classroom, Skype, GoToMeeting, etc. Nevertheless, the internet infrastructure of the countries and the level of students and educators' having technical equipment determined whether the education will continue online or not. For example, Gimenez, Gavira ve Bonacelli (2020) reported that the Brazilian federal higher education system has not been able to maintain educational activities, leaving over 60 % of students without classes. Many students did not have the access to the technology needed to attend online classes (computers, high-speed internet, etc.). Distance learning showed profound digital inequality in Brazil, making it impossible for many students to follow the classes properly.

Onyema et al. (2020) surveyed the effects of COVID-19 on education in Saudi Arabia, Nigeria, India, and Bangladesh. According to the results, educational activities seemed badly affected in these countries. Pandemic decreased the educational opportunities especially for students who are underprivileged or in rural areas. More than 70 % of the respondents of the survey agreed that inadequate facilities such as lack of computer, internet facility, were the major factors that limited their engagement in online education. Similarly, poor electricity service, unavailability and accessibility issues, network issues, etc. also created many problems for education in these countries. Bania ve Banerjee (2020) state that digital impossibilities in India have caused higher education enrollment rates to decline. In urban areas in India, only 42 % of households have an internet connection and in rural areas, this rate is less than 15 %. The poorest households cannot afford a smartphone or computer. The authors underline that the pandemic has revealed the deeply rooted inequality and hierarchy between the rich and poor in the Indian education system. Thus to eliminate this inequality, they suggest that internet and technology services should be considered as a necessity and not a luxury in their country.

In countries where the majority of students have access to distance education, this changed learning environment had different effects on students in terms of various factors. For example, Godonoga ve Gruszka (2020) surveyed the satisfaction levels of students on the readiness of their institutions for distance learning in Poland during the COVID-19 outbreak. According to survey results, satisfaction levels were lowest among specializations that require practical, creative, or lab-based work and highest among specializations that are based on verbal and social communication. Instructors' self-motivation was identified as a key enabler of a successful implementation of distance learning while instructors' lack of experience with e-learning and technology is seen as a key barrier to it. The authors also criticized that the lack of a coherent national strategy to help higher education institutions cope with the crisis led to a state of confusion and uncertainty for universities. Because responsibility for devising a solution was delegated to the universities, disparities in readiness across institutions have affected the satisfaction levels of students in different directions. Adedoyin and Soykan (2020: 6) also highlighted that the compatibility of distance learning with social science and humanities has been proved effective while it is contested its compatibility with sports sciences, engineering and medical sciences where hands-on practical experiences are required as part of instructional activities has been resulted ineffective.

On the other hand, there are also studies revealing that pandemic positively affected the success level in higher education. For example, Gonzalez et al. (2020) analyzed the effects of COVID-19 confinement on the learning performance of students in higher education in Spain, Madrid, and showed that there is a positive effect of confinement on students' performance. They explained this improvement in their scores with changes in students' learning strategies during the isolation. Before the confinement, students did not study continuously. Yet with the measures adopted to slow down the outbreak of the pandemic, their habits of studying changed to a more continuous basis, and the efficiency of learning has improved.

In summary, with the COVID-19 pandemic, higher education had to experience widespread distance education all over the world. Although this new education model has been adapted rapidly in developed countries, it has also been observed that it has sometimes become an obstacle to access to education especially in developing and less developed countries. In countries where adaptation is achieved successfully, it can be a factor that can increase student success but on the other hand it cannot be effectively and efficiently applied in some disciplines and this compatibility gap is yet to be filled. In this context, studies that country-specific and/or indigenous to different disciplines on this subject should be carried out in the future.

3. The Effects of COVID-19 on Higher Education in Turkey

Turkey is a country where the youthful population has a high proportion of the total population. As of last year, the young population in the 15–24 age group was calculated as 12.9 million. This corresponds to 15.6 % of Turkey's total population, which is 83 million (TÜİK, 2020). The total number of students in tertiary education is 7.9 million in the period of 2019–2020 academic year.

Table 2: Number of Students in Turkish Higher Education

	Public University	Foundation University	Total
Associate's degree	2.845.301	157.663	3.002.964
Bachelor's degree	4.145.428	393.498	4.538.926
Master's degree	239.072	57.929	297.001
Doctoral degree	90.648	10.594	101.242
Total	7.320.449	608.123	7.940.133

Source: YÖK (2020a). Yükseköğretim Bilgi Yönetim Sistemi, https://istatistik.yok.gov.tr/.

As can be seen from Table 2, approximately 7.9 million university students in Turkey continue their education within 209 universities. Higher education is mostly provided by the public sector in Turkey. 92.2 % of the students are enrolled in 129 public universities and the rest of them are students of 78 foundation universities.

A central public institution in Turkey named YOK (the Council of Higher Education in Turkey) is responsible for the strategic planning of higher education, the coordination between universities, and most importantly establishing and maintaining quality assurance mechanisms for all higher education institutions. During the outbreak in the spring semester, all universities in Turkey have simultaneously implemented the measures determined and coordinated by YOK. By the call of YOK on February 4, all higher education institutions have taken necessary and precautionary measures for the Coronavirus outbreak. On March 6, measures regarding the international mobility of students and academicians were announced. On March 11, the day when the first coronavirus case was confirmed in the country, a meeting was held in the YOK building with the participation of rectors and it has been decided that every university would establish a "Coronavirus Board" and be in connection with YOK directly and constantly. As of March 16, education at all universities was suspended for a week and the opportunities and capacities of universities for distance education were determined in the meantime. As of March 23, many higher institutions in Turkey have started to distance education (YOK, 2020b).

Two years ago, YOK started intensive programs for academics and students through the "Digital Transformation Project at Universities." With the aim of increasing social justice, 6,000 lecturers from 16 universities in economically underdeveloped regions took preparation courses in digital course material preparation, and a digital competency course was put on the curriculum of more than 50,000 students for credit. In the light of these experiences, YOK was able to organize the education of distance educators in universities immediately after transition to distance education.

Considering the youth population in Turkey, in addition to formal education, distance and open education applications are also applied widely in universities and 128 universities currently have distance education centers. All digital courses in the universities' course pools were opened to access through the interface, called YOK Courses (Courses of Higher Education Institutions), created on March 23 to meet the content needs of universities, and it was decided to add digital course materials of other universities to this pool. As of April 29, YOK also made a 6 GB distance education support internet quota for all higher education students to use when reaching the "YOK Courses" platform. It was noted that the course content, links, or other directions provided by universities via Zoom, Teams, YouTube, and similar tools would be excluded from this supported quota and therefore, these usages will be charged by deducting from the quota of students' internet packages belonging to their operators (YOK, 2020c). In this context, some public and foundation universities (for example, Marmara University, Boğaziçi University, Istanbul City University, Mardin Artuklu University, etc.), which have the financial opportunity, started to provide monthly internet scholarships to their students to avoid problems in terms of internet quota.

In addition to these, YOK announced additional measures to heal the aggrievement of students in higher education regarding internships, professional exams, etc. It was also decided that if they request, the students from all levels of universities would freeze their enrollments in the spring semester of the 2019–2020 academic year without any reduction in their maximum duration (YOK, 2020b).

Prof. Saraç (2020), the president of YOK, states that although some students living in rural areas have had problems accessing the system due to problems with internet connections and facilities, local municipalities and authorities are trying to find solutions to the problem. Otherwise, the online education system is working appropriately in Turkey.

4. An Analysis of the Effects of COVID-19 on Students' Achievement Levels

Istanbul Medeniyet University is one of the public universities in Turkey, which was found on July 21, 2010. It has 7554 students in the 2019–2020 academic year, 1264 of them are students of the Faculty of Political Sciences. In line with the decisions taken by YOK, Istanbul Medeniyet University has started distance education as of March 23. In this teaching process, the Edmodo learning management system and Zoom virtual classroom creation applications were used in addition to the existing UZEM (Distance Education Center) infrastructure.

In the Faculty of Political Sciences, a survey was conducted in April 2020, to determine the technological needs of the students after the transition to distance education. 570 students of the faculty answered the survey, which includes questions about the technological and spatial opportunities of the students. At the end of the academic year, the students' fall and spring semester GPAs, and the answers given to the survey were gathered and the effect of the COVID-19 on students' achievement levels was analyzed.

In this part of the study, firstly, we compare the students' average scores before and after COVID-19 and we examine whether there is a statistically significant difference between them. Afterwards, taking advantage of the survey conducted with students in the COVID-19 period, we examine whether there is a statistically significant difference between the factors that may affect the GPA of the students in the spring semester when COVID-19 showed its effect and distance education applications were initiated. In order to carry out the relevant analyzes, we first examined whether the GPA series that indicate the success of the students showed normal distribution or not with the Kolmogorov-Smirnov and Shapiro-Wilk test (Alpar, 2017: 105).

Graph 1 shows how GPA values in the fall semester are distributed with histogram representation.

When the histogram distribution is examined, it is seen that the GPA values are not normally distributed. However, we applied the normality tests to confirm this assumption.

The assumptions regarding normality testing are as follows:

H_0: Data has a normal distribution.
H_A: Data does not have a normal distribution.

Although both tests give the same results, the Kolmogorov-Smirnov test statistic value is taken as the basis and the null hypothesis is rejected (p=,000) because the number of observations is higher than fifty (Table 3). It is concluded

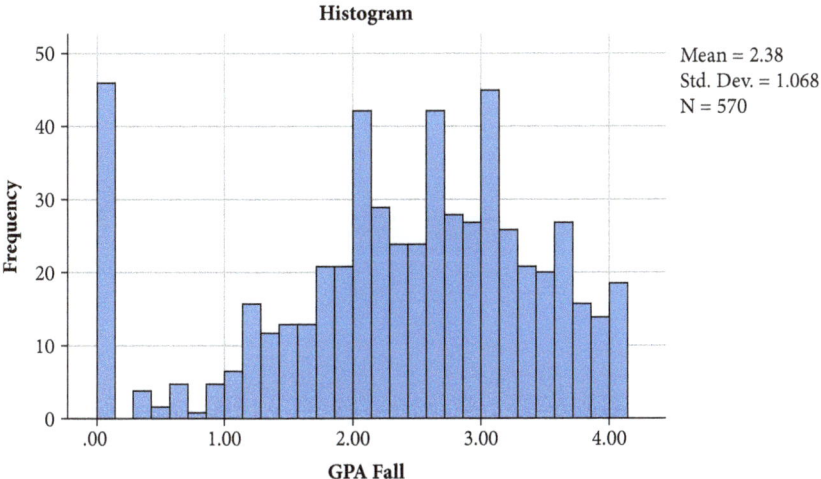

Graph 1: Distribution of GPA in the Fall Semester

Table 3: Test of Normality for GPA Values in the Fall Semester

	Kolmogorov-Smirnov[a]			Shapiro-Wilk		
	Statistic	df	Sig.	Statistic	df	Sig.
GPA Value (Fall)	,076	570	,000	,939	570	,000

a Lilliefors Significance Correction.

that the "GPA Value" variable in the fall semester is not suitable for normal distribution.

Graph 2 shows how GPA values in the spring semester are distributed with histogram representation:

When the histogram distribution is examined, it is seen that the GPA values are not normally distributed. However, we again applied the normality tests to confirm this assumption. The assumptions regarding normality testing are the same.

We take the Kolmogorov-Smirnov test statistic value from Table 4 as the basis and the null hypothesis is rejected (p=,000). We conclude that the "GPA Value" variable in the Spring Semester is not suitable for normal distribution.

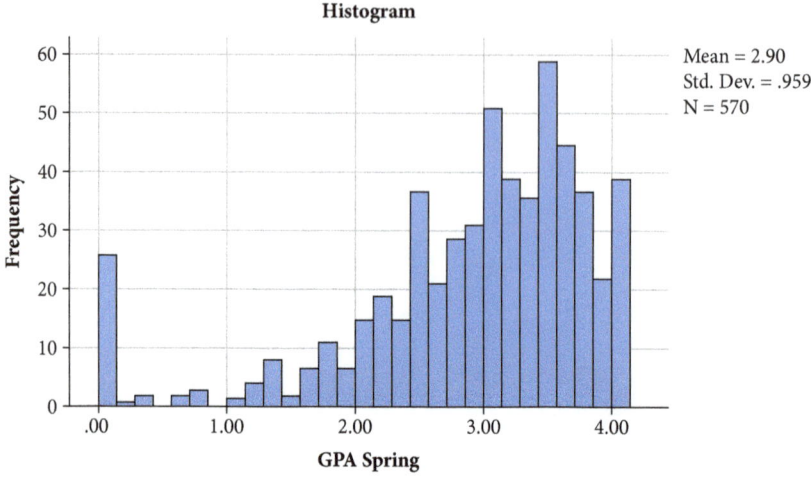

Graph 2: Distribution of GPA in the Spring Semester

Table 4: Test of Normality for GPA Values in the Spring Semester

	Kolmogorov-Smirnov[a]			Shapiro-Wilk		
	Statistic	df	Sig.	Statistic	df	Sig.
GPA Value (Spring)	,125	570	,000	,859	570	,000

a Lilliefors Significance Correction.

The findings show that both GPA series are not normally distributed. In this case, the normality assumption, which is the prerequisite of parametric tests, cannot be achieved. For this reason, in the next sections of this study, to compare the means of dependent groups the Wilcoxon Signed-rank test will be used and to compare the means of independent groups the Mann-Whitney U (1947) and Kruskall-Wallis (1952) tests will be used.

4.1. Comparison of Students' Achievement Levels between Two Semesters

We start by viewing the descriptive statistics about GPA in both semesters:

As can be seen from Table 5, the mean value of the GPA in the fall semester is 2,38 and the median value is 2,56. On the other hand, the mean value of the

Effects of COVID-19 on Turkish Higher Education

Table 5: Descriptives of GPA in the Fall and Spring Semester

		Fall Semester		Spring Semester	
		Statistic	Std. Error	Statistic	Std. Error
Mean		**2,3816**	,04475	**2,8955**	,04016
95 % Confidence Interval for Mean	Lower Bound	2,2938		2,8166	
	Upper Bound	2,4695		2,9743	
5 % Trimmed Mean		**2,4255**		**2,9934**	
Median		**2,5650**		**3,1300**	
Variance		1,141		,919	
Std. Deviation		1,06831		,95888	
Minimum		,00		,00	
Maximum		4,00		4,00	
Range		4,00		4,00	
Interquartile Range		1,32		1,08	
Skewness		-,696	,102	-1,444	,102
Kurtosis		-,096	,204	1,957	,204

GPA in the spring semester is 2,89 and the median value is 3,13. If we compare the 5 % trimmed means, the trimmed mean value of the GPA in the fall semester is 2,42 and the trimmed mean value of the GPA in the spring semester is 2,99.

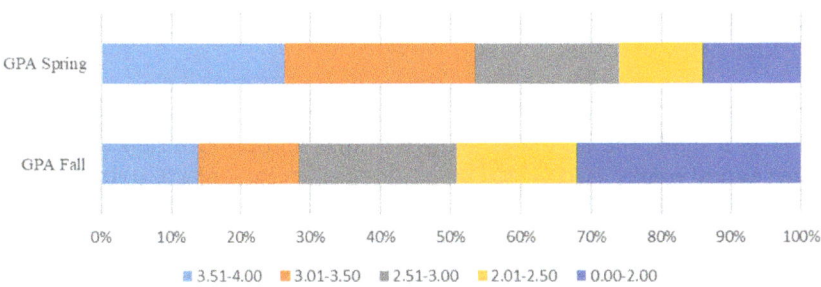

Graph 3: Distribution of GPA According to Different Semesters

By looking at the mean and median values from Tables 4–5 and by examining the relationship between the semesters and GPA categories from Graph 3, it can be said that students' achievement levels are higher in the period of distance learning which came with the COVID-19 outbreak. However, we can statistically test whether the GPA values of students differ in two different semesters.

To analyze the effect of COVID-19 on students' achievement levels between two semesters, we performed a Wilcoxon Signed Rank Test, which compares two related samples that cannot be assumed to be normally distributed. Because in the previous section of this study, we found that GPA series are not normally distributed. In the analysis related to this subject, the same students were involved in both samples and their average scores are compared before and after COVID-19 and the distance learning experience that came with it.

The assumptions regarding the Wilcoxon Signed Rank Test are as follows:

H_0: There is a significant difference between the means.
H_A: There is no significant difference between the means.

Table 6: Wilcoxon Signed Rank Test for GPA Values of Two Semesters-1

Ranks				
		N	Mean Rank	Sum of Ranks
GPA Fall - GPA Spring	Negative Ranks	420[a]	287,08	120573,50
	Positive Ranks	119[b]	209,72	24956,50
	Ties	31[c]		
	Total	570		

a GPA Fall < GPA Spring.
b GPA Fall > GPA Spring.
c GPA Fall = GPA Spring.

Table 6 shows the number of negative ranks and positive ranks obtained based on test results. Accordingly, the GPA Spring values of 420 students were higher than their GPA fall values. The opposite is true for 119 students. 31 students have the same GPA value in both semesters.

Table 7 shows that according to the Wilcoxon Signed Rank Test, the H_0 hypothesis (p = 0,000) can be rejected. There is a statistically significant difference between the GPA Values of the spring and fall semesters. We can say that students' achievement levels are higher in the spring semester.

Table 7: Wilcoxon Signed Rank Test for GPA Values of Two Semesters-2

Test Statistics[a]	
	GPA Fall – GPA Spring
Z	–13,217[b]
Asymp. Sig. (2-tailed)	,000

a Wilcoxon Signed Ranks Test.
b Based on positive ranks.

4.2. Comparison of Students' Achievement Levels amongst Themselves in the Spring Semester

In this section of the study, we examined how COVID-19 and distance learning affect the success level of students among themselves with the help of various independent factors. On this occasion, we aim to determine the new negativities caused by COVID-19 in terms of equal opportunity in education. We asked our students about their methods of connecting to classes, their possibilities of using technological devices, their internet quota, and the places where they access the lessons. According to the answers obtained from these questions, we analyzed whether there was a difference between the students in terms of GPA.

In the previous section, we found that GPA values of the Spring Semester are not normally distributed. Therefore, to analyze the effect of COVID-19 on students' achievement levels amongst themselves; we performed the Kruskall-Wallis and the Mann Whitney U tests, which compare unrelated samples that cannot be assumed to be normally distributed.

4.2.1. Comparison of Students' Achievement Levels According to the Connection Method

The distribution of the answers given to the question asked to the students about "how they connected to the lesson during the distance education period" is as follows:

Table 8 shows 61.8 % of the students participating in the survey connect to lessons from their homes via Wi-Fi, while 25.6 % of them connect by phone, 12.6 % of them do not have internet access at home and connecting to lessons from outside of the home.

In order to match the answers with the GPA values more easily, we created five GPA categories. By classifying the answers in terms of these GPA categories, we obtain the following crosstable.

Table 8: Frequency of Answers about Connection Method

	Frequency	Percent	Cumulative Percent
Connecting with Wi-Fi at home	352	61,8	61,8
Connecting with smartphone at home	146	25,6	87,4
Does not have internet access at home, using the internet of relatives	43	7,5	94,9
Does not have internet access at home, cannot connect	29	5,1	100,0
Total	570	100,0	

Considering the spring semester GPAs of the students participating in the survey who connect to distance education lessons with Wi-Fi access at home, 54.9 % of them have a GPA above 3.00, and 24.5 % of them have a GPA below 2.50. 56.1 % of the students who connect to the lessons by phone at home have a GPA above 3.00 and 28 % have a GPA below 2.50. 48.9 % of the students who access the lessons by using the internet of their relatives have a GPA above 3.00 and 28 % of them have a GPA below 2.50. Only 31 % of the students who do not have internet access at home have a GPA above 3.00, while 37.9 % of them have a GPA below 2.50 (Table 9).

As can be seen in Graphic 4, when we examine the relationship between the opportunities of students regarding the connection method and their GPA categories, it can be said that the success rate decreases as the connection becomes more difficult. Students who are connecting to lessons from their home easily have higher GPAs comparing with the total.

We can also statistically test whether the GPA values of students differ in terms of different connection methods with the Kruskal-Wallis method. The assumptions regarding the Kruskal-Wallis Test are as follows:

H_0: The distribution of GPA Value is the same across categories of Connection Method.

H_A: The distribution of GPA Value is not the same across categories of Connection Method, at least one is different.

The Kruskal-Wallis test results outlined in Table 10 demonstrate that the H_0 hypothesis (p = 0.223) cannot be rejected. Therefore, no statistically significant difference is detected between the methods of connection to lessons and GPA values.

Table 9: Cross-Table of Answers about Connection Method and GPA Category

		GPA Category					Total
		3,51–4,00	3,01–3,50	2,51–3,00	2,01–2,50	0–2,00	
Connecting with Wi-Fi at home	Count	97	96	73	47	39	352
	Percent	*27,6 %*	*27,3 %*	*20,7 %*	*13,4 %*	*11,1 %*	*100 %*
Connecting with smartphone at home	Count	38	44	24	16	24	146
	Percent	*26 %*	*30,1 %*	*16,4 %*	*11 %*	*16,4 %*	*100 %*
Does not have internet access at home, using the internet of relatives	Count	10	11	10	2	10	43
	Percent	*23,3 %*	*25,6 %*	*23,3 %*	*4,7 %*	*23,3 %*	*100 %*
Does not have internet access at home, cannot connect.	Count	5	4	9	4	7	29
	Percent	*17,2 %*	*13,8 %*	*31 %*	*13,8 %*	*24,1 %*	*100 %*
Total	Count	150	155	116	69	80	570
	Percent	*26,3 %*	*27,2 %*	*20,4 %*	*12,1 %*	*14 %*	*100 %*

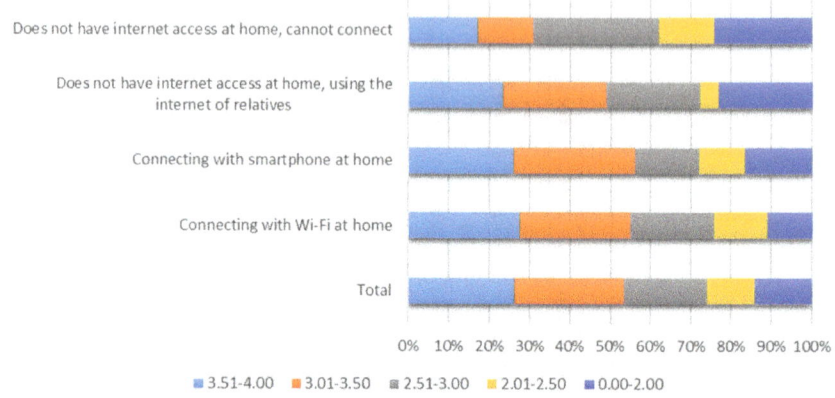

Graph 4: Distribution of GPA According to Connection Method

Table 10: Kruskal-Wallis Test Results for Connection Method

Total N	570
Test Statistic	4,378[a,b]
Degree Of Freedom	3
Asymptotic Sig.(2-sided test)	,223

a The test statistic is adjusted for ties.
b Multiple comparisons are not performed because the overall test does not show significant differences across samples.

4.2.2. Comparison of Students' Achievement Levels According to Internet Quota

The distribution of the answers given to the question asked to the students about "the amount of internet quota on their smartphones during the distance education period" is as follows:

Table 11: Frequency of Answers about Internet Quota

	Frequency	Percent	Cumulative Percent
0–2 GB	66	11,6	11,6
2–5 GB	196	34,4	46,0
5 GB and more	308	54,0	100,0
Total	570	100,0	

Table 11 shows 11.6 % of the students participating in the survey have an internet quota between 0 and 2 GB, while 34.4 % of them have 2–5 GB, and 54 % of them have internet access more than 5 GB on their smartphones. By classifying the answers in terms of the GPA categories, we obtain the following crosstable:

Table 12: Cross-Table of Answers about Internet Quota and GPA Category

		GPA Category					Total
		3,51–4,00	3,01–3,50	2,51–3,00	2,01–2,50	0,00–2,00	
0–2 GB	Count	13	14	16	8	15	66
	Percent	*19,7 %*	*21,2 %*	*24,2 %*	*12,1 %*	*22,7 %*	*100,0 %*
2–5 GB	Count	57	55	36	19	29	196
	Percent	*29,1 %*	*28,1 %*	*18,4 %*	*9,7 %*	*14,8 %*	*100,0 %*
5 GB and more	Count	80	86	64	42	36	308
	Percent	*26,0 %*	*27,9 %*	*20,8 %*	*13,6 %*	*11,7 %*	*100,0 %*
Total	Count	150	155	116	69	80	570
	Percent	*26,3 %*	*27,2 %*	*20,4 %*	*12,1 %*	*14,0 %*	*100,0 %*

Considering the spring semester GPAs of the students participating in the survey who have an internet quota between 0 and 2 GB, 40.9 % of them have a GPA above 3.00, and 34.8 % of them have a GPA below 2.50. 57.2 % of the students who have an internet quota between 2 and 5 GB have a GPA above 3.00 and 24.5 % have a GPA below 2.50. 53.9 % of the students who have internet access opportunities more than 5 GB have a GPA above 3.00 and 25.3 % of them have a GPA below 2.50 (Table 12).

As can be seen in Graphic 5, when we examine the relationship between the students' internet quotas and their GPA categories, it can be said students who have more internet use opportunities have higher GPAs, and students who have limited internet use opportunities have lower GPAs comparing with total.

We can also statistically test whether the GPA values of students differ in terms of different internet quotas with the Kruskal-Wallis method. The assumptions regarding the Kruskal-Wallis test are similar to the section before.

The Kruskal-Wallis test results in Table 13 prove that the null hypothesis ($p = 0.045$) can be rejected. There is a statistically significant difference between internet quotas of students and the GPA values. Then we examine the paired comparison results to determine from which category the difference originated.

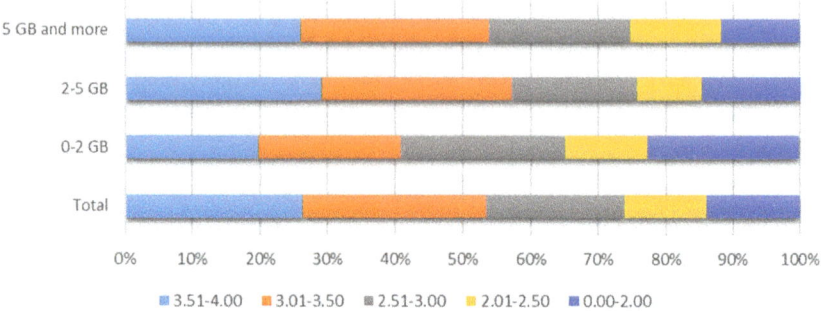

Graph 5: Distribution of GPA According to Interned Quota

Table 13: Kruskal-Wallis Test Results for Internet Quota

Total N	570
Test Statistic	6,195[a]
Degree of Freedom	2
Asymptotic Sig.(2-sided test)	,045

a The test statistic is adjusted for ties.

When we evaluate the results of the pairwise analysis, the average GPA values of the students with internet quota between 0 and 2 GB are found to be statistically significantly lower than those with 2–5 GB internet quota and 5 GB and above (Table 14). In other words, the achievement levels of students with lower internet access opportunities are lower than the others.

4.2.3. Comparison of Students' Achievement Levels According to Technological Device Owning

The distribution of the answers given to the question asked to the students about "the possibilities of using smartphones, personal computers, shared computers, tablets, and similar technological devices while connecting to lessons during the distance education period" is as follows:

Table 15 shows 29.3 % of the students participating in the survey does not have any device except a smartphone, while 26.3 % of them does not have a personal computer but sharing a computer or tablet with household, 32.1 % of them have a personal computer, and 12.3 % of the students are able to use

Table 14: Pairwise Comparisons of Internet Quota

Sample 1-Sample 2	Test Statistic	Std. Error	Std. Test Statistic	Sig.	Adj. Sig.[a]
0–2 GB-5 GB and more	-45,161	22,328	-2,023	,043	,129
0–2 GB-2–5 GB	-58,248	23,427	-2,486	,013	,039
5 GB and more-2–5 GB	13,087	15,041	,870	,384	1,000

Each row tests the null hypothesis that Sample 1 and Sample 2 distributions are the same.
a Asymptotic significances (2-sided tests) are displayed. The significance level is 0,05.

Table 15: Frequency of Technological Device Owning

	Frequency	Percent	Cumulative Percent
Does not have any. Connecting with a smartphone.	167	29,3	29,3
Does not have a personal computer. Using a shared computer or tablet at home	150	26,3	55,6
Personal computer only	183	32,1	87,7
Personal computer plus shared computer or tablet at home.	70	12,3	100,0
Total	570	100,0	

shared computer or tablet besides their personal computer. By classifying the answers in terms of the GPA categories, we obtain the following crosstable:

Considering the spring semester GPAs of the students participating in the survey who does not have any technological device except smartphone, 43.4 % of them have a GPA above 3.00, and 34.4 % of them have a GPA below 2.50. 60.1 % of the students who do not have a personal computer but can access a shared computer or tablet to connect to lessons have a GPA above 3.00 and 22.3 % of them have a GPA below 2.50. Considering the students who have a personal computer, 57.4 % of them have a GPA above 3.00 and 25.3 % of them have a GPA below 2.50. 51.4 % of the students are able to use shared computer or tablet besides their personal computer have a GPA above 3.00 and 25.7 % of them have a GPA below 2.50 (Table 16).

As can be seen in the Graphic 6, when we examine the relationship between the students' technological devices and their GPA categories, it can be said students who have more opportunities using them have higher GPAs, and students who have limited opportunities have lower GPAs comparing with total.

When we statistically test whether the GPA values of students differ in terms of technological device owning with the Kruskal-Wallis method, the results are:

The test results outlined in Table 17 shows the null hypothesis ($p = 0.014$) can be rejected. There is a statistically significant difference between students' technological device owning status and the GPA values. Then we examine the paired comparison results to determine from which category the difference originated.

When we evaluate the analysis results presented in Table 18, the average GPA values of the students who stated that they don't have the opportunity of using a computer or similar device and connecting to lessons only with their

Table 16: Cross-Table of Answers about Technological Device Owning and GPA Category

		GPA Category					Total
		3,51–4,00	3,01–3,50	2,51–3,00	2,01–2,50	1,51–2,00	
Does not have any. Connecting with a smartphone.	Count	36	36	37	21	36	166
	Percent	21,7 %	21,7 %	22,3 %	12,7 %	21,7 %	100,0 %
Does not have a personal computer. Using a shared computer or tablet at home.	Count	53	58	32	22	19	184
	Percent	28,8 %	31,5 %	17,4 %	12,0 %	10,3 %	100,0 %
Personal computer only.	Count	43	43	31	15	18	150
	Percent	28,7 %	28,7 %	20,7 %	10,0 %	12,0 %	100,0 %
Personal computer plus shared computer or tablet at home.	Count	18	18	16	11	7	70
	Percent	25,7 %	25,7 %	22,9 %	15,7 %	10,0 %	100,0 %
Total	Count	150	155	116	69	80	570
	Percent	26,3 %	27,2 %	20,4 %	12,1 %	14,0 %	100,0 %

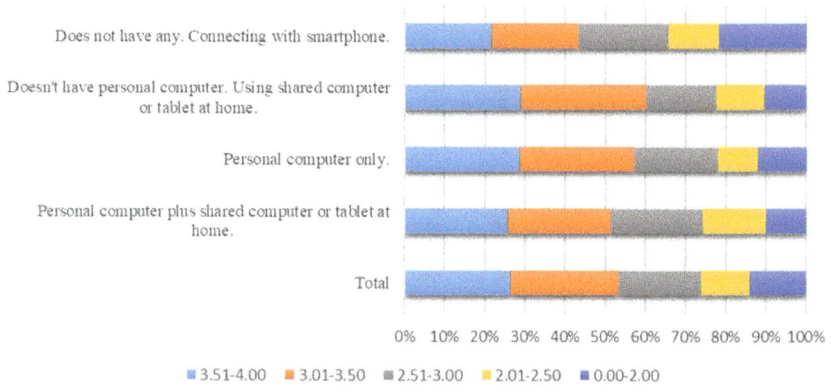

Graph 6: Distribution of GPA According to Technological Device Owning

Table 17: Kruskal-Wallis Test Results for Technological Device Owning

Total N	570
Test Statistic	10,691[a]
Degree Of Freedom	3
Asymptotic Sig.(2-sided test)	,014

a The test statistic is adjusted for ties.

smartphones, were statistically significantly lower compared to the GPAs of the students who have a personal computer or have access to a shared computer or tablet. In other words, the achievement levels of students with fewer opportunities to use technological devices are lower than the others.

4.2.4. Comparison of Students' Achievement Levels According to Spatial Opportunities

The distribution of the answers given to the question asked to the students about "the place they connected to lessons during the distance education period" is as follows:

Table 19 shows 50.9 % of the students participating in the survey have their own room, while 21.8 % of them do not have their own room but can stay alone when connecting to lessons. 25.4 % of the students are not able to stay alone when connecting to lessons and 1.9 % of them are connecting to lessons

Table 18: Pairwise Comparisons of Technological Device Owning

Sample 1-Sample 2	Test Statistic	Std. Error	Std. Test Statistic	Sig.	Adj. Sig.[a]
Does not have any. Connecting with a smartphone – Personal computer plus shared computer or tablet at home.	-33,630	23,459	-1,434	,152	,910
Does not have any. Connecting with a smartphone – Personal computer only.	-47,000	18,544	-2,534	,011	,068
Does not have any. Connecting with a smartphone – Doesn't have a personal computer. Using a shared computer or tablet at home.	-53,844	17,621	-3,056	,002	,013
Personal computer plus shared computer or tablet at home – Personal computer only.	13,370	23,827	,561	,575	1,000
Personal computer plus shared computer or tablet at home – Doesn't have a personal computer. Using a shared computer or tablet at home.	20,215	23,116	,874	,382	1,000
Personal computer only – Doesn't have a personal computer. Using a shared computer or tablet at home.	6,845	18,108	,378	,705	1,000

Each row tests the null hypothesis that the Sample 1 and Sample 2 distributions are the same.
a Asymptotic significances (2-sided tests) are displayed. The significance level is ,05.

Table 19: Frequency of Spatial Opportunities

	Frequency	Percent	Cumulative Percent
Own room, alone	290	50,9	50,9
Other rooms, alone	124	21,8	72,6
Other rooms, not alone	145	25,4	98,1
Other places, not home	11	1,9	100,0
Total	570	100,0	

somewhere else than home, like internet cafes, etc. By classifying the answers in terms of the GPA categories, we obtain the following crosstable:

Considering the spring semester GPAs of the students participating in the survey who have own room, 53.1 % of them have a GPA above 3.00, and 24.9 % of them have a GPA below 2.50. 58.1 % of the students who do not have own room but can use a room alone when connecting to lessons have a GPA above

Table 20: Cross-Table of Answers about Spatial Opportunities and GPA Category

		GPA Category					Total
		3,51–4,00	3,01–3,50	2,51–3,00	2,01–2,50	1,51–2,00	
Own room, alone	Count	74	80	64	35	37	290
	Percent	25,5 %	27,6 %	22,1 %	12,1 %	12,8 %	100,0 %
Other rooms, alone	Count	40	32	18	16	18	124
	Percent	32,3 %	25,8 %	14,5 %	12,9 %	14,5 %	100,0 %
Other rooms, not alone	Count	35	40	30	16	24	145
	Percent	24,1 %	27,6 %	20,7 %	11,0 %	16,6 %	100,0 %
Other places, not home	Count	1	3	4	2	1	11
	Percent	9,1 %	27,3 %	36,4 %	18,2 %	9,1 %	100,0 %
Total	Count	150	155	116	69	80	570
	Percent	26,3 %	27,2 %	20,4 %	12,1 %	14,0 %	100,0 %

3.00 and 27.4 % of them have a GPA below 2.50. Considering the students who cannot stay alone when connecting to lessons, 51.7 % of them have a GPA above 3.00 and 27.6 % of them have a GPA below 2.50. Only 36.4 % of the students who connect to lessons somewhere else than home have a GPA above 3.00 and 27.3 % of them have a GPA below 2.50 (Table 20).

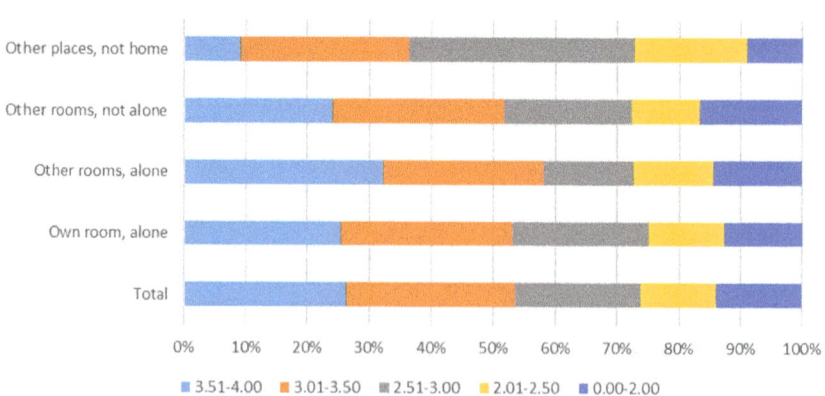

Graph 7: Distribution of GPA According to Spatial Opportunities

When we examine the relationship between the students' spatial opportunities and their GPA categories from Graph 7, it can be said students who have more opportunities to stay alone have slightly higher GPAs, and students who cannot stay alone in the home when connecting to lessons have lower GPAs comparing with total.

When we statistically test whether the GPA values of students differ in terms of spatial opportunities with the Kruskal-Wallis method, the results are in Table 21.

Table 21: Kruskal-Wallis Test Results for Spatial Opportunities

Total N	570
Test Statistic	,898[a,b]
Degree Of Freedom	3
Asymptotic Sig.(2-sided test)	,826

a. The test statistic is adjusted for ties.
b. Multiple comparisons are not performed because the overall test does not Show significant differences across samples.

According to the Kruskal-Wallis test, the H_0 hypothesis (p = 0.826) cannot be rejected. Therefore, no statistically significant difference is detected between spatial opportunities and GPA values.

4.2.5. Comparison of Students' Achievement Levels According to Gender

Finally, in this part of the study, it was analyzed whether inequality of opportunity emerged in terms of gender in the COVID-19 period. The distribution of the GPAs of the students according to gender during the distance education period is as follows:

Considering the spring semester GPAs of the female students, 59.6 % of them have a GPA above 3.00, and 23.4 % of them have a GPA below 2.50. 47.2 % of the male students have a GPA above 3.00 and 29.2 % of them have a GPA below 2.50 (Table 22).

When we examine the relation between the students' gender and their GPA categories from Graph 8, it can be said that female students have higher GPAs comparing with the male.

We can statistically test whether the GPA values of students differ in terms of gender with the Mann-Whitney U method. The assumptions regarding the Mann-Whitney Test are as follows:

Table 22: Cross-Table of Genders and GPA Category

		GPA Category					Total
		3,51–4,00	3,01–3,50	2,51–3,00	2,01–2,50	1,51–2,00	
Female	Count	78	93	48	31	36	286
	Percent	27,3 %	32,5 %	16,8 %	10,8 %	12,6 %	100,0 %
Male	Count	72	62	67	39	44	284
	Percent	25,4 %	21,8 %	23,6 %	13,7 %	15,5 %	100,0 %
Total	Count	150	155	115	70	80	570
	Percent	26,3 %	27,2 %	20,2 %	12,3 %	14,0 %	100,0 %

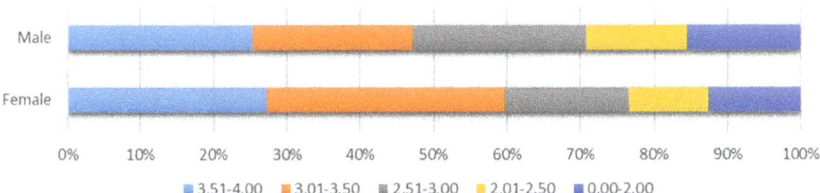

Graph 8: Distribution of GPA According to Gender

H_0: The distribution of GPA Value is the same across categories of Gender.
H_A: The distribution of GPA Value is not the same across categories of Gender.

Table 23: Mann-Whitney Test Results for Gender

Mann-Whitney U	36028,000
Wilcoxon W	76498,000
Z	-2,333
Asymp. Sig. (2-tailed)	,020

According to the test results outlined in Table 23, the null hypothesis (p = 0.020) can be rejected. There is a statistically significant difference between female and male students' GPA values. The GPA values of female students are statistically significantly higher than male students.

CONCLUSION

Higher education institutions all over the world and in Turkey were forced to move to distance education applications instead of face-to-face education during the spring semester due to the outbreak of COVID-19. In this study, we examined how pandemic and distance education practices affected students' achievement levels in Turkish Higher Education. We utilized from the survey that has a sample consisting of 570 students of the Faculty of Political Sciences, Istanbul Medeniyet University to search for factors, which may affect the students' achievements during the spring period that we have confronted with outbreak. We also examined if there was a significant difference between the students' success grades in the fall and spring semesters.

We determined a significant difference between the achievement levels of the students during the face-to-face education and the distance education period.

The results show that there is a positive effect of the COVID-19 confinement on students' achievement levels. This difference may be due to the fact that distance education techniques provide students with new and flexible learning opportunities. That is to say, students can both access the lessons by spending less time and they can watch the lessons asynchronously whenever and wherever they choose. This may be a factor that increases student success. On the other hand, with the transition to distance education, systems for measuring and evaluating student success in lessons have moved away from the old way of written and simultaneous exams and more flexible measuring systems like homework, presentations, etc. are widely used. This may be another factor that increase the success level of the students, too. As Gonzales et al. (2020) have argued, since distance education is a form of learning that students encounter for the first time, they may have followed classes in a more continuous and focused way to make sure they did everything right in the process and avoid loss of academic term.

It is worthy to analyze further if the positive effect of COVID-19 on students' achievements is related to the new learning methodology, or the new assessment process. Besides, it is stated that distance education can be applied more effectively and efficiently in the field of social sciences compared to other disciplines. Our research sample consisted of students from the Faculty of Political Sciences. Considering this difference, the effect of distance education on students from other disciplines as sports, engineering, medicine, tourism, etc. should be investigated separately.

During the distance education period, there was no inequality of opportunity for students in terms of the connection method and the place where they attend the course. A great majority of the students stated that they can connect to the lessons somehow and this situation did not reveal a difference in terms of success levels. Nevertheless, it should be kept in mind that the survey, whose results were used in this study, was also conducted online. Therefore, it is useful to interpret the results obtained with caution. Having more comprehensive data on the applications of distance education in the country, YOK states that there are problems in terms of internet access especially in rural areas of the country. When we examine the achievement levels of students in terms of gender, there is no gender inequality in terms of success grades, even the average grades of female students is higher than male students.

We determined that the opportunities of students to use technological devices and the amount of internet quota they have are the significant factors affecting the level of success among students during the pandemic. For this reason, the scope of the internet package support application implemented by

YOK should be expanded and it should be used when connecting to courses from various platforms other than the "YOK Courses Platform." Measures to be taken in this direction are important in terms of reducing this inequality of opportunity. In primary and secondary education in Turkey, the government decided to distribute tablet computers to students who are thought to be in need in the fall semester of the 2020–2021 academic year. Some criteria are determined among the needy students, such as family income level, the number of siblings at school age, attendance at face-to-face education, special education needs, and these students were prioritized based on official data. The government should implement similar practices in higher education institutions in order to guarantee equal opportunities in education for university students.

Decisions concerning higher education in Turkey are determined and coordinated by YOK. The advantage of having a central public institution is that YOK carried out a national strategy to help and coordinate higher education institutions to cope with the crisis. Collecting educational materials in a common pool and making them accessible to all students with internet support has relatively helped to reduce the inequalities that may arise in terms of students studying at different universities during the distance education period.

YOK have taken steps regarding distance education before the pandemic period, led to the opening of distance education centers in most public universities, and stated that 30 % of the courses could be given through distance learning methods. With the pandemic period, these initiatives were accelerated, additional distance education centers were established to cover all public universities, and the rate of courses that can be continued with distance learning was increased to 40 % in September 2020 (YOK, 2020d). This situation shows that the government and YOK have a tendency to give more weight to distance education.

The government should come together with YOK and representatives of universities and they need to draw on the lessons during the pandemic to understand what worked well in higher education and should plan an effective and efficient strategy for the distance education model of the future. As can be seen from the findings of the study, apart from the advantages it provides, distance education also brings its own inequalities of opportunity. These inequalities such as internet access and computer ownership are reflections of the inequalities of income distribution in society. Although the pandemic imposed widespread implementation of distance education as a necessity, it appears to deepen existing inequalities in education and add new ones. If there is a goal to increase the scope of distance education in universities in Turkey, the government has an important role to play in providing equal opportunities for students in higher education and must ensure that all students have sufficient technical device and internet connection to access the online lessons.

REFERENCES

Adedoyin, O. B. and Soykan, E. (2020). COVID-19 pandemic and online learning: The challenges and opportunities. *Interactive Learning Environments*, DOI:10.1080/10494820.2020.1813180

Alpar, R. (2017). Uygulamalı çok değişkenli istatistik yöntemler (5. b.). Ankara: Detay Yayıncılık.

Bania, J. and Banerjee, I. (2020). Impact of COVID-19 pandemic on higher education: A critical review. Global University Network for Innovation (GUNI), Retrieved December 10, 2020, from http://www.guninetwork.org/files/guni_impact_of_covid_19_pandemic_on_higher_education_a_critical_review_india.pdf

Bowen, J. A. (2012). *Teaching naked: How moving technology out of your college classroom will improve student learning.* Jossey-Bass, San Francisco; John Wiley & Sons, Hoboken.

China Daily (2020, January 26). China's State Council extends spring festival holiday. Retrieved December 10, 2020, from https://www.chinadaily.com.cn/a/202001/27/WS5e2e0f0ea31012821727356b.html

Di Pietro, G.; Biagi, F.; Costa, P.; Karpiński, Z. and Mazza, J. (2020). *The likely impact of COVID-19 on education: Reflections based on the existing literature and international datasets.* EUR 30275 EN, Publications Office of the European Union, Luxembourg, ISBN 978-92-76-19937-3, doi:10.2760/126686, JRC121071.

Gimenez, A. M. N.; Gavira, M. O. and Bonacelli, M. B. M. (2020). Adaptation and future challenges for public universities in Brazil in the face of the COVID-19 pandemic. Retrieved December 4, 2020, from http://www.guninetwork.org/files/gimenez_gavia_bonacelli_brazil.pdf

Godonoga, A. and Gruszka, D. (2020). A new vision for higher education in Poland and beyond. Retrieved November 23, 2020, from http://www.guninetwork.org/files/a_new_vision_for_he_in_poland_and_beyond_-_guni_reflection_article_-_godonoga_and_gruszka.pdf

Gonzalez, T.; de la Rubia, M. A.; Hincz, K. P.; Comas-Lopez, M.; Subirats, L.; Fort, S. and Sacha, G. M. (2020). Influence of COVID-19 confinement on students' performance in higher education. *PLoS ONE*, 15(10), e0239490. Retrieved December 16, 2020, from https://doi.org/10.1371/journal.pone.0239490

Gruber, J. (2013). *Public finance and public policy.* Worth Publishers, New York.

IAU (International Association of Universities) (2020). *The impact of COVID-19 on higher education around the world*. IAU Global Survey Report. Retrieved August 28, 2020, from https://www.iau-aiu.net/IMG/pdf/iau_covid19_and_he_survey_report_final_may_2020.pdf

Kruskal, W. H. and Wallis, W. A. (1952). Use of ranks in one-criterion variance analysis. *Journal of the American Statistical Association*, 47(260), 583–621.

Mann, H. B. and Whitney, D. R. (1947). On a test whether one of two random variables is stochastically larger than the other. *The Annals of Mathematical Statistics*, 18, 50–60.

Montenegro, C. E. and Patrinos, H. A. (2014). *Comparable estimates of returns to schooling around the world*. World Bank, Policy Research Working Paper, No: 7020.

OECD (2008). Ten steps to equity in education. Retrieved December 2, 2020, from http://www.oecd.org/education/school/39989494.pdf

Onyema, E. M.; Eucheria, N. C.; Obafemi, F. A.; Sen, S.; Atonye, F. G.; Sharma, A. and Alsayed, A. O. (2020). Impact of coronavirus pandemic on education. *Journal of Education and Practice*, 11 (13), 108–121.

Pedro, Francesc (2020, May 6). UNESCO's framework for the day after COVID-19 in higher education. Retrieved November 12, 2020, from http://www.guninetwork.org/report/unescos-framework-day-after-COVID-19-higher-education

Rashid, S. and Yadav, S. S. (2020). Impact of COVID-19 pandemic on higher education and research. *Indian Journal of Human Development*, 14(2), 340–343. Doi:10.1177/0973703020946700.

Reddy, V.; Soudien, C. and Winnar, D. L. (2020, May 6). Impacts of school closures on education outcomes in South Africa. Retrieved November 18, 2020, from https://theconversation.com/impact-of-school-closures-on-education-outcomes-in-south-africa-136889

Saraç, Yekta (2020, April 18). Preparing a national roadmap for online higher education. Retrieved September 12, 2020, from https://covid19.yok.gov.tr/Documents/AnaSayfa/Preparing-a%20national-roadmap-for-online-higher-education-UWN.pdf

Strielkowski, W. (2020). COVID-19 pandemic and the digital revolution in academia and higher education. *Preprints 2020*, 2020040290 (doi: 10.20944/preprints202004.0290.v1).

TÜİK (2020, November 14). Nüfus ve demografi. Retrieved September 24, 2020, from https://data.tuik.gov.tr/Kategori/GetKategori?p=nufus-ve-demografi-109&dil=1

Ulbrich, H. (2003). *Public finance in theory and practice*. Thomson, South-western.

UNESCO (2020a). COVID-19 impact on education. Retrieved September 27, 2020, from https://en.unesco.org/covid19/educationresponse

UNESCO (2020b, March 6). 10 Recommendations to plan distance-learning solutions. Retrieved September 28, 2020, from https://en.unesco.org/news/COVID-19-10-recommendations-plan-distance-learning-solutions

UIS (UNESCO Institute for Statistics) (2020). Enrollment level by education. Retrieved September 27, 2020, from http://data.uis.unesco.org/

WHO (2020, March 11). *WHO Director-General's opening remarks at the media briefing on COVID-19-11 March 2020*. World Health Organization, Geneva, March 11, 2020. Retrieved August 29, 2020, from https://www.who.int/director-general/speeches/detail/who-director-general-s-opening-remarks-at-the-media-briefing-on-COVID-19---11-march-2020

YOK (2020a). Yükseköğretim Bilgi Yönetim Sistemi. Retrieved November 14, 2020, from https://istatistik.yok.gov.tr/

YOK (2020b, April 21). Turkish higher education in days of pandemic. Retrieved November 14, 2020, from https://covid19.yok.gov.tr/Sayfalar/HaberDuyuru/opinion-turkish-higher-education-in-days-of-pandemic.aspx

YOK (2020c, April 29). Üniversite öğrencilerine ücretsiz 6 gb'lik "uzaktan eğitime destek" kotasi. Retrieved November 14, 2020, from https://www.yok.gov.tr/Sayfalar/Haberler/2020/ogrencilere-egitime-destek-kotasi.aspx

YOK (2020d). Yükseköğretim kurumlarında uzaktan öğretime ilişkin usul ve esaslar. Retrieved November 14, 2020, from https://www.yok.gov.tr/Documents/Kurumsal/egitim_ogretim_dairesi/Uzaktan_ogretim/yuksekogretim_kurumlarinda_uzaktan_ogretime_iliskin_usul_ve_esaslar.pdf

Erşan Sever[*]
Merve Ay[**]

The Global Economy during COVID-19 Pandemic: Realizations and Predictions

Abstract The COVID-19 crisis, which has been severely hitting the world economy for more than a year, has left the whole world to deal with first health, then economic, and lastly social problems. In that regard, the COVID-19 crisis has outpaced the 1929 Depression, which was the biggest contraction in the world economic history. This study discusses the macroeconomic effects of the COVID-19 outbreak on the global economy. In this context, we discuss the mechanisms by which a pandemic in the health field slows down the functioning of the economy. Then, we analyze the effects of the crisis on households. The effects of the pandemic are discussed in a group of countries that differ according to their level of development. Struggling with the COVID-19 crisis, all countries have intervened in the market through monetary and financial instruments. Countries' monetary policy decisions affect other countries' macroeconomic outlook. Therefore, in this study, the monetary and fiscal policy decisions taken by country groups during the pandemic are discussed according to their development levels. With the increasing spread of the pandemic, supply and demand shocks are seen within countries and thus economic contractions occur. Since this contraction influences all large and narrow scale businesses within a short period, the companies dismissed workers which resulted in an alarming increase in unemployment rates all over the world. With the weakening of international trade in this process, the world economy has experienced a recession that cannot be recovered for many years.

Keywords: COVID-19 pandemic, global macroeconomic outlook, economic recession.

INTRODUCTION

In addition to posing a threat to global public health, the COVID-19 pandemic has also shocked supply and demand in markets, leading to a sudden contraction of the global economy. The contraction in total global supply, accompanied

---

[*] Prof., Aksaray University, Faculty of Economics and Administrative Sciences, Department of Economics, esever@aksaray.edu.tr
[**] Res. Asst., Aksaray University, Faculty of Economics and Administrative Sciences, Department of Economics, mervekaya@aksaray.edu.tr

by a weakness in domestic and international demand, has deepened the impact of the crisis in all sectors. On the other hand, the course of the pandemic also continues to cause uncertainty in the health, social and economic spheres (OECD, 2020). To respond to the pandemic, countries have taken a variety of measures, such as curfews, quarantine, temporary closure of workplaces, and travel restrictions as allowed by their economic conditions. Depending on the course of the pandemic and the economic conditions in countries, these measures have time to time been tightened or eased. However, the tight grip of the pandemic and lack of widespread vaccination have made the burden on governments unbearable, which has lead some countries to opt for herd immunity. In addition, many countries have been intervening in their markets via economic stimulus, support, and bailout packages, as well as through monetary instruments to stimulate their economies and minimize the negative impact of the pandemic on companies and employment in the face of the pessimistic outlook caused by the pandemic.

Despite all measures, international organizations note that the world economy is experiencing the deepest crisis since the Great Depression in the 1930s. According to the World Trade Organization (WTO), the recession caused by the COVID-19 pandemic in global trade has more devastating effects than the one experienced during the 2008 crisis. In this regard, the measures taken during the global economic crisis in 2008 pale in comparison with those taken in response to the pandemic in 2020. Nouriel Roubini states that the impact of the COVID-19 pandemic on global macroeconomic indicators will have more rapid and deeper effects than the 2008 global crisis and even the Great Depression of 1929. In these two major crises, the stock market depreciated by more than 50 %, credit markets were frozen, mass bankruptcies took place, unemployment rates rose above 10 %, and GDP depreciated by more than 10 %. While these downfalls took place within three years, the macroeconomic and financial impacts of the COVID-19 pandemic emerged over the course of three weeks (Roubini, 2020).

Currently, there are various expectations that the ways of social life, governance, communication, production and trade will change after the COVID-19 pandemic. In this study where we will analyze the global macroeconomic crisis caused by the pandemic, we will focus on the impacts of the COVID-19 pandemic on the global growth performance, financial markets, labor market, and international business operations, respectively, and on predictions.

1. The Ways the COVID-19 Pandemic Impacts the Economy

The COVID-19 pandemic will have direct and indirect costs on the global economy in the short and long term. Figure 1 shows the ways the pandemic will directly and indirectly affect the economy and the resulting losses. Direct costs include costs of treatment, testing, and vaccination, which place an additional burden on households, companies, and the public, and supplementary payments made to healthcare workers' salaries. Direct costs also include research and development costs of new treatments and vaccines. On the other hand, referring to hospitals for test and treatment, time spent, transportation costs, and additional hygiene expenses make up additional direct costs, which were not previously an expense item for households (Rima, 2020).

Indirect costs are all additional costs associated with the economic impact of sickness and behaviors adopted to prevent sickness. Productivity losses caused by the inability of employees to continue working due to sickness and death can be listed as an indirect cost item. In addition to the loss of wages, there are also opportunity costs. On the other hand, the spillover effects of preventive measures taken by the public, companies, and households on the economy are an indirect cost item. The spillover effect of the combination of causes such

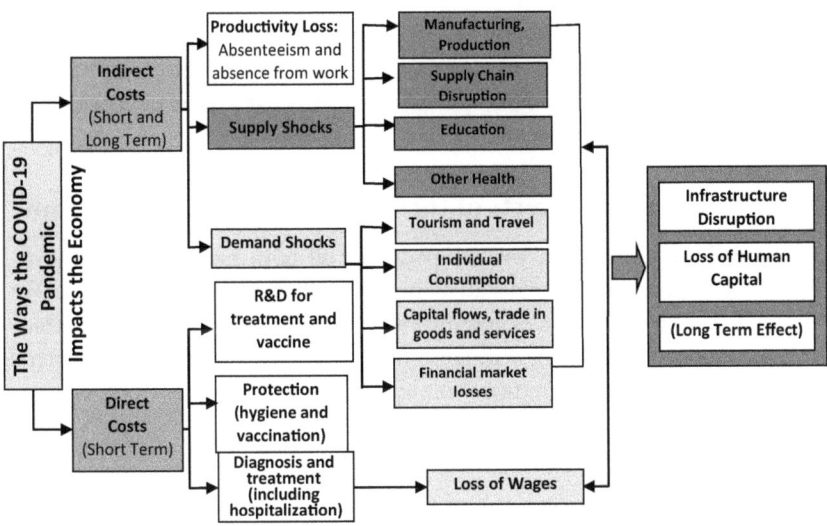

Figure 1: The Ways the COVID-19 Pandemic Impacts the Economy
Source: (Evans and Over, 2020); (Rima, 2020).

as social distancing, isolation, quarantine, and disease and measures taken to prevent them ultimately lead to supply and demand shocks in the economy (Rima, 2020). As noted by Nourel Roubini (2020), the impact of the 2008 global crisis on commodity and financial markets emerged in three months, while the global and destructive impact of the COVID-19 pandemic on the economy, causing supply and demand shocks via the ways explained above surfaced within only three weeks. Another factor that triggers supply shocks is that some businesses, hotels, restaurants, etc. are considered "non-essential" by governments. Demand shocks have been caused by the near-end of consumption, travel, transport, and other non-essential spending (Rima, 2020; Evans and Over, 2020). In other words, since these services constitute sectors of high demand and income flexibility, they are the first ones to be abandoned in a crisis. The contraction in supply and demand experienced here spreads to other sectors of the economy due to spillover effects, making the entire economic outlook negative.

In the short term, the loss of goods and services caused by supply and demand shocks due to the pandemic has also led to the disruption of the supply chain, which is an important element of production. On the other hand, increased government spending on healthcare has caused the budget allocated to other public activities, especially education, to shrink. The fact that all educational institutions, from preschool to higher education, have been offering their services remotely for more than a year has led to unrecoverable productivity losses in educational services. Given the fact that students are human capital, it is clear that a year's loss of human capital will cause a huge loss on countries' economic growth in the long term.

2. Macroeconomic Effects of the Pandemic on Global Economy

Countries have announced various packages on both national and international levels to minimize the negative impact of the COVID-19 pandemic. The effects of these packages on economic variables such as growth, foreign trade volume, monetary indicators, interest rates, employment levels, the general level of prices, and capital markets will be discussed below.

2.1. Impact on Global Economic Growth

In its Global Economic Outlook of October, IMF projected that the global economy will contract by 4.4 %, while in its updated January 2021 report, it revised expectations and projected the contraction to be 3.5 % (see Table 1). The

Table 1: Growth Forecasts for Country Groups

	Realized	Estimated	Projection		Based on October 2020 Forecast	
	2019	2020	2021	2022	2021	2022
Global	2.8	-3.5	5.5	4.2	0.3	0.0
Advanced Economies	1.6	-4.9	4.3	3.1	0.4	0.2
Emerging Markets and Developing Economies	3.6	-2.4	6.3	5	0.3	-0.1
Low-Income Developing Countries	5.3	-0.8	5.1	5.5	0.2	0.0

Source: (IMF, 2021).

growth forecast by country groups in Table 2 reflects a stronger-than-expected recovery across the regions in the second half of the year. In addition to additional policy measures announced at the end of 2020 that the US and Japan will offer more support to global economy in 2021–2022, the discovery of an effective vaccine and vaccination efforts revised expectations to an upward trend. In light of these expectations, the global economy is expected to recover and grow by 5.5 % in 2021 and 4.2 % in 2022 (IMF, 2021: 5). Table 1 shows the growth figures of country groups. The COVID-19 pandemic most prominently demonstrated its negative impact in the second quarter of 2020, when isolation measures were tightened. While there was some recovery in the third quarter, there was a slowdown in economic activity in the fourth quarter due to the increase in the number of cases and deaths, although not as much as in the second quarter.

An important question is which countries have suffered more damage due to the economic crisis caused by the COVID-19 pandemic. According to Table 1, it is safe to say that the economies of developed countries have felt the impact of the crisis the most. Developed economies are expected to contract by 4.9 % in 2020. It is not surprising that the economies of the most developed countries have been hit the hardest by the pandemic due to globalization and faster integration into the world economy. The G7 countries, namely the United States, China, Japan, Germany, Britain, France, and Italy, which have been hit the hardest by the pandemic, together make up 60 % of global revenue, 65 % of global production, and 41 % of global exports. China, Korea, Japan, Germany, and the United States are also an important part of global value chains. For this reason, problems that take place in these countries lead to supply chain transmissions in almost all countries, which means that if these economies sneeze, it is certain that the rest of the economies will catch a cold (Baldwin and Weder di Mauro, 2020:2).

The economy of the US, which has reported most deaths due to COVID-19, has also ended 2020 with a recession. As in developed countries, the US economy, which had struggled with low economic growth before the pandemic, will shrink by 3.5 % in 2020, according to IMF estimates. The Japanese economy, which is another developed one, has experienced a recession that has not been recorded since the Second World War, contracting by 28.1 % annually in the second quarter (Bank of Japan, 2020: 7). Japan, which recorded the lowest industrial production index (37.8 %) in June, has shown a V-shaped recovery following this date (Investing, 2020a).

According to Table 1, emerging markets and developing economies are expected to contract by 2.4 % and low-income emerging economies by 0.8 %. There are also projections that emerging markets and developing economies will recover faster during normalization thanks to widespread vaccination and global monetary expansion due to ease of funding. Based on these projections, it is safe to say that a V-shaped recovery is expected on a global scale.

IMF projects that emerging markets and developing economies will contract by 2.4 % by the end of 2020. As the pandemic spread to other countries and plunged the global economy into recession, China was able to reduce the number of cases and deaths through quarantine and other measures and revive its economic activities after April 2020. This performance by China has led to positive economic growth projections for the end of 2020. China, which has the most robust economic activity among developing countries, contracted by 6.8 % in the first quarter of 2020, for the first time since 1992, and achieved positive economic growth figures in the second and third quarters by reducing the number of cases and deaths. Thus, China is expected to grow by 1.9 % in 2020, 8.1 % in 2021 and 5.6 % in 2022. China's economic recovery in the first quarter of 2020 has been delayed beyond the second quarter for the rest of the world. The world economy is expected to achieve positive growth starting from the third quarter of 2021.

Experts debate about how long it will take to vaccinate the entire world population. Without a doubt, the less developed countries will have access to widespread vaccination at the latest. The economic activities of these countries prior to the pandemic, in other words, their economic values pale in comparison with emerging market economies. Therefore, the loss caused by the pandemic in these countries is not as critical as in developed countries. For this reason,

Table 2: GDP Growth Rates of Selected Countries (%)

Country	2019*	Estimate 2020	Projection 2021	Projection 2022	Country	2019*	Estimate 2020	Projection 2021	Projection 2022
Argentina	−2,1	−10,4	4.5	2.7	Malaysia	4.3	−5,8	7	6
Australia	1.9	−2,9	3.5	2.9	Mexico	−0,1	−8,5	4.3	2.5
Brazil	1.4	−4,5	3.6	2.6	Netherlands	1.7	−4,1	3	2.9
Canada	1.9	−5,5	3.6	4.1	Nigeria	2.2	−3,2	1.5	2.5
China	6	2.3	8.1	5.6	Pakistan	1.9	−0,4	1.5	4
Egypt	5.6	3.6	2.8	5.5	Philippines	6	−9,6	6.6	6.5
France	1.5	−9,0	5.5	4.1	Poland	4.5	−3,4	2.7	5.1
Germany	0.6	−5,4	3.5	3.1	Russia	1.3	−3,6	3	3.9
India	4.2	−8,0	11.5	6.8	S. Arabia	0.3	−3,9	2.6	4
Indonesia	5	−1,9	4.8	6	S. Africa	0.2	−7,5	2.8	1.4
Iran	−6,5	−1,5	3	2	Spain	2	−11,1	5.9	4.7
Italy	0.3	−9,2	3	3.6	Thailand	2.4	−6,6	2.7	4.6
Japan	0.3	−5,1	3.1	2.4	Turkey	0.9	1.2	6	3.5
Kazakhstan	4.5	−2,7	3.3	3.6	UK	1.4	−10,0	4.5	5
Korea	2	−1,1	3.1	2.9	USA	2.2	−3,4	5.1	2.5

Source: (IMF, 2021).

the countries whose economic activity contracted the least during the pandemic have been low-income developing countries. IMF predicts that the countries in this category will shrink by 0.8 % by the end of the year.

Table 2 shows realized economic growth in 2019, estimations for 2020, and projections for 2021 and 2022 of selected economies based on IMF's 2021 global economic outlook report. As seen on the table, the highest contractions in 2020 are expected to take place in Spain, Argentina, and the UK. Economies impacted by the pandemic a little less include France, India, Italy, Mexico, the Philippines, and South Africa. These economies are projected to achieve negative growth by 8 to 10 %. On the other hand, China, Egypt, and Turkey are expected to grow positively by the end of 2020, although they have also been negatively affected by the pandemic.

Economic uncertainty in emerging markets and developing countries, excluding China, continues due to the fact that their healthcare systems are disrupted as the pandemic continues to spread and economies depend on external financing, tourism, and aid. In Asia, where the vast majority of developing countries and especially large countries such as India and Indonesia are located, the pandemic has yet to be contained (IMF, 2020c: 11).

Russia, which is another developing country, survived the economic impact of the COVID-19 pandemic in the first quarter with less damage than other countries. In the first quarter of 2020, it recorded a growth rate of 1.6 % compared to the same quarter of the previous year. But although production in manufacturing, retail, wholesale trade, and finance did not decelerate, the lack of foreign demand caused GDP to contract in the second quarter, as the impact of the pandemic began to be felt much more in the second quarter. Another factor that dealt a blow to the Russian economy in the second quarter was the sharp drop in world oil demand, which led to a fall in oil prices due to a lack of reduction of oil supply. In addition, major contractions were observed in the industrial production index, and capacity utilization rate (Department of Strategy and Budget of the Presidency of Turkey, 2020: 20). IMF estimates the Russian economy to contract by 3.6 % by the end of the year (IMF, 2020c: 11).

On the other hand, based on the growth projection for 2021, it is projected that the economy that will exhibit the highest growth performance will be India as response efforts make progress and normalization begins. India is expected to be followed by China with a growth rate of 8,1 %, and Malaysia with a growth rate of 7 %. Turkey is projected to grow by 6 % in 2021. It is also predicted that the growth performance expectations of countries for 2022 will slow down slightly compared to the previous year.

Chart 1 shows the course of consumption and investment expenditures, which are the most important components of national income to ensure an exit from the global economic crisis that began in 2020. In terms of their contribution to growth, excluding private investments in China, recovery in the US, Australia, the Euro Zone, India, Japan, Korea, Turkey, and New Zealand realized above expectations following the contraction in the second quarter of 2020. As can be seen from Chart 1, consumption expenditures support global growth more than investment expenditures do due to the increase in deferred consumption expenditures (IMF, 2021: 2).

Despite negative developments such as the faster spread of the COVID-19 virus mutations from the beginning of 2021, acceleration of vaccination efforts in countries consolidates expectations of positive development in the upcoming periods. It should also be noted that important duties fall upon policymakers to minimize problems relating to global vaccine distribution and limit the damage caused by the sharp decline in the economy.

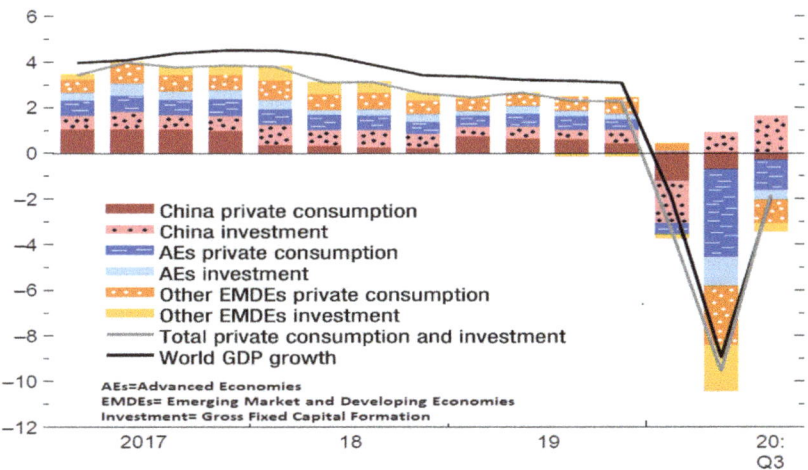

Chart 1: Contribution of Global Consumption and Investment Expenditures to GDP Growth
Source: (IMF, 2021).

2.2. Impact on Financial Markets and Inflation

The high number of cases and deaths reported from around the world has triggered contractions in the goods and services market and financial markets, and a mood of uncertainty emerged on a global scale. While governments intervene in this mood of uncertainty through monetary and financial instruments, the lack of widespread vaccination continues to threaten the global economy. While the financial decisions of the US, China, and European countries, which hold a large share in the world economy, will mainly affect their own economic outlook, their financial decisions will play a decisive role in the world economy. Nowadays, the policy interest rates of countries remain the most emphasized policy argument. Even though the policy interest rates adopted by developing countries, particularly during the pandemic, have been high compared to developed countries, the global unease directed global capital to developed countries that are considered to be safe harbors with low-risk premium. Thus, the global capital has followed a reverse path. Even in terms of the outcome of the policy interest rate alone, the COVID-19 pandemic has painted a grimmer picture than the 2008 global crisis. This has led to an upward spiral on the interest rates, exchange rates and inflation of developing countries with high-risk premiums. According to Yeldan (2020), there are three indicators to look for the value of local currency during the pandemic. These are the interest rate, which plays a decisive role in the choice between consumption and savings, the inflation rate, which reflects the depreciation of money in the face of imbalances in the goods and labor market, and the exchange rate, which shows the exchange value of national currency versus foreign currency. This chapter deals with the macroeconomic course of country groups based on these three indicators.

Central banks in developed and developing countries have made comprehensive asset purchases, restructured the debts of institutions, and offered loan support to debtors of various sizes to minimize the economic damage caused by the pandemic and to stimulate markets. Following the decline in the number of cases in July, financial conditions have signaled a recovery on a global scale. On the other hand, the disagreement between financial markets and the real economy requires unprecedented policy support (Acemoğlu et al., 2020). Given monetary policy decisions taken to respond to the pandemic, we can see that almost all countries have taken measures to increase market liquidity. In particular, expansionary policies of developed economies that increase market liquidity affect the global economic outlook.

Before addressing the monetary policy decisions taken by the US economy in response to the pandemic, we must briefly touch upon its experience following the 2008 crisis to better understand the country's current monetary policies. FED, the main goal of which is to maximize employment and ensure price stability, has been trying to move the unemployment rate below 6.5 %, and the inflation rate above 2 % and to protect its economy from the pressure of deflation since the 2008 global crisis. To this end, FED increased market liquidity through purchasing bonds and bills (FED, 2020a: 23). This way, it increased the loan volume by keeping interest rates close to zero and adopted traditional monetary policy methods in which it sought to protect households from savings. As a result of these traditional methods, the US has managed to lower the unemployment rate and grow, but has not been able to achieve the desired increase in the inflation rate (Stiglitz, 2020). Households have delayed their consumption with the expectation that prices will not increase in the country, and shifted their savings to developing countries with high interest rates. This can be one of the reasons behind the long-standing low growth rates in the US.

Struggling with low growth and deflation until the COVID-19 pandemic, the US experienced a dramatic decline in economic activity as the pandemic spread all across the country starting in March. In the US, the supply shock disrupted the supply chain, damaged consumer confidence, and increased country and loan risk premiums. Weak demand and historically-low oil prices led to a downward movement in the consumer price index in the US. Chart 2

The Global Economy during COVID-19 Pandemic 135

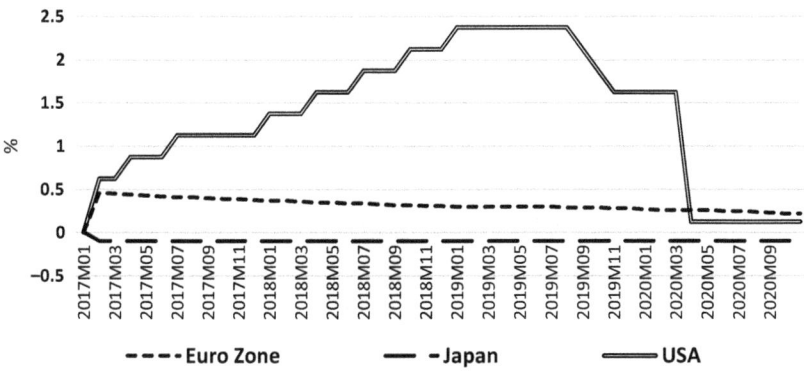

Chart 2: Policy Interest Rates of Selected Countries/Country Groups
Source: (IMF, 2021).

shows the US interest rates, even the speculation of which causes major impact in global markets, and policy interest rates in the Euro Zone and in Japan. The FED, which had a policy interest rate of 1.63 before the pandemic, first lowered it by 50 basis points and then by 100 basis points in March 2020, as the pandemic increased economic risks, pulling the interest rate between 0 to 0.25 and ensuring a high monetary expansion. FED kept interest rates between 1.00 and 1.25 even during the 2008 global crisis (FED, 2020b: 1). Japan has kept interest rates at negative levels for many years in order to discourage its people from saving and stimulate consumption. Interest rates in Japan remain at 0.10 % during the pandemic. Another group of countries that kept interest rates close to zero before the pandemic is the Eurozone. The interest rate, which was 0.26 % before the pandemic, fell to 0.22 % in October 2020.

Chart 2 shows the course of monthly policy interest rates in the last three years of emerging economies, including China, Mexico, Brazil and Turkey. According to the chart, the most consistent country in terms of policy interest rates over the past three years has been China. Trade wars with the US before the pandemic and the economic recession after it did not make China alter the interest rate, which was kept at 4.40. The economy of China, which was the first country to face the devastating consequences of the pandemic and therefore to have its economic activity slow down rapidly, faces a worse situation than the one during the global crisis of 2008. China's central bank (PBOC) kept policy interest rates steady, while in March it reduced the reverse repo rate to 2.40 from 2.20, making a 20-basis point cut. On the other hand, it adopted a monetary

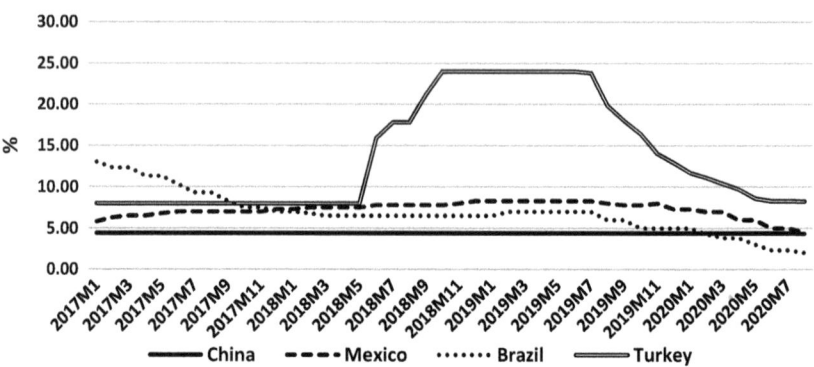

Chart 3: Policy Interest Rates in Selected Developing Countries
Source: (IMF, 2020b)

expansionary policy with the liquidity it offered to the market by making cuts on required reserve ratios. However, compared to economies similar in size, it is safe to say that PBOC adopted a more cautious monetary expansionary policy (Presidency of Strategy and Budget of the Turkish Presidency, 2020: 17–18).

As seen in Chart 3 the Mexican policy rate, which moved around 8 % before the pandemic, began to fall starting from the first months of 2020 and reached 4.50 % in August. The Brazilian policy interest rate, which was around 15 % in the first months of 2017, decreased to 8 % in the first months of 2018 and to 5 % in the last months of 2019. The downward trend continued due to the expansionary monetary policies adopted following the pandemic and remained around 2 % in August. Among developing countries, the country with the most unstable interest rate is Turkey. Since 2015, Turkey has been increasing M1 money supply. This trend gained momentum in March, when the pandemic spread to Turkey. Rapid credit expansion limited the disinflationist pressure of negative demand conditions (TCMB, 2020b: 1; 2020c: 7). The policy rate, which was around 8 % until May 2018, rose up to 24 % due to high exchange rates in June 2018, then went into a downward trend. To limit the negative impact of COVID-19 on the Turkish economy and to ensure cash flow for households, companies, financial markets, and credit channels, CBT reduced the policy rate to 9,75 % in Mart, and to 8,25 % in August. It was then raised to 10,25 % in September to counter the increasing exchange rate (TCMB, 2020a).

Disagreeing with Saudi Arabia over oil production, Russia experienced a dramatic revenue loss for oil as Saudi Arabia's continued oil production reduced

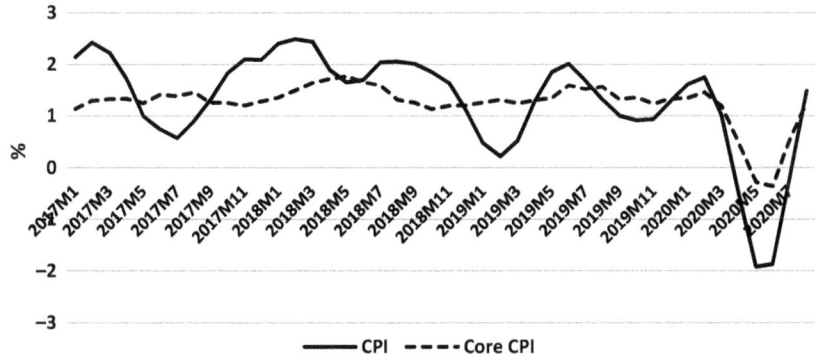

Chart 4: CPI and Core Inflation Figures in Advanced Economies
Source: (IMF, 2020b).

prices. This has been one of the factors negatively affecting the Russian economy during the pandemic. The Central Bank of Russia predicts that its economy will contract by 3.9 to 4.2 % by the end of 2020. It is projected that suppressed demand and the weakening of the Ruble will result in higher-than-expected inflation in 2021. It is projected that investment and consumption expenditure indicators will lead to the weakening of domestic demand, prolonging economic recovery. In order to support markets, the Bank offered housing loan support and loan to small and medium-sized enterprises at a rate of 2 %. The Central Bank of Russia has gradually lowered the policy interest rate since the second quarter of 2019 to 4.2 %, which was around 7 % in 2019. This credit expansion indirectly affected the prices in the credit market. The Bank plans to increase market liquidity by the end of 2020 by increasing money supply by 14 to 17 % compared to the previous year (Bank of Russia, 2020).

Damaging other macroeconomic indicators, the COVID-19 pandemic has also had a devastating effect on the already-problematic inflation, especially in developed countries. Chart 4 shows the monthly realized inflation in developed countries over the past three years. While there was a weak inflation before the pandemic around 0 to 2 % despite monetary expansions, it realized at around -2 % due to weak demand caused by the infection's spread to developed countries such as the US, Europe, and Japan in April and May. Demand revived and inflation surpassed negative rates and reached 1.5 % in August as a result of a decrease in the number of cases and easing of containment measures starting from July 2020 (European Central Bank, 2020b).

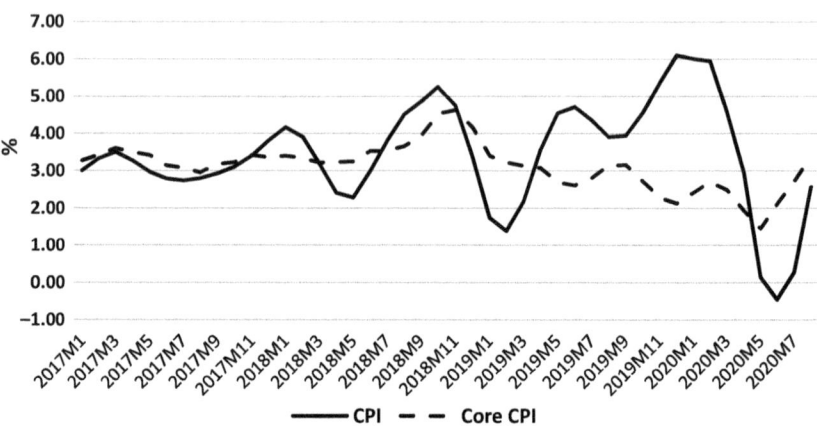

Chart 5: CPI and Core Inflation in Emerging Markets and Developing Countries
Source: (IMF, 2020b)

Chart 5 shows the average inflation rate of emerging markets and developing countries. Accordingly, in the last quarter of 2019, inflation in developing countries remained at 5 %, while since February 2020, when the pandemic in China began to spread, inflation has started to decline in developing countries. Emerging markets and developing countries saw a deflation of -0.46 % in June. Even though the number of cases in these countries has been stable since July, the revival in demand and deferred demand due to the easing of precautionary measures have raised the general level of prices to a positive level. According to IMF, year-end inflation expectations for 2020, 2021, and 2022 in emerging markets and developing economies are 5 %, 4.7 %, and 4 %, respectively.

As the prices of products such as medical supplies have increased in developed economies, commodity prices have caught an upward trend after hitting bottom in April. However, due to weak aggregate demand in developed economies, inflation has not been able to reach a level at which it will bring economic growth. That is why in developed economies, inflation remains in the same course it was in before the pandemic (IMF, 2020b: 23).

Production, which has been unable to reflect increasing costs during the pandemic on customers due to lack of demand, will include this delayed price increase on products when the pandemic ends and economy starts to recover. Consumers, who have delayed their demands due to restrictions during the pandemic, will stimulate the aggregate demand as the pandemic wears off. This is expected to result in significant increase in the general level of prices after the pandemic. On the other hand, it is likely that inflation expectations will rise rapidly if governments run a fiscal deficit if central banks fund governments instead of maintaining price stability. In developed countries, the inflation expectation for 2020 is 0.8 %, while for 2021 this expectation goes up to 1.6 %. If economic recovery continues, this expectation is projected to be 1.9 % in 2022 (IMF, 2020a: 15–16).

Along with challenges relating to interest rates and inflation indicators, the exchange rate serves as a pivotal macroeconomic indicator for emerging markets with external deficits and a high debt burden. Therefore, the most regarded currency on a global scale is the US Dollar. US Dollar index refers to the average value of the US Dollar relative to a basket of foreign currencies consisting of Euro, Yuan, Yen, Sterling, Krona, and Franc. Due to uncertainty caused by COVID-19, the US Dollar index was around 103,5 in March 2020 and fell to 91,123 following a downward trend until January 2021. Behind the downward trend of the US Dollar index, especially since June, lies the efforts of the US to prevent further depreciation of the currencies of developing countries. Since the depreciation in developing countries caused global trade to suffer by reducing imports of these countries, the US opted for increasing the reserve of the US Dollar in the global market through purchasing bonds from other countries' central banks and swap deals (FED, 2020a).

A very important macroeconomic indicator for countries is the value of the national currency against reserve currencies. The flow of reserve currencies to developed countries during the pandemic, unlike in the 2008 global crisis, has put depreciation pressure on the currencies of developing countries. Currencies of many emerging markets started to recover between April and June following a blur in the market and violent pressure in March. The Chinese Yuan, which was around 6,80 against the US Dollar at the beginning of the pandemic, rose to 7,14 until May as the virus spread within the country and put the economy into recession. It appreciated against the US Dollar until February 2020 to around 6,47 as China went into recovery as the virus started to spread outside of China. In this process, as mentioned above, China appreciated its currency without making any changes to policy interest rates. Other Asian currencies remained stable on a real effective exchange rate basis. In contrast, the Russian Ruble depreciated due to geopolitical factors, and the national currencies of countries such as Argentina and Brazil also depreciated due to the pandemic and external factors or due to their financial situation.

Turkey, which has a high foreign debt obligation, experienced a sharp loss of foreign demand as the impact of the pandemic deepened in European countries, of which Turkey is a very important exporter. Turkey's total exports reduced by 19 % compared to March 2019, 43 % compared to April 2019, and 41 % compared to May 2019. Considering the loss of tourism revenues as a result of travel restrictions, Turkey saw a significant loss in foreign exchange earnings. This has led the currency to set on an upward trend starting from August. While the US Dollar liquidity offered by the US to the market flowed to developing countries, which offered higher interest rate opportunities, when economic activity was high, the risk and uncertainty brought about by the pandemic shifted reserve currencies to developed countries, appreciating the US Dollar in developing countries. Due to concerns over the disruption of the global trade balance, FED decided to make swap deals with foreign countries.

Starting from the first chapter of this study, we have noted that the COVID-19 pandemic primarily impacted the commodity market through supply and demand shocks. Negative expectations in the commodity market have forced governments to intervene in the market via monetary and fiscal policies. The ongoing pessimistic expectations led to a succession of shocks in labor markets and the whole world experienced high unemployment rates. The loss of income caused by unemployment has created a vicious cycle and negatively impacted commodity and money markets. In capital markets, the other side of this vicious cycle, the impact of COVID-19 becomes clear in only a day.

The effects of the panic caused by the pandemic in global capital markets are demonstrated in Chart 6. Following the first deaths relating to the virus in the US, the US and UK stock markets suffered their biggest lost in history since Black Monday in 1987. On March 16, 2020, the Nasdaq and Dow Jones indices experienced a decline of up to 30 % compared to the previous month. On the other hand, Tokyo Stock Exchange's Nikkei index declined by 7 % in a single day. This triggered a wave of fear and panic across all markets (Reuters, 2021). Following the decline caused by the first shock, recovery began in the following months. Expansionary policies adopted by countries increased liquidity in international markets, which has supported the upward movement of capital markets, especially recently. During this period, the appreciation in the stock value of companies operating in the healthcare industry is noteworthy.

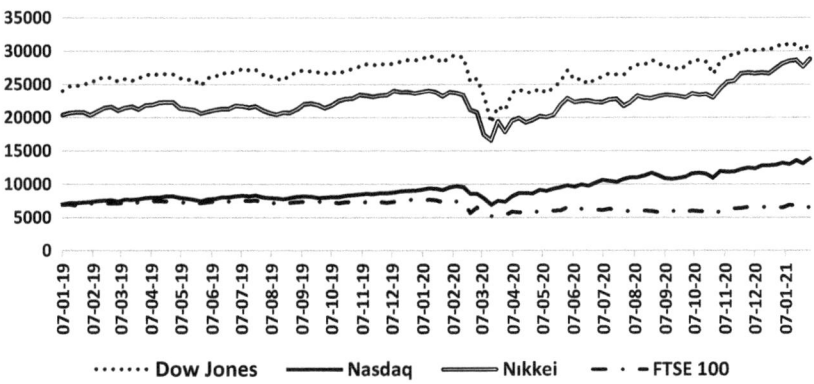

Chart 6: Stock Market Indices of Developed Countries
Source: (Yahoo Finance, 2021).

2.3. Impact on the Labor Market

The slowdown in economic activity leads to lower income levels and increased poverty. In particular, long-term unemployment can lead to loss of skills and a decline in future earnings by weakening human capital. According to the human capital theory, improving cognitive skills through education leads to better productivity and income. A trained labor force can easily adapt to the changing needs of employers and novel technologies and get better information about job opportunities than family, friends, ads, old employers, the radio, and employment agencies. This gives the trained labor force leverage in responding to a crisis. However, the picture becomes much clearer after a crisis when income equality between the trained and skilled labor force and others deepens.

According to real-time surveys conducted in the UK, US, Germany, Japan and Canada, the COVID-19 pandemic has caused an increase in income inequality, as expected. In these countries, young, less-educated, women, and minority workers have been affected by COVID-19 much more. Based on the labor market data of the US and the UK, it is expected that this pandemic, which has impacted the world much deeper and twenty times faster than the Great Depression, will raise the poverty rate by creating an army of unemployed (Fasih et al., 2020: 4).

During the pandemic, those doing per diem work without social security have been more likely to be laid off (officially or de facto). With layoffs during

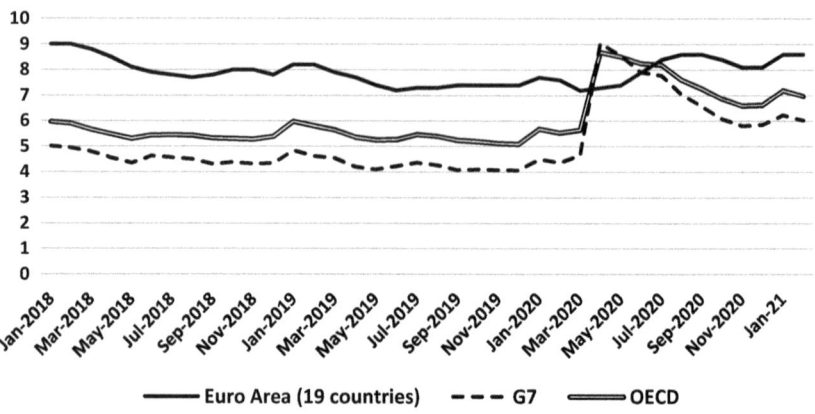

Graph 7: Change in Unemployment Rates (%)
Source: (OECD, 2021)

the pandemic, the number of people with a daily income of less than USD 1.90 has reached 90 million worldwide. The pandemic has hit the segments of society that are economically more vulnerable, in particular young men and women in the labor force. Low-income workers are more likely to lose their jobs than those with high income. A similar situation applies in emerging markets and developing countries. Unregistered workers, which are higher in numbers in these economies, in times of crisis, they are more likely to be laid off and deprived of social benefits. Since the burden of crisis is unevenly distributed among sectors, the labor force with the heaviest burden has been the workers in accommodation, food and beverage, transport, retail and wholesale services (Brussevich et al., 2020: 19–20).

The developments in unemployment rates in the Euro area, G7, and OECD countries are presented in the Chart 7 show the impact of the global pandemic on unemployment. The unemployment rate among G7 countries increased by 92 % in April compared to the previous month and by 52 % for OECD countries. In the following months, expansionary monetary and fiscal policies, easing of restrictions, and new approaches to working helped unemployment indicators in these countries to have a slower acceleration. However, as of November 2020, unemployment rates are higher than in the prepandemic period. The increase in the unemployment rate in Euro area countries (19 countries) maintained an upward trend from April to July, and then entered a weak downward trend.

Table 3: Change in Working Hours Compared to Previous Quarter

	2020	2020 Q1	2020 Q2	2020 Q3	2020 Q4
Global	-% 8,8	-%5,2	-% 18,2	-% 7,2	-% 4,6
Low-Income Countries	-% 6,7	-%2,5	-% 13,4	-% 7,6	-% 3,3
Lower Middle-Income Countries	-% 11,3	-%2,5	-% 29	-% 9,3	-% 4,5
Upper Middle-Income Countries	-% 7,3	-%8,4	-%11,5	-% 5,6	-% 3,9
High-Income Countries	-% 8,3	-%3,4	-% 15,8	-% 7,3	-% 7

Source: (ILO, 2021).

In many countries, unemployment rate indicators can be misleading because of how unemployment rates are calculated. During the pandemic, many people are unable to work even though they are employed, many do not seek jobs after being laid off due to despair (not included in active labor force), and many are not considered unemployed because they work part-time. Due to the pandemic, the whole world is facing this picture. To assess unemployment and income loss during the pandemic more accurately, it is better to interpret the indicator of working hours (Lee, Schmidt-Klau and Verick, 2020: 2).

Table 3 shows the change in working hours by country groups. According to ILO estimates, in 2020, 8.8 % of global working hours were lost compared to the last quarter of the previous year. This is equivalent to 255 million full-time jobs. Working hour loss is particularly high in Latin America and the Caribbean, Southern Europe and South Asia. When we compare the crises in 2020 and 2008, it is striking that the crisis caused by the pandemic has had a more negative impact on macroeconomic indicators. Likewise, working hour loss in 2020 is nearly four times higher than in the global financial crisis of 2008 (ILO, 2021: 1). Following worldwide lockdowns and intense restrictions, the loss of working hours reached a peak in the second quarter of 2020. In the second quarter of 2020, the loss of working hours has been by 18.2 % worldwide, which is estimated to be equivalent to 525 million full-time jobs. Considering working hours in country groups, we can say that upper-middle income countries suffered more by the COVID-19 pandemic in terms of loss of working hours in the first quarter of 2020, while the biggest loss was suffered by lower-middle income countries in the second, third, and fourth quarters.

ILO has developed three scenarios about the labor market for future expectations covering pandemic and no-pandemic possibilities (see Table 4). Under this scenario, global working hour loss will be 90 million full-time jobs by

Table 4: Working Hours Loss for 2020 and Scenarios for 2021

	2020 Q4	Base Year 2021	2021 Pessimistic Scenario	2021 Optimistic Scenario
Global	-% 4,6	-% 3	-% 4,6	-% 1,3
Low-Income Countries	-% 3,5	-% 1,8	-% 3,4	-% 1,1
Lower Middle-Income Countries	-% 4,7	-% 2,6	-% 4,7	-% 1,2
Upper Middle-Income Countries	-% 3,8	-% 2,9	-% 4,2	-% 1,1
High-Income Countries	-% 7	-% 4,7	-% 5,7	-% 1,8

Source: (ILO, 2021).

declining by 3 % in 2021 assuming a 48-hour work week (compared to Q4 of 2020). Based on country groups, it is expected that working hours in low- and middle-income countries will recover strongly in the first quarter of 2021 compared to the last quarter of the previous year. The lack of alternative sources of income and widespread poverty force people to engage in any economic activity to survive. High-income and upper-middle-income countries are expected to face a challenging first quarter, however, it is possible to see a relatively strong recovery in the second half of the year if a critical proportion of the population gets vaccinated (ILO, 2021: 11).

According to Table 4, the world will expect a pessimistic scenario if mass vaccination remains slow and the confidence indices of consumers and firms weaken as a result of chronic negative expectations raised because of the pandemic. If the pessimistic scenario becomes the reality, the labor market will experience a quite slow recovery in 2021. In this case, the working hour loss would be as high as 4.6 % compared to the last precrisis quarter, which would be equivalent to 130 million full-time jobs. On the other hand, if the optimistic scenario realizes, a strong recovery in working hours is expected in 2021 thanks to the containment of the pandemic and increase in consumer and business confidence. However, even in this scenario, there will be a 1.3 % gap of global working hours in 2021, which would correspond to 36 million full-time jobs assuming a 48-hour work week (ILO, 2021: 12).

Within this framework, it is safe to say that the COVID-19 pandemic will have negative consequences for unemployment and income distribution, even if the optimistic scenario occurs, and this situation will persist for some time. On the other hand, the emergence of new working arrangements and lines of business with the pandemic and political decisions can alleviate the severity of these negative consequences. Speeding up vaccination efforts as more and more vaccines get approval is a critical turning point in the fight against the pandemic. If stable and accurate policies are adopted, we can hope that the labor market will benefit from these developments, both from a health and economic point of view, along with the recovery of economic activity in the coming period.

The findings of empirical literature addressing the negative consequences of the pandemic on the labor market coincide with the reports of organizations such as IMF, ILO, and OECD. Within this framework, Béland et al. (2020) found that COVID-19 has increased unemployment and reduced working hours and labor force participation in the US, but not had a significant impact on wages. Disadvantaged groups in terms of gender, age, race, and educational level are affected by the pandemic more. Based on these findings, it is safe to say that COVID-19 exacerbates inequality in the labor force. The study also found that workers, who were forced to work in close contact with others, were more susceptible to the economic challenges brought about by the pandemic compared to those working under social distancing or isolation measures. Rodriguez et al. (2021) found that social distancing and quarantine measures taken to contain the spread of COVID-19 led to wage losses in European countries, triggering poverty and income inequality.

Future expectations point to a significant recovery in 2021 as uncertainties will clear away thanks to more vaccines being approved all over the world. However, there are also problems that have yet to be clarified and responded to. It is unclear at what rate the infection will slow down after vaccination. It is also not clear how vaccination will take place on a global scale, especially in underdeveloped countries. It is not certain to what extent and how long governments will continue to implement incentive policies, which have been widely used in response to the pandemic.

2.4. Impact on International Trade

The global economy is built on the specialization of labor among countries. According to the comparative advantages theory, which constitutes the basis of the international system of exchange of goods and services, the specialization of labor maximizes the total output and increases prosperity. However, the COVID-19 pandemic has shown that the net benefits of the system also bring about costs. The pandemic has affected world trade from both supply and demand fronts. Many governments ordered the closure of non-essential production sites, while numerous companies took such measures voluntarily (e.g.,

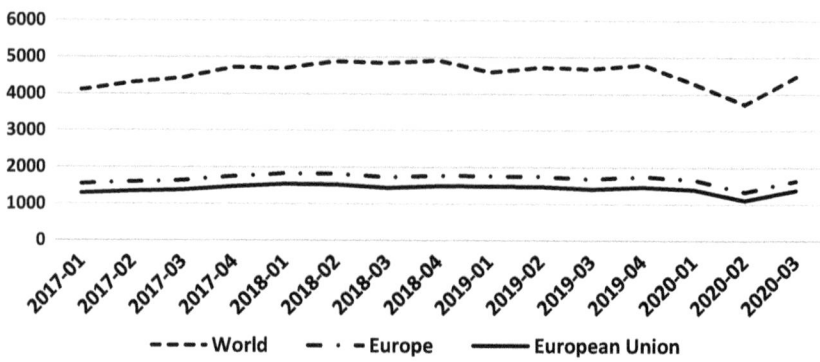

Chart 8: Global Export (USD Billion)
Source: (WTO, 2021)

due to a decline in labor supply) or reduced production due to interruptions in the supply chain. However, the impact of the COVID-19 vaccine has been felt the most by the international service industry. International tourism, civil aviation, and containerization have been hit the most (Gruszczynski, 2020: 339–340).

The first disruption to the supply chain occurred as a result of factory closures in China to slow down the spread of COVID-19. This eventually led to shortages of parts and equipment in sub-sectors, namely automotive, chemical, computer equipment, garment and textile, machinery, metal and metal products industries, and precision instrument-related sectors. The successive effects of these shortages echoed in many other countries, causing some establishments to slow down production or suspend operations altogether. In addition, the negative shock to labor supply brought about by nation-wide bans and restrictions to cross-border movements of people resulted in critical supply shortages for agricultural products and many other industrial products, especially in developing countries and emerging economies (ILO, 2020: 2).

Chart 8, which shows the effect of the COVID-19 pandemic on export, demonstrates that this effect is clear in the first and second quarters of 2020. Compared to the last quarter of 2019, world exports decreased by 25.5 %, European countries by 23.6 %, and European Union by 23.6 %. However, there is a recovery trend in the third quarter of 2020. Compared to previous periods, there is an increase in the share of exports of food products and healthcare equipment in international trade. Clearing of some uncertainties thanks

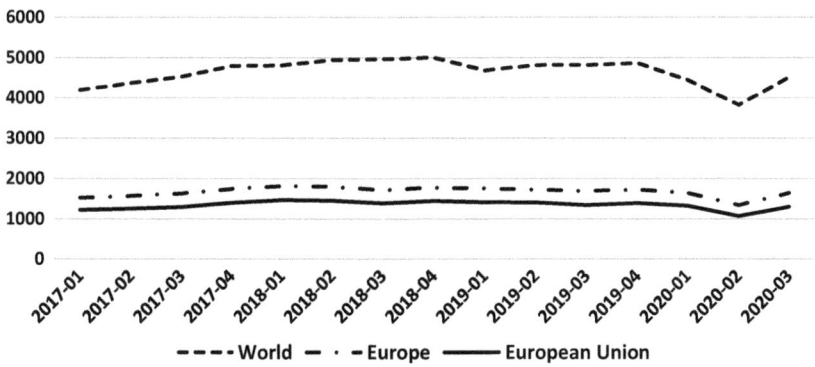

Chart 9: Global Import (USD Billion)
Source: (WTO, 2021)

to more rapid vaccination in countries will pave the way for more positive developments in the coming quarters.

During the pandemic, there has been a loss of income since individuals have worked less due to quarantines and restrictions. If this loss of income is not compensated by public policies, it is inevitable that there will be a decrease in total demand. In addition, during times of heightened uncertainty, individuals tend to save more and spend less. Another reason behind the decline in demand is the deferral of non-essential spending (consumer durables) due to concerns over getting infected. In addition, an increase in import demand can be expected due to increased demand for hygiene support (Kazunobu and Hiroshi, 2020: 4).

Chart 9 shows the change in imports on a global scale and in Europe. The COVID-19 pandemic impacted global imports predominantly in the first and second quarters of 2020. Compared to the last quarter of 2019, world imports decreased by 21,5 %, European imports by 22,2 %, and European Union imports by 22,5 %. On the other hand, there are positive signals towards recovery in the third quarter of 2020. It is safe to say that this has been made possible by the easing of restrictions and the increase in deferred consumption demand due to expansionary monetary and fiscal policies (European Central Bank, 2020a: 14).

Although there has been a significant reduction in the volume of international trade in the short-term following the COVID-19 pandemic, we can expect global trade to return to its previous level with the containment of the pandemic thanks to vaccination efforts in the medium and long term. The positive direction obtained in the third quarter of 2020 indicates this expectation. The COVID-19 pandemic has also shown that it is necessary to diversify suppliers to minimize risks in countries' supply chains. The supply shocks that have been experienced intensify the projection that businesses will shift to a production model that further reduces labor dependence and uses information technologies more intensively in the future.

CONCLUSION

The COVID-19 pandemic, which is considered to be the deepest crisis facing the world economy after the depression of 1929, has took the lives of 2.28 million people worldwide according to official figures and continues to wreak havoc on world economy. The cost of restrictive measures adopted across the globe such as quarantine, curfews, and social distancing has led to a decline in total supply, disrupted the distribution chain, and suspended production altogether in some sectors, such as tourism while the significant contraction in demand brought countries to the brink of deflation. The most important outcome of supply and demand contractions has been unemployment. Developed countries have supported households through unemployment benefits while this support has been limited in developing countries with higher rates of informal employment. According to figures released by official organizations, the world economy, which is in recession, is expected to contract by 3.5 % by the end of 2020.

In addition to financial support packages offered by governments in response to the pandemic, monetary policy decisions adopted by central banks have played a pivotal role in the recovery of economies. Central banks have fought the pandemic through asset purchases, liquidity support to financial institutions, swap deals and credit flows. Especially in developing countries, economies have been intervened through treasury bills, state-guaranteed bonds, and mortgage-based support packages. Despite inflation pressures to be faced in the coming period due to deferred demand, developed and developing countries have adopted monetary expansionary policies. While developed economies have not experienced inflation, emerging and developing economies, such as India and Turkey, witnessed signs of inflation. Developed economies have reduced interest rates to 0.25 to 0.50 %, which were already around 0 to 2 % due to weak economic growth before the outbreak. In developing countries, interest rates have been lowered to recover weakening economies. In this process, the US Dollar, which is the reserve currency, depreciated by 4 %, and the currencies of developing countries also depreciated against the real effective exchange rate.

Undoubtedly, many academic studies have been published on the impact of the COVID-19 pandemic on various fields of science. Here, it is safe to say that the experience gained through remote working and the developed technological infrastructure has brought and will bring significant changes in the way we work. New practices to be accompanied by Industry 4.0 are expected to have both a positive and negative impact on the labor market. This process has had a particularly negative impact on the labor force, which has a low educational level, lacks social security, and works on wage. On the other hand, the educated and skilled labor force has started to shift to new lines of business. After these developments, the income gap between the qualified and unqualified workforce has grown even more.

However, contractions in supply and demand due to various reasons, such as uncertainty and containment measures, had a negative impact on international trade in goods and services. In particular, international tourism, air travel, and containerization were among the sectors that have been hit the hardest by the pandemic. Following short-term contractions, international trade has shown signs of recovery thanks to policies adopted and clearing of uncertainties. Achieving results from vaccinate development efforts and acceleration of vaccination in response to the pandemic clears uncertainties about the future and reinforces expectations that the virus will be contained soon. Within this framework, we can expect positive developments in international trade in goods and services in the coming period. Also, in terms of supply chains, we expect companies to adopt a multidimensional approach to minimize risks in the future.

Achieving the desired economic, social and health-related progress in the coming period can only be made possible by containing the COVID-19 pandemic. In this context, global actors in the fields of health, economy, and politics should take a precise and decisive approach towards the desired implementation of vaccination, especially in less developed countries. It is safe to say that there is no other way to stop the ever-spreading virus than to come up with a global solution.

REFERENCES

Acemoğlu, D., Demiralp, S., Taymaz, E. and Yımaz, K. (2020, June 12). COVID-19 Salgınının İktisadi Analizi. (K. Yımaz, Röportaj Yapan) Bilim Akademisi. Retrieved December 20, 2020, from https://bilimakademisi.org/COVID-19-salgininin-iktisadi-analizi12-haziran-bilim-akademisi-webinari/

Baldwin, R. and Weder di Mauro, B. (2020). *Economics in the Time of COVID-19*. London: Centre for Economic Policy Research Press.

Bank of Japan. (2020, October). *Financial System Report*. Retrieved January 06, 2021, from https://www.boj.or.jp/en/research/brp/fsr/data/fsr201022a.pdf

Bank of Russia. (2020, October). *Monetary Policy Report*. Bank of Russia. Retrieved January 05, 2021, from http://www.cbr.ru/eng/about_br/publ/ddkp/longread_4_32/page/

Béland, L.-P., Brodeur, A. and Wright, T. (2020). The Short-Term Economic Consequences of COVID-19: Exposure to Disease, Remote Work and Government Response. *IZA Discussion Paper No: 13159*.

Brussevich, M., Dabla-Norris, E. and Khalid, S. (2020). *Who Will Bear the Brunt of Lockdown Policies? Evidence from Tele-workability Measures Across Countries*. IMF Working Papers, 20(88).

Caycho-Rodríguez, T., Tomás, J. M., Barboza-Palomino, M., Ventura-León, J., Gallegos, M., Reyes-Bossio, M. and Vilca, L. W. (2021). Assessment of fear of COVID-19 in older adults: Validation of the fear of COVID-19 scale. International Journal of Mental Health and Addiction, 1–15.

Department of Strategy and Budget of the Presidency of Turkey (2020). *Dünya Ekonomisindeki Son Gelişmeler (Ocak-Haziran)*.

European Central Bank. (2020a). *Economic Bulletin*. Issue: 6. Retrieved January 03, 2021, from https://www.ecb.europa.eu/pub/economic-bulletin/html/eb202103.en.html

European Central Bank. (2020b). *ECB Staff Macroeconomic Projections for the Euro Area*. Retrieved January 03, 2021, from https://www.ecb.europa.eu/pub/projections/html/ecb.projections202009_ecbstaff~0940bca288.en.html

Evans, D. and Over, M. (2020, March 12). *The Economic Impact of COVID-19 in Low- and Middle-Income Countries*. Center For Global Development. Retrieved December 30, 2020, from https://www.cgdev.org/blog/economic-impact-COVID-19-low-and-middle-income-countries

Fasih, T., Patrinos, H. A. and Shfiq, M. N. (2020, May 20). *The Impact of COVID-19 on Labor Market Outcomes: Lessons from Past Economic Crises*. World Bank. Retrieved December 29, 2020, from https://blogs.worldbank.org/education/impact-COVID-19-labor-market-outcomes-lessons-past-economic-crises

FED. (2020a, March 19). Central bank Liquidty Swaps. *Sections: FED*. Retrieved November 11, 2020, from https://www.federalreserve.gov/monetarypolicy/central-bank-liquidity-swaps.htm

FED. (2020b). *Monetary Policy Report*. June 12, 2020. Retrieved December 20, 2020, from https://www.federalreserve.gov/monetarypolicy/2020-06-mpr-summary.htm.

Gruszczynski, L. (2020). The COVID-19 Pandemic and International Trade: Temporary Turbulence or Paradigm Shift? *European Journal of Risk Regulation, 11*(2), 337–342.

ILO. (2020). *The Effects of COVID-19 on Trade and Global Supply Chains.* ILO, Geneva.

ILO. (2021). *ILO Monitor: COVID-19 and the World of Work. Seventh edition.* ILO, Geneva.

IMF. (2020a). *A Crisis Like No Other, An Uncertain Recovery.* International Monetary Fund. World Economic Outlook. Retrieved November 10, 2020, from https://www.imf.org/~/media/Files/Publications/WEO/2020/Update/June/English/WEOENG202006.ashx?la=en.

IMF. (2020b). *Global Financial Stability Report.* IMF, Washington.

IMF. (2020c). *World Economics Outlook.* IMF, Washington.

IMF. (2021). *World Economic Outlook Update.* International Monetary Fund, Washington.

Investing. (2020a, September 17). Japonya Merkez Bankası Para Politikasını Değiştirmedi. Retrieved December 10, 2020, from https://www.ekoturk.com/haber/japonya-merkez-bankasi-para-politikasini-degistirmedi/

Investing. (2020b, February 03). *Japan Manufacturing Purchasing Managers Index (PMI).* Retrieved December 30, 2020, from https://www.investing.com/economic-calendar/manufacturing-pmi-202

Kazunobu, K. and Hiroshi, M. (2020). Impacts of COVID-19 on International Trade: Evidence from the First Quarter of 2020. *IDE Discussion Paper No. 791.*

Lee, S., Schmidt-Klau, D. and Verick, S. (2020). The Labour Market Impacts of the COVID-19: A Global Perspective. *The Indian Journal of Labour Economics, 63*(1), 11–15.

OECD. (2020). *Economic Outlook, Interim Report.* Retrieved January 01, 2021, from https://www.oecd.org/economic-outlook/

OECD. (2021). *OECD. Stat.* OECD. Retrieved April 10, 2021 from https://stats.oecd.org/

Reuters. (2021, January 27). US Stocks-S&P, Dow slide after Boeing results; Nasdaq fall cushioned by Microsoft. Retrieved February 07, 2021, from https://www.reuters.com/article/usa-stocks-idUSL4N2K23MU

Rima, S. (2020, April 7). *The economic impact of COVID-19.* Centre for Tropical Medicine and Global Health, Nuffield Department of Clinical Medicine, University of Oxford: https://www.tropicalmedicine.ox.ac.uk/news/the-economic-impact-of-COVID-19

Roubini, N. (2020). *NourielRoubini.com*. A Greater Depression? Retrieved December 29, 2020, from https://nourielroubini.com/a-greater-depression/

Stiglitz, J. E. (2020). *Deficit Lessons for the Pandemic From the 2008 Crisis*. The American Prospect. Retrieved December 29, 2020, from https://prospect.org/economy/deficit-lessons-pandemic-2008-crisis/

TCMB. (2020a). *Finansal İstikrar Raporu*. Ankara: TCMB. Retrieved November 13, 2020, from https://www.tcmb.gov.tr/wps/wcm/connect/832a5718-f26c-4869-8480-ab366e1b1eae/F%C4%B0R31_T%C3%BCmMetin.pdf?MOD=AJPERES&CACHEID=ROOTWORKSPACE-832a5718-f26c-4869-8480-ab366e1b1eae-nqFxO1W

TCMB. (2020b). *Makroekonomik Görünüm*. Ankara: TCMB. Retrieved November 13, 2020, from https://www.tcmb.gov.tr/wps/wcm/connect/b1111141-446b-4cc0-90f6-b3913b61ddf6/bolumII-26.pdf?MOD=AJPERES&CACHEID=ROOTWORKSPACE-b1111141-446b-4cc0-90f6-b3913b61ddf6-mhbTNTn

WTO. (2021, January 31). *Data*. World Trade Organization. Retrieved February 12, 2021, from https://data.wto.org/Yahoo Finance. (2021). Stock Market Indices. Retrieved February 5, 2021, from https://finance.yahoo.com/world-indices

Yeldan, E. (2020). *Türk Lirası'nı ve TC Merkez Bankası'nı Anlamak*. Yazarlar: Cumhuriyet Gazetesi: (12.08.2020). Retrieved December 27, 2020, from https://www.cumhuriyet.com.tr/yazarlar/erinc-yeldan/turk-lirasini-ve-tc-merkez-bankasini-anlamak-1757744

Mithat Arman Karasu[*]

The COVID-19 Pandemic and Its Effects on Urban Life

Abstract The COVID-19 outbreak that appeared in China in December 2019 spread to the entire world within a short period of time. Together with the COVID-19 outbreak, social lives in cities are being suspended, travels within and outside the countries are being restricted, movements of certain age groups and individuals with chronic diseases are being restricted, partial or complete curfews are being imposed, education in schools are being interrupted, working hours are being made flexible, or the model of working from home is preferred. Culture, art and sports activities are being suspended and production in factories is interrupted. All these negative occurrences are deeply affecting cities.

In the frame of this study, the effects of the COVID-19 outbreak will be examined under four headlines, namely, the cultural and psychosocial, economic, architectural, and design, and technology. Staying at home for long periods of time and being unable to socialize in urban locations can have permanent effects on human psychology. The uncertainty caused by the outbreak, death anxiety, and losing loved ones are not psychological problems that can be coped with easily. The measures taken and bans brought are forcing cities to "suspend the urban life."

As regards the economy, the COVID-19 outbreak has created damages that are more permanent than those created by the 2nd World War. The outbreak is making the operation of economic functions that cities have throughout the history. The COVID-19 outbreak will result in some changes in city planning and home designs. While working from home has become important, the question of how suitable are houses for working from home still waiting to be answered. The obligation of social distance and the instantaneous data flow required by the outbreak gives way to new techno-solutions in the urban space.

Keywords: the COVID-19 outbreak, pandemic, city, urban life, virus

INTRODUCTION

Certain events pose great political, economic, cultural and social challenges during the time in which they take place, have consequences that will leave a

---

[*] Prof., Harran University, Faculty of Economics and Administrative Sciences, makarasu@harran.edu.tr

mark on the future and go down in history. The COVID-19 pandemic is one of those events and has already been embedded in history. It has been a test for the whole world. The healthcare and education systems of countries, hundreds of different sectors that make up the global economy, technological infrastructure, sense of solidarity and unity of societies, and psychological endurance of individuals have been traveling through a tunnel. However, the light at the end of the tunnel is nowhere to be seen.

Due to the global transportation network, COVID-19 has spread extremely rapidly. The plague in 14th century took 40 years to spread all over the world, the Spanish flu in 1918 in 2 to 3 years while COVID-19 in only months. COVID-19, which emerged in Wuhan, Hubei in China on December 31, 2019, was reported from 196 countries as of May 25, 2020. As the outbreak became more widespread, the World Health Organization (WHO), on January 30, 2020, declared that the outbreak constituted a Public Health Emergency of International Concern, and declared it a global epidemic (pandemic) on March 11, 2020 after a surge in the number of deaths.

The fragility of global solidarity has become much clearer during the pandemic when globalization was interrupted and nation-states got back on the scene. The reputation and credibility of international organizations, especially the World Health Organization, have been questioned. Faced with shortages of masks, drugs, and ventilators, each country turned back to its own territory and a colonial-era-like competition came to a head among states (Aydınlı, 2020: 38). Medical intelligence between states has become increasingly strategic (Seren, 2020: 86).

Undoubtedly, cities are the settlements hit the hardest by the pandemic. Cities where a large number of people live in a narrow area at a relatively high population density, a large number of public activities take place, communication and transport systems operate non-stop within a network are ideal places for an outbreak to spread. The COVID-19 pandemic emerged in one city and has spread all over the world by means of the global transportation networks between cities. On the other hand, lockdowns, curfews for certain age groups, and bans on economic and cultural activities have brought urban life to a standstill. In other words, while cities spread outbreaks, ironically, outbreaks render cities dysfunctional.

The purpose of this study is to find an answer to the question of what the COVID-19 pandemic has changed in urban life and how. The first chapter of this study will deal with how outbreaks and health-related problems shaped cities in history. The second chapter will cover the effects of the COVID-19 pandemic on cities in terms of cultural and psychosocial, economic, planning and design, and technology. Without a doubt, the impact of the COVID-19 pandemic today will give us a clue on how the cities will be shaped in the future.

1. Cities and Outbreaks in History

The historical development of cities largely coincides with the spreading of outbreaks and diseases around the world. Moreover, the introduction of certain diseases to humanity was the result of sedentism and the domestication of some animals. The frequency of contact between animals and humans through animal feeding, milking, helping give birth, shearing, living under the same roof, using manure, etc. greatly increased the variety of infectious diseases (TÜBA, 2020: 29). The number of such diseases, known in medicine as "zoonosis," is around 200. With the domestication of animals, animal diseases such as rabies, measles, anthrax, smallpox, malaria, plague, etc. also began to appear in humans. More than 90 % of infectious diseases in humans are of zoonotic origin, and many of them have ceased to be zoonotic, jumping from human to human (TÜBA, 2020: 31).

With sedentism, humans started to come in more contact with diseases and diseases started to transmit to humans more easily. In a way, cities served as a hotbed for outbreaks and infectious diseases. Sedentism boosted agricultural production. Storing surplus produce brought disease-spreading rodents closer to humans. The fact that the cities are areas where people lived collectively in a narrow area surrounded by walls led to faster contamination of the surrounding water resources and raised the problem of having to remove or destroy large amounts of waste. Standing and unused water resources have become an ideal habitat for disease-carrying parasites and mosquitos.

In the face of outbreaks throughout history, cities were only able to adopt temporary measures, and there were insufficient efforts to diagnose or eradicate diseases due to the lack of modern medical facilities to understand why outbreaks spread and how they emerged. The plague that broke out in 1345 was thought to have been caused by the conjunction of Mars, Saturn and Jupiter (Genç, 2011: 126). It has often been told that outbreaks are the result of annoying divine forces (Yıldırım, 2020: 1337).

Dumping the dead, who were about to stink, into death pits outside cities was commonplace. Quarantine, which means 40 days in Italian, was first imposed by the Venetians. Lack of urban planning, lack of separation of activities in public spaces, inadequacies in terms of public sanitation and hygiene, failure to dispose of waste, and difficulty in accessing high-quality drinking water combined with improvidence and social neglect during outbreaks made their spread and mass deaths inevitable.

Different diseases have caused outbreaks many times in history. In fact, human history is the history of outbreaks and wars waged against them. While outbreaks strengthened people's immune systems, ironically, mutated diseases caused newer and deadlier outbreaks (Lai, Webster, Kumari, Sarkar, 2019: 1). The first large-scale outbreak in history was the Plague of Justinian in the 6th century BC. The plague, which is named for the Byzantine emperor Justinian who contracted the disease, is presumed to have originated in Asia. It reached India and then Egypt through trade routes, and then all the way to Constantinople via merchant ships.

Constantinople was the city that hit the hardest by the plague, rendering the capital of the Byzantine Empire a dead city (Ahsan, 2020: 1). The plague took the lives of thousands of people every day and reduced Constantinople's population by 35 to 45 %. In addition, as a result of the disruption of the supply chain due to the plague, there was a shortage in the city, which led residents to starve and fell victim to the disease. Between its emergence and eradication, which took 50 years, the Plague of Justinian is estimated to have reduced the population of the Byzantine Empire by 25 % (Pamuk, 2020: 35).

The weakening of the Byzantine Empire after the plague created a serious political vacuum. This vacuum was filled by the ever-strengthening Muslim armies. Following the plague, the Islamic Civilization was able to expand much faster, shifting the regional leadership from Constantinople to Baghdad for some time (Little, 2012: 43). Constantinople's influence in geography will only be possible after the looting of Baghdad and the Ottoman Empire making Constantinople its capital following the Mongolian invasion.

Another plague that left a mark in history and had serious consequences was the plague pandemic of 1348 called the "Black Death." The pandemic, which emerged in China in 1330, reached Crimea in 1346, and Cairo in 1355. The Black Plague was influential until 1600, ultimately reaching England via merchant ships (Yıldırım, 2020: 1334). The plague claims the lives of one in three people in Europe. The population of the European continent fell significantly. 75 to 100 million people died in Europe between 1347 and 1357 (Tekeli, 2020: 62). Globally, the pandemic took the lives of around 200 million people (Little, 2012: 19).

People were desperate in the face of the Black Plague. Since the cause of the disease was unknown, the only thing left people to do was to dispose of the dead. In Italy, upon official instructions, the belongings and beds of plague victims were buried and their homes were disinfected with smoke and cleaned with vinegar. After the Black Plague, inoperative trade routes changed eating habits, getting people to eat rabbits, deer, fish, and weed (Genç, 2011: 136).

The Black Plague was highly influential over the history of the continental Europe. A large number of people of working age died during the pandemic, which caused by a contraction in the labor market, resulting in a significant increase in wages (Ortaylı, 2020: 49). This increase in wages, which continued for several decades after the pandemic, also increased the prices of finished goods. Thus, while the income of agricultural producers and landowners decreased, the income of labor increased. While the share of agricultural products in city economy decreased, the share of finished goods and luxury consumer goods increased. International trade, which declined after the fall of the Roman Empire, began to rise again in Europe. The labor contraction and high wages caused by the Black Plague paved the way for industrial capitalism to take hold in Britain and the Netherlands later on. The same plague epidemic had a negative impact on Italy, Spain and the Eastern Mediterranean (Pamuk, 2020: 38–47).

As with the present-day COVID-19 pandemic, the Black Plague weakened social relations within the community. Fathers, children, spouses, and siblings were forbidden to see one another. With the plague, public confidence in the church was shaken. The failure of church members to provide a satisfactory answer about the causes and consequences of the plague reduced confidence in the church, and religion was questioned. Some blamed the Jewish for the pandemic, claiming that they spread the plague. As a result of these claims, thousands of Jewish people were burned, put to the sword, and hanged. 2,000 Jewish people were burned alive in Strasbourg (Genç, 2011: 143). Perhaps the most important cultural outcome of the plague was the development of national languages. Lack of Latin-speaking clergymen paved the way for the development of national languages.

Plague outbreaks continued throughout the 15th century. There were outbreaks in Bursa in 1429, Thessaly in 1466, and later in Macedonia and Thrace. The plague, which emerged in Venice in 1478, jumped to Constantinople in 1492. Unable to return to Constantinople upon the news of the plague, Bayezid II was trapped in Adrianople. In this outbreak, 56 thousand people died in Constantinople (Tekeli, 2020: 63).

Cholera started to become more influential as the plague grew weaker. The first cholera outbreak broke in Calcutta, India in 1816 and spread to China and the Middle East. It reached the American continent via British merchant fleets, resulting in more than 100 thousand deaths. The second cholera outbreak occurred between 1829 and 1851. Active in Asia, America and Europe, this outbreak took the lives of 100 thousand people. Another similar outbreak occurred in Afghanistan, Russia and India between 1852 and 1860, killing 1 million people.

The first smallpox outbreak broke out in China in 161 AD and spread to the Roman Empire in the Mediterranean basin, killing one third of those who were infected. Another outbreak emerged between 310 and 312, this time killing 40 % of those who were infected. The outbreak spread to Asia and Africa through caravans and developed into a childhood disease over time. It killed a considerable number of people in Europe and in the Americas in the 17th and 18th centuries. In a similar way, typhus killed thousands of people over the course of the 18th century. The typhus outbreak that broke out due to a slave uprising in Haiti in 1793 spread to the United States, and forced 20 thousand Americans, including President Washington to migrate from Philadelphia (Genç and Akyürek, 2020: 51).

Both cities and diseases underwent a significant change with the Industrial Revolution. Commercial, religious and military functions of cities changed with the Industrial Revolution, and mass production became the main function of cities. Wanting to work in factories, millions of people flocked from villages to cities. The urban population of London reached 2 million in 1851 from 880 thousand in 1801. The population of Manchester increased from 70 thousand in 1801 to 300 thousand in 1851. While there were only two cities in Great Britain with a population of over 100 thousand, this number reached ten in 1850. In Great Britain, the leading country of the Industrial Revolution, the number of workers reached 3.3 million in 1841 from 1.7 million in 1800 (Beaud, 2003: 135).

This rapid increase in urban population, combined with numerous environmental problems caused by the Industrial Revolution, rendered made cities convenient for outbreaks. Another reason why cities became favorable for outbreaks was the exploitation of workers brought about by the Industrial Revolution and the widespread poverty caused by the unfair distribution of income. In 1834, 13 % of those working in the British cotton industry were children, and 75 % were at the hunger threshold (Beaud, 2003: 141–143). Long working hours, child labor, lack of public health services, malnutrition, occupational accidents, lack of sanitary housing, crowded slums, etc. made cities very hard to live in.

Widespread use of railways and steamships after the Industrial Revolution increased the mobility of people and goods, facilitating the spread of outbreaks. Mass production caused by the Industrial Revolution increased the trade of both raw materials and finished goods between countries, facilitating the transport of diseases. Coming in contact with different human races, diseases became more resistant.

New solutions were introduced for all the problems brought about by the Industrial Revolution. The first solution was urban planning. In the modern sense, it was first applied to the cities of the Industrial Revolution. Municipal organizations were started to be established in order to prevent lack of planning and solve urban problems. The planning allowed different activities carried out in cities to be divided into specific areas. Building of wide roads and parks, relocating industrial facilities to outside of city centers, introduction of sanitary and technical standards for residential buildings, separation of drinking water and sewer systems, and planned removal of waste led the way to cities that are more resilient to diseases.

The first health law in the UK was enacted in 1832. New improvements were introduced for employees between 1838 and 1845, and the Public Health Act entered into force in 1847. The first municipal organization to conduct development and infrastructure services of cities was established in England in 1835. After the cholera outbreak in France in 1850, the first health law was enacted. In 1838, *Meclis-i Tahaffuz* (Quarantine Assembly) was established in the Ottoman Empire, and the municipal organization was established İN 1855 (Tekeli, 2020: 66).

Due to the fact that cleaning materials cheapened and became more accessible to the public, the state took over the provision of healthcare services, and preventive public health services became more widespread thanks to the Industrial Revolution, the number of diseases reduced and living conditions improved. Undoubtedly, another factor that fed into the increase in the quality of life was the progress in the field of medicine after the Industrial Revolution. The discovery of microorganisms, vaccination, the availability of antibiotics, hygiene and sanitation measures reduced outbreaks considerably. On the other hand, interventional medical procedures and medical interventions gave way to resistant microorganisms, rapidly increasing the number of healthcare-associated infections. Virus-borne outbreak started to become more frequent (TÜBA, 2020: 33).

The Spanish Flu, which took place between 1918 and 1920, was the most influential of these outbreaks. The Spanish Flu, which emerged during the First World War and was the most devastating event known to mankind, took hold of the whole world. The virus, which infected about 500 million people, killed 50 million people in 18 months. Young people and adults were more susceptible to the flu. States lost far more people to the pandemic than they lost in the war.

The Spanish Flu was the first example to show us how transport networks in modern world can play a key role in the spread of outbreaks.

Another type of the Spanish Flu pandemic emerged as the "Hong Kong flu" in 1968 and the "Asian Flu" in 1975. More than 1 million people died because of the Hong Kong Flu. The flu pandemic, which coincided with the Vietnam War, spread rapidly in the United States after American soldiers returned home. Similar to the Hong Kong Flu, the Asian Flu took the lives of more than 4 million people. The pandemic in China continued for 10 years (Yıldırım, 2020: 1339).

Pandemics like these occur today in increasing numbers. The HIV (human immunodeficiency virus) collapses the immune system in humans, causing AIDS. It is known to have first appeared in 1960 in monkeys. In 2017, 940 thousand HIV-related deaths and 1.8 million new cases of HIV infection were identified. The "Swine Flu," which emerged in 2009, transmitted from pigs and poultry. The pandemic, which spread to 191 countries, was detected in 800 thousand people and killed around 9 thousand. Another outbreak that spread to West Africa from a small village in Guinea in 2014, was caused by the Ebola virus. The Ebola virus causes complications such as viral hemorrhagic fever in humans and non-human primates. It was largely limited to the African continent. Other virus-borne outbreaks were SARS in 2003, MERS in 2012, and Zika in 2015 in Brazil.

Increasing transportation opportunities, global trade and supply chains, global tourism activities, growing human population, and settlements close to animal habitats make it easier for diseases to jump from animals to humans and to turn into outbreaks. The frequency of outbreaks is gradually increasing. We are experiencing a new outbreak every 10 to 15 years. This frequency was 80 to 100 years before the Industrial Revolution (UCLG, 2020: 7). Even illegal animal trafficking alone increases the risk of viruses spreading and mutating by up to ten times (aa.com.tr, 25.11.2020). Cities are more susceptible to outbreaks than ever before in history. Modern medical facilities are not very successful in preventing outbreaks. The most recent virus-borne pandemic experienced by humanity has been the COVID-19 pandemic.

2. COVID-19 Pandemic and Its Impact on Cities

The Coronavirus, which originated in Wuhan, Hubei Province, China, on December 31, 2019, has already spread to the entire world. As of December 5, 2020, the total number of COVID-19 cases worldwide reached 66 million and the death toll to1.5 million. As it has been the case throughout history, cities have been hit the hardest by the COVID-19 pandemic. COVID-19 took cities captive (Candan, 2020: 1).

The COVID-19 pandemic is reshaping cities, and new rules and practices are being introduced with the support of law enforcement. On the other hand, it is unclear whether these new rules will turn into a behavioral pattern in society. Variables such as the duration of the COVID-19 pandemic, the area it will spread to, and its impact on society will show us that. During the SARS pandemic in the Far East in 2003, people were forced to wear masks. After the pandemic, 23 % of people made it a habit to wear masks (Kye and Hwang, 2020: 3). Due to increased radioactive contamination after the Chernobyl accident, some people in Turkey stopped drinking tea. The same behavioral changes can also happen today.

The effect of pandemics on urban areas is determined not only by their characteristics, but also by the characteristics of the area. Tens of variables such as the density of residential areas, means, and volume of urban transportation, the closeness of residential areas, types of residences (apartment building or detached), types of land use, the width of streets (Stier, Berman, Bettencourt, 2020: 7–9), distribution of urban public areas, the situation of green and recreational areas, the rate of disadvantaged groups (elderly, disabled, chronically ill, etc.) within the urban population, the volume of urban economy, its structure and level of global integration, and the topography and climate of the city are influential over the transmission of outbreaks in cities (Lai, Webster, Kumari, Sarkar, 2019: 1–3).

We can examine the effects of the COVID-19 pandemic on cities in four aspects. The first one are cultural and psycho-social effects. The second is economic, the third is planning and design-related effects. The final one is its effects on technological developments in cities.

2.1. Cultural and Psychosocial Effects

With the COVID-19 outbreak, public areas in cities such as restaurants, stadiums, cafeterias, theater halls, museums, coffee shops, etc. are shut down, travels within and between countries are restricted or banned altogether, movements of certain age groups and individuals with chronic diseases are restricted, partial or complete curfews are imposed, education in schools are suspended, working hours are made flexible, or working from home is preferred. Places of worship are closed, cultural, art and sports events are suspended, all economic activities are restricted (excluding essential services), and production in ports, loading stations, and factories are halted. Subway, tram, bus, and train services, which are the lifeblood of cities, are suspended.

However, a city is a combination of all these activities. A city cannot be without cultural, art, sports, tourism, recreational, or entertainment activities. The anxiety, fear, and uncertainty caused by the COVID-19 pandemic force cities to take a break on urban life. This is the most critical cultural negativity caused by the pandemic in cities.

Cultural, arts, and sports events separate cities from the countryside. Cities where a large number of people coexist are a melting pot for identities. Restaurants, cafeterias, theater halls, museums, coffee shops, etc. are indispensable not only for the urban economy but also for the socialization of urbanites. COVID-19 measures turn cities into prisons made up of thousands of separate cells, morphing them into "dead cities" (Ergönül, 2020: 7). As noted by Dinç, urban areas are divided into small boxes (Dinç, 2020: 32).

With the pandemic in cities, bans and measures that are called the "new normal" are introduced. People find it difficult to adapt to these new rules imposed on cities. Habits, behavioral patterns, and the usual activities of cities are suspended, and we are shaped by new behavioral patterns. Some of these new behavioral patterns are wearing a mask, social distancing, focusing on domestic activities, and overdoing cleaning and hygiene. The motto of "life is on the streets" has lost its validity and been replaced by "home is the safest place." Being a part of urban life, and being caught up in the flow of the city does not seem very appealing, at least during the pandemic (Hasgül, 2020: 22).

People, who were locked in their houses, have been unable to engage in physical and sports activities. However, these activities are important for the physical and mental development of people and an integral part of daily urban life. It was found that physical and sports activities decreased by 30 to 35 % worldwide with the pandemic, and people staying at home gained weight by 8 to 11 % (Nieuwenhuijsena, 2020: 2).

The new normal imposes its own rules. Eating in a restaurant, for example, has new rules. Numerous rules, such as wearing a mask, layout of tables, seating distance of customers, disposable plates, forks, knives, etc. have turned a simple and ordinary activity into a problematic and sometimes risky one with safety rules. Similarly, wedding ceremonies are held at a certain time and with fewer participants. Sports events take place without spectators, museums offer virtual exhibits. Even funerals are subject to strict rules. All this change is the consequence of the new normal.

Pandemics like COVID-19 exhaust psychological capital by causing uncertainty in public, leading to intense and widespread anxiety and fear. However, psychological capital is indispensable for a person. Psychological capital includes four resources: a) self-efficacy describing the struggle against problems, b) optimism describing the belief in success, c) hope encouraging constant positive thinking, and d) resilience describing the perseverance and determination to achieve goals. The psychological capital created by all these factors is necessary to maintain life (Genç and Akyürek, 2020: 54).

The psychological effects caused by the pandemic can be grouped under three categories. These are social relationships, uncertainty, and resentment towards life. Social relationships are meaningful mental, emotional and physical activities for people. They give people physical and emotional immunity. The isolation brought about by the pandemic means the elimination of this immunity. The uncertainty and anxiety caused by the pandemic wear people down significantly. Uncertainty leads to instant reactions, and panic in people, and undermines the power of rational decision-making. COVID-19 brings people face to face with death and the loss or illness of loved ones or familiar faces creates a heavy psychological pressure (Taştan, 2020: 11–13).

Along with the pandemic, various restrictions have been introduced about children's access to public places where they can play freely, causing them to feel restricted and isolated. The removal of children's immediate surroundings, friends, and school environment, which play an important role in their socialization, development, and transformation into adults, brings about psychological challenges.

A study conducted on 3000 children in Luxembourg, Germany, Switzerland and Brazil found that children's rate of satisfaction with life decreased significantly with the COVID-19 pandemic. The level of satisfaction with life, which was 95 % before the pandemic, decreased to 53 % afterward. The study also found a decrease in the rate of satisfaction of children with school. In Germany, the school satisfaction rate, which was 90 % before the pandemic, fell to 50 % afterward (Gazete Duvar, 26.11.2020).

With the pandemic, both solidarity and segregation are happening in urban areas at the same time. On one hand, problems and uncertainty bring people together. People help those who are isolated, especially the elderly, and offer financial assistance to their family members much more. Neighborly relations are getting stronger. On the other hand, increased anxiety and uncertainty trigger negative behavior in some people such as not caring, self-preservation, panic, aggression, etc. (Taştan, 2020: 17–19). The possibility of infecting others, and forced social distancing drive people away from each other.

Having to stay at home more during the pandemic, brings out activities that were previously put off or overlooked. As people spend more time at home, they call their relatives, play with their children, read books, discover new hobbies, watch movies that have not been watched, cook, etc. Increased fear and anxiety will increase adherence to religion. Religious life and its rituals will be more involved in daily life (Karakaş, 2020: 553).

With the pandemic, the dose of violence and types of crime have changed. According to the Turkish National Police data, the number of public order incidents such as murder, extortion, theft, pickpocketing, stealing, etc. fell to 11,578 in March 2020 compared to 13,538 in March 2019. Among public order incidents, the only increase has been in acts of domestic violence. The number of domestic violence incidents increased by 38.2 % in March 2020, compared to March 2019. Cases of burglary, pickpocketing, and theft have decreased.

2.2. Economic Effects

The most significant downside brought about by the COVID-19 pandemic in urban areas has been its impact on the economy. Commercial networks connecting cities have become inoperable. The global supply chain, which is the foundation of today's industrial production, has been cut off due to both travel restrictions and lockdowns. Being the center of production and consumption throughout history, cities are no longer able to perform this function in a healthy way due to pandemic-related measures and practices.

The economic crisis caused by the COVID-19 pandemic can easily be the greatest economic crisis in human history. The UN declared the COVID-19 pandemic the greatest disaster since World War 2. The President of the EU Commission Von Der Leyen said it was an economic disaster great enough to require a second Marshall Plan, while OPEC's Secretary-General called it an "invisible monster."

The economic crisis caused by the COVID-19 pandemic is different from other economic crises. First of all, the pandemic that has led to this economic crisis is on a global scale, and it has spread very rapidly (Voyvoda and Yeldan, 2020: 189). For this reason, the economic outcomes of the pandemic have been observed in a very short time and commonly. The pandemic is present in every country, developed and less developed. Although the US and EU countries have been more affected, there has been no country that the pandemic has not reached and affected economically (Tunalı, 2020: 26).

The pandemic is taking place at a time when the world economy is fully integrated. The world economy operates through global supply chains made up of millions of producers connected by complex networks. There are 8000 suppliers working in the toy industry in China alone (Karagöz, 2020: 73). According to

2015 data, 52 % of the world's foreign trade takes place between these supply chains (Yazgan, 2020: 151). This chain of production would collapse if the pandemic halts transportation and communication.

Another distinctive feature of the economic crisis induced by the pandemic is that it affects the economy on both supply and demand fronts. Which renders the entire economic system dysfunctional (Tunalı, 2020: 26). Quarantine measures and fear and anxiety among people cause people to stay away from public places, inducing a change in their consumption habits. Due to increasing economic uncertainty, all consumption items and service demand in cities are suspended, except for essential food and health expenditures (Koru, 2020: 92).

In a study covering 24 countries, GDP losses of countries were calculated and seven different scenarios were proposed. According to the most optimistic scenario, the world economy will experience a loss of USD 2,400 billion in GDP. However, if the pandemic spreads even more, this loss is estimated to reach USD 9,200 billion (Mckibbin and Fernando, 2020: 23–40).

In April 2020, the IMF announced that the world economy would contract by 3 %, developed economies by 6 %, and developing countries by 1 % (bbc.co.uk, 08.06.2020). The World Bank estimates a contraction of 5.2 % worldwide in 2020, 7 % in developed countries and 2.5 % in developing economies (World Bank, 2020: 2). Due to the economic crisis caused by the COVID-19 pandemic, 195 to 200 million people are at risk of losing their jobs (Demirbaş and İncekara, 2020: 62). It is estimated that the income loss of informal workers worldwide is 60 % (Omay, 2020: 164).

A variety of industries that are operational in cities have been affected by the pandemic in different ways. Airline freight transportation decreased by 19 % and passenger transportation by 63 %. According to a report by the World Tourism Council, 100 to 120 million people are at risk of losing their jobs in the tourism industry, which is likely to experience a USD 2.1 trillion loss in revenues. Following the declaration of a pandemic by the World Health Organization on March 11, 35 % of bookings made up to the month of July were canceled (wttc.org. 08.07.2020). As a result of the measures implemented in the first 20 days of March 2020, international flights decreased by 99 %, and the amount of fuel used in such flights fell by 95 % (IMF, 2020: 6).

Compared to April 2019, there was a 60 % decline in the textile and ready-to-wear industry in April 2020 in Turkey. The retail sales volume index declined by 19.3 %. In the retail industry, food sales increased by 12.5 %, while non-food sales declined by 36.7 %. While there was a 52 % decline in the home appliances sector, the sharpest decline was experienced by the tourism industry. Compared to April 2019, there was a decline by 93.9 % in April 2020 (Adıgüzel, 2020: 211).

Curfews, restricted travel, closure of shopping malls, closure of schools, etc. introduced to contain the spread of the virus have brought not only the economy, but also social life to a standstill, and have made the impact of the pandemic more pronounced. The cancellation of cultural and art events has brought artists, actors, and musicians to the brink of financial destruction (UCLG, 2020: 33). Street artists, pantomime and graffiti artists have been out of business for months (Pratt, 2020: 1). The pandemic is expected to have long-term, permanent and widespread negative consequences on production and employment.

It is highly likely that all this adversity will give way to new challenges and costs for cities. The death of hundreds of thousands of people, millions of people being under house arrests, planes that are unable to lift off, cancelled vacation plans, children being away from school, companies going bankrupt, workers being laid off and suffering loss of income have been the negative and unwanted consequences of the COVID-19 pandemic. After the pandemic, it would not be surprising to see widespread unemployment, a considerable decline in production, increasing poverty, and mass bankruptcies in cities.

The COVID-19 pandemic has made the existing class segregation in cities more pronounced. As the chairperson of the board of directors of TUSIAD said, the COVID-19 pandemic has deepened the existing income inequality, leading to a dramatic rise in inequality and poverty (cumhuriyet.com.tr, 03.12.2020). With the pandemic, a clear separation has emerged between those who stay home and those who cannot. The upper and middle-income groups living in residence and apartment buildings have been able to work from home while low-income groups living in slums have had to work outside their homes.

The existing inequality in society has also become more evident in the education system. Students who lack a computer, Internet connection, or a separate room to study at home are unable to make the best use out of distance education. Distance education is severely problematic, especially in poor families with many children.

Disadvantaged groups such as the elderly, pensioners, the homeless, migrants, etc. are disproportionally affected by the COVID-19 pandemic. People who lack social security, have difficulty accessing healthcare services, are forced to work outside both have to take on the health risks posed by the COVID-19 pandemic, and face with the social and economic problems it brings such as low wages, unemployment, mandatory leave, etc. Moreover, even if the pandemic ends, budget cuts, contraction of public services, reduction in wages, and forced informal work are some of the possible threats awaiting the poor (Baker, Cira,

Lall, 2020: 11–16). The dire economic situation and growing concerns about the future posed by the pandemic ring the bell for tough times for the poor.

2.3. Planning and Design Effects

The COVID-19 pandemic has once again revealed the heavy toll of unhealthy urbanization. Residential areas that lack zoning and cultural and recreational areas and are dense and cramped, are very suitable for outbreaks to spread. Quarantining of huge apartment complexes and residential buildings the size of ten villages are the bitter consequences of a dense and cramped settlement (Candan, 2020: 2). Instead of high-density cities, urban areas with more green space, breathable houses, green roads, and the importance of environmentally-friendly municipalities have become clearer with the pandemic (Seçkin, 2020: 39). Considering Turkey, the bitter consequences of rent-based urbanization are evident in the COVID-19 pandemic, as in every earthquake.

With the pandemic, the importance of the principle of access to public service within walking distance advocated by urban planning has been understood. Cities that are within walking distance of healthcare facilities, educational institutions or parks can more easily fight the pandemic. Providing healthcare services at the neighborhood level both reduces contact during the pandemic and relieves the burden of public transport, which plays an important part in the spread of the virus.

The pandemic will introduce changes to the design of living spaces in cities. Housing without a garden or a green space will become more and more unpopular. The pandemic has shown the value of small spaces at homes that allow people to breathe. The design of areas without any traffic or slower traffic stands out. There will be more need of space where children can play and the elderly can walk around and stretch their legs (Tuna, 2020: 15).

With the pandemic, people are expected to escape from densely-populated urban areas, where social distancing is challenging and public transportation is a must, to outside of cities. A new movement of *suburbanization* in cities seems inevitable. With the dissemination of working from home and being able to meet all needs online reduce the need for urban areas; increasing health risks make it possible for the popularization of settlements similar to E. Howard's Garden City model (Kunzmann, 2020: 24–25).

Without a doubt, these design changes will popularize slow city, healthy city, or ecological city models even more. The COVID-19 pandemic has demonstrated the value of environmentally and pedestrian-friendly, sustainable, and green cities with social and cultural areas even more. Crowded, dense, and cramped design of cities, unplanned spaces, environmental pollution, and lack of proper disposal of urban waste turn cities into hotbeds for diseases. For this reason, environmental solutions and planning focused on public interest are the best measures to adopt in urban space against pandemics and diseases.

Some changes should also be expected in indoor designs. With the pandemic, people spending more time at home eat more frequently and spend more time in their kitchens. Between March and September 2020, the sales of bread makers increased by 770 % (ntv.com.tr., 03.10.2020). It is possible that kitchens will be designed more spaciously, tying kitchens and living rooms together. It is possible to include dining corners in kitchens or to join them with balconies.

Larger living rooms, adding a room suitable for working to home design, having a separate room for children where they can play and attend courses are some of the features sought in post-pandemic home designs. Children's rooms should not be designed without a balcony (Tuna, 2020: 16). For better ventilation of houses, skylights, horizontal and vertical pivot openings, sash windows and internal and external transom windows should again be included in design and application taking into consideration the wind direction.

LEED, WELL, and Fitwell, etc. building certification programs will now be more health-focused. Building designs that will reduce the chances of a possible future outbreak or better protect individuals against them will undoubtedly of significance (Özdemir, 2020: 9). Design details such as access to and the entrance of buildings, open spaces, indoor environment, working areas, common areas, emergency procedures, etc. should be more outbreak-responsive.

2.4. Technological Effects

The use artificial intelligence-powered intelligent urban systems in city services, which started to take effect in the 1990s, reached its peak after the COVID-19 pandemic (Kunzmann, 2020: 22). Perhaps in the history of cities, technology has never been so involved in daily life. There are several reasons why technology has become more involved in urban life with the pandemic.

The first one has been the measures and bans to contain the spread of the pandemic. Strict measures are adopted to prevent the pandemic. Implementation of these measures in cities where millions of people live is possible only through technology. In China, there are systems that can remotely measure fever, calculate the number of passengers on the bus, and track it. Facial recognition systems that can identify patients with high fever are increasingly being used in train stations, shopping malls or parks. There are smart cards that warn people when they get too close to each other and social distance is violated. Moreover, these smart cards can track who came close with whom, where the holder went, and came into contact with and submit this information to an information center (Özdemir, 2020: 65).

The Municipality of Moscow has made it mandatory to receive a QR code. In Turkey, a new application was developed that generates a HES (Life Fits Home) code. A technology company announced that a chip was ready that is inserted under the skin and can track people (Erciyes and Genç, 2020: 5). Medical supplies are transported by autonomous vehicles operating unmanned in China. Food distribution, cleaning of squares and disinfection are carried out by robots.

The flow of information about the pandemic is extremely important when accurate and instantaneous information is of vital importance. Millions of data processed about the pandemic must be processed instantly and accurately and shared with the public (Acet, 2020: 58). Processing of numerous data, an "information cloud," is only possible via artificial intelligence technology. Rumors and disinformation create anxiety and fear among people as much as the pandemic. Therefore, processed, instantly shared, and accurate information is of great importance (Polat, 2020: 80).

Geographic Information Systems (GIS) and maps were used for the first time in Italy during the pandemic, and location-based transmission maps were shared with the public. These maps raised critical awareness to better understand the spread of the disease and the danger it poses (Karagülle, 2020: 52).

Another reason for the popularization of technology in daily life in cities is the new behavioral patterns brought about by the "new normal" that came about with the pandemic. As banknotes are used less and less, cryptocurrencies and contactless credit cards become more widespread. Digital life turns into an important alternative in business, education, and entertainment; it is becoming possible to maintain a life without leaving the house for high-income families with digital facilities at home.

As people stay at home more and more, interest in the digital is growing. According to a study conducted on this subject, the use of social media increased by 67 %. Netflix viewership increased by 51 %, TV viewership by 45 %, and WhatsApp and Messenger use by 45 %. Money spent on computers and video games increased by 35 %. Staying home fuels the desire to consume (bbc.co.uk, 15.12.2020). E-commerce is experiencing its golden age while the entire economy collapses. Between March and October in Turkey, there was a 4-fold increase in e-commerce sales (aa.com.tr, 10.10.2020). Worldwide, e-commerce grew by 21 %, while in developed countries where the Internet is widespread, such as the UK, this increase reached 116 % (bbc.co.uk, 04.09.2020).

The growing e-commerce market leads to serious competition, with most stores setting up free home delivery networks.

The number of users of applications such as Zoom, Slack, etc. that allow remote access increased from 6 million before the pandemic to 108 million two months after it. Through digital applications, people can receive education, hold meetings, visit museums, and organize cultural and art events. These applications offer solutions to psychosocial problems that develop because of the pandemic such as loneliness, disconnection from social relationships, etc. (Akca and Küçükoğlu, 2020: 75).

Social distancing, the obligation to reduce contact, and lockdowns force people to work from home. Working from home has increased the need for social media, and there has been a digital transformation (Karlı and Çelikyay, 2020: 329). On the other hand, working from home causes people to move away from the city and close up in their homes. At home, there are fewer possibilities to socialize. Moreover, working from home reduces productivity. According to a study conducted in Turkey, only 38.2 % of employees said that working at home had a positive impact on them (Akca and Küçükoğlu, 2020: 79).

CONCLUSION

In cities, the COVID-19 pandemic has had devastating cultural, psychosocial, and economic consequences. Thousands of people have been laid off, urban life has come to a standstill, and businesses have been driven into bankruptcy. Cities have been under the surveilled by cameras and thermal devices.

Despite its negative consequences, the COVID-19 pandemic also offers a window of opportunity for humanity. All this negativity makes it possible to transition into a new era. This negativity should be perceived as lessons learned by the pandemic and guide us in building new cities of the future.

Unfair income distribution in cities, growing inequality, ignoring the principle of public interest in planning, urban building density created for the purpose of rent, social segregation and racism, privatization of education and healthcare services, and neoliberal policies that promote growth despite the environment have become untenable in the face of the pandemic.

As in COVID-19, solving pandemics before they create critical consequences requires an urban society that is more environmentally friendly, has social concerns, is open to participation, and targets quality of life instead of growth. Smart city technologies should contribute to this goal. Zoning plans should not be used for brand city competitions or grand flashy projects but for the sake of public interest and the future of society. Cities should be transformed into areas where there is quality of life for all.

This city model is also craved today. The New Urban Agenda, which was released during the Habitat III Summit, common objectives of humanity were listed as: environmentally-friendly cities, involvement of all spheres of society in governance, proper meeting of essential humanitarian needs such as health, education, and housing, and alleviation of poverty (UN, 2017).

The Millennium Development Goals, declared by the UN in 2000 include the same goals. Less poverty and higher quality of life are key goals for the UN. The Aalborg Charter of 1994, published by the EU, and the Leipzig Charter of 2007 aim for Sustainable Cities, emphasizing that a high-quality and environmentally-friendly urban life is an achievable goal for all. To conclude, the city model that we should aim for after the pandemic is already a goal included in many international documents. What is left for us is to take the first step.

REFERENCES

Acet, E. A. (2020). Pandemi kadar tehlikeli bir gerçek infodemi. *Spektrum*, Haziran, 57–59.

Adıgüzel, M. (2020). COVID-19 Pandemisinin Türkiye ekonomisine etkilerinin makroekonomik analizi. *İTÜ SBD*, COVID-19 Özel Sayı, 191–221.

Ahsan, M. (2020). Strategic decisions on urban built environment to pandemics in Turkey: lessons from COVID-19. *Journal of Urban Management*, 9(3), 281–285.

Akca, M. and Küçükoğlu, M. (2020). COVID-19 ve iş yaşamına etkileri: evden çalışma. *JIMEP Dergisi*, 8(1), 71–81.

Aydınlı, E. (2020). Salgınlar ve uluslararası sistemin dayanıklılığı. U. Ulutaş (Ed). *COVID-19 Sonrası Küresel Sistem: Eski Sorunlar, Yeni Trendler* (35–44). Ankara: T.C. Dışişleri Bakanlığı Stratejik Araştırmalar Merkezi.

Baker, J., Cira, D. and Lall, S. (2020). *COVID-19 and the urban poor addressing those in slums*. Washington, DC: World Bank Group.

Beaud, M. (2003). *Kapitalizmin tarihi 1500–2010*. Çev. Fikret Başkaya. İstanbul: Yordum Kitap.

Candan, T.K. (2020). Pandemi, kent, mekân, yaşam ve gelecek. *Gazete Duvar*, 08.05.2020.

Demirbaş, D. and İncekara, A. (2020). Blokzincir ve COVID-19 küresel salgın ilişkisi. D. Demirbaş ve V. Bozkurt (Ed). *COVID-19 Pandemisinin Ekonomik, Toplumsal ve Siyasal Etkileri* (53–68). İstanbul: İstanbul Üniversitesi Yayını.

Dinç, S. (2020). Localaşan yeni mekânsallıklar. *Spektrum*, Haziran, 31–35.

Erciyes, E. and Genç, M. (2020). COVID-19 salgınının toplumsal değişim ile güvenlik ortamına etkisi ve kolluğa önerileri. *Güvenlik Bilimleri Dergisi*, 9(1), 1–14.

Ergönül, Ö. (2020). Sürdürülebilir mekânların pandemiye karşı değerlendirilmesi. *Spektrum*, Haziran, 7–11.

Genç, C. and Akyürek, S. (2020). COVID-19: kaçınılmaz değişim alarmı! ya insan ya da insan! *Kayseri Üniversitesi SBD*, 2(1), 48–63.

Genç, Ö. (2011). Kara ölüm: 1348 veba salgını ve ortaçağ Avrupa'sına etkileri. *Tarih Okulu*, 10, 123–150.

Hasgül, E. (2020). Salgın Öncesinde ve Sonrasında Konut Mekanındaki Mekan Kullanım Pratiklerinin Fiziksel ve Sosyal Dönüşüm Süreci, *Spektrum*, Haziran, 19–21.

IMF (2020). *World economic outlook*, Washington, DC: IMF Yayını.

Karagöz, F. (2020). Pandeminin küresel tedarik zincirlerinin işleyişine etkisi ve muhtemel sonuçları üzerine bir değerlendirme. D. Demirbaş ve V. Bozkurt (Ed). *COVID-19 Pandemisinin Ekonomik, Toplumsal ve Siyasal Etkileri* (69–86). İstanbul: İstanbul Üniversitesi Yayını.

Karagülle, D. (2020). Mekâna bağlanmak, *Spektrum*, Haziran, 51–56.

Karakaş, M. (2020). COVID-19 salgınının çok boyutlu sosyolojisi ve yeni normal meselesi. *İstanbul Üniversitesi Sosyoloji Dergisi*, 40(1), 541–573.

Karlı, R. and Çelikyay, S. (2020). Akıllı kentlerin gelişiminde COVID-19 etkisi. *Van Yüzüncü Yıl Üniversitesi SBE Dergisi*, Salgın Hastalıklar Özel Sayısı, 321–338.

Koru, A.T. (2020). COVID-19 ve küreselleşmenin geleceği. Ö.F. Çolak (Ed). *Salgın Ekonomisi* (87–114). Ankara: Efil Yayınları.

Kunzmann, K.R. (2020). Smart Cities after COVID-19: Ten Narratives. *disP-The Planning Review*, 56(2), 20–31.

Kye, B. and Hwang, S. (2020). Social trust in the midst of pandemic crisis: implications from COVID-19 of South Korea. *Research in Social Stratification and Mobility*, 68, 1–5.

Lai, K., Webster, C., Kumari, S. and Chinmoy, S. (2019). The nature of cities and the COVID-19 pandemic. *Current Opinion in Environmental Sustainability*, 20, 1–5.

Little, L.K. (2012). Plague and the end of antiquity: the pandemic of 541–750. Cambridge: Cambridge Üniversitesi Yayını.

Mckibbin, W. and Fernando, R. (2020). *The global macroeconomic impacts of COVID-19: seven scenarios*, Sidney: Avustralya Ulusal Üniversitesi CAMA Yayını.

Nieuwenhuijsena, M. (2020). COVID19 and the city; from the short term to the long term. *Environmental Research*, 191, 1-3.

Omay, U. (2020). COVID-19 salgını sonrası çalışma hayatı: güncel sorunlar, öngörüler ve öneriler. D. Demirbaş ve V. Bozkurt (Ed). *COVID-19 Pandemisinin Ekonomik, Toplumsal ve Siyasal Etkileri* (153-170). İstanbul: İstanbul Üniversitesi Yayını.

Ortaylı, N. (2020). Pandemi ve gelecek, *Psikeart*, 71, 48-53.

Özdemir, G. A. (2020). Pandemide yeni nesil teknolojinin önemi. *Spektrum*, Haziran, 63-69.

Pamuk, Ş. (2020). Tarihte küresel salgınlar ve iktisadi etkileri. Ö.F. Çolak (Ed). *Salgın Ekonomisi* (35-54). Ankara: Efil Yayınları.

Polat, İ. (2020). COVID-19, blokzincir ve akıllı şehirler. *Kent Dergisi*, 2, 79-81.

Pratt, Andy (2020). COVID – 19 impacts cities, cultures and societies. *City, Culture and Society*, 21, 1-2.

Seçkin, P. (2020). Salgın koşullarında peyzaj tasarımında değişen konfor arayışları. *Spektrum*, Haziran, 37-41.

Seren, M. (2020). Medikal istihbaratın yükselişi. U. Ulutaş (Ed). *COVID-19 Sonrası Küresel Sistem: Eski Sorunlar, Yeni Trendler* (86-91). Ankara: T.C. Dışişleri Bakanlığı Stratejik Araştırmalar Merkezi.

Stier, A., Berman, M. and Bettencourt, L. (2020, March 29). COVID-19 attack rate increases with city size. Retrieved October 1, 2020, from https://www.medrxiv.org/content/10.1101/2020.03.22.20041004v2

Taştan, C. (2020). *Kovid-19 salgını ve sonrası psikolojik ve sosyolojik değerlendirmeler*. Ankara: Polis Akademisi Yayını.

Tekeli, İ. (2020). Salgınlar ve kentler sarmalında dünyanın geldiği nokta: COVID-19. Ö.F. Çolak (Ed). *Salgın Ekonomisi* (54-90). Ankara: Efil Yayınları.

Tuna, R. (2020). Yaşam mekânlarımız nasıl değişecek? *Spektrum*, Haziran, 15-19.

Tunalı, Ç.B. (2020). COVID-19 pandemisinin ekonomik büyüme üzerindeki etkisi. D. Demirbaş ve V. Bozkurt (Ed). *COVID-19 Pandemisinin Ekonomik, Toplumsal ve Siyasal Etkileri* (25-34). İstanbul: İstanbul Üniversitesi Yayını.

TÜBA (2020). *COVID-19 küresel salgın değerlendirme raporu*, Ankara: TÜBA Yayınları.

UCLG (2020). *Culture, cities and the COVID-19 pandemic*. UCLG Kültür Komitesi Yayını.

UN (2017). *New urban agenda*. Quito: BM Yayını.

Voyvoda, E. and Yeldan, E. (2020). COVID-19 salgınının Türkiye ekonomisi üzerine etkileri ve politika alternatiflerinin makroekonomik genel denge analizi. Ö.F. Çolak (Ed). *Salgın Ekonomisi* (190–232). Ankara: Efil Yayınları.

World Bank (2020). *Global economic prospects*, June 2020.

Yazgan, M. E. (2020). Koronavirüs sonrası dünyada dış ticareti ne bekliyor? Ö.F. Çolak (Ed). *Salgın Ekonomisi* (142–163). Ankara: Efil Yayınları.

Yıldırım, S. (2020). Salgınların sosyal-psikolojik görünümü: COVID-19 (koronavirüs) pandemi örneği. *Turkish Studies*, 15(4), 1331–1351.

Abdullah Çelik*
Ali Burak Aksungur**

Administrative Measures Adopted in Response to the COVID-19 Pandemic and Their Effects

Abstract Coronaviruses that emerged at the beginning of the 21st century caused various respiratory diseases in the human body. On the other hand, COVID-19, the new type of coronavirus that emerged at the end of 2019, spread to the world in a short time and became a pandemic. Thus, COVID 19 significantly affected social and economic life. Governments had to take some administrative measures in order to mitigate the effects of the pandemic.

The main tools of combating the pandemic in Turkey have been administrative measures. In this context, restrictions on social, cultural and sports activities, transition to distance education model, tax and credit delays, obligation to wear face masks, curfew restrictions, stay at home calls, isolation and quarantine, intercity travel restrictions, flexible working practices were applied.

Administrative measures taken during the pandemic process have been great importance for the protection of public health as well as for the social and economic sustainability. In this process, it has been observed that digital services have gained an essential role in ensuring the continuity of public services.

Keywords: COVID-19, pandemic, public administration, administrative measures

INTRODUCTION

Throughout history, pandemics have caused various destructions, leading to famine and death. Viruses, defined as "parasites that are smaller-in size than bacteria, are required to enter a host cell to survive, and can only be seen via an electrone microscope" (Turkish Language Association, 2020), have had a significant impact on humans and societies, and still maintain their destructive effects today.

---

* Prof., Harran University, Faculty of Economics and Administrative Sciences, Department of Public Administration, acelik@harran.edu.tr
** Res. Asst., Harran University, Faculty of Economics and Administrative Sciences, Department of Public Administration, aliburakaksungur@gmail.com

At the beginning of the 21st century, a family of viruses were discovered, called the Coronaviruses, which enter human body and cause respiratory disease. Among this family of viruses, SARS-CoV, MERS-CoV, and SARS-CoV-2 have been observed to transmit to humans, causing respiratory illness and even death (Unhale et al., 2020: 109). Compared to other Coronaviruses, the virus causing COVID-19 has been found to have some differences and to be transmitted between humans easier than SARS-CoV. As a matter of fact, it has been found that COVID-19 can spread from one person to another as a result of a cough or sneeze during face-to-face communication (Heymann, 2020: 543–544). The virus' ability to spread this fast has led the disease it causes to transmit all over the world in a short period of time, making COVID-19 the main agenda of 2020.

This study deals with administrative measures adopted by central the government during the COVID-19 pandemic in the fields of health, education, work, and disadvantaged groups, and the effectiveness of these measures.

1. COVID-19 Pandemic across the World

The disease, which was first identified in Guangdong, China in 2002 as a respiratory disorder with an unknown cause and was called SARS (severe acute respiratory syndrome), shows similarities with the symptoms caused by the COVID-19 virus (WHO, 2020). The SARS-CoV virus caused 744 deaths in a total of 8096 cases, resulting in a mortality rate of around 10 % (Wang, Horby, Hayden, Gao, 2020: 471).

In April 2012, another disease showing symptoms similar to those caused by the SARS virus was identified in Saudi Arabia. This disease, called MERS (Middle East Respiratory Syndrome), was alto detected in numerous countries such as Qatar, Jordan, the United Arab Emirates, the United Kingdom, France, Germany, Italy and Tunisia (Zhao et al., 2013: 2). The MERS virus caused 2500 deaths and 875 deaths worldwide with a mortality rate of 35 % (Weston and Frieman, 2020: 1).

Following the SARS pandemic in 2002 and the MERS pandemic in 2012, the novel Coronavirus, known as nCoV, SARS-CoV-2, and COVID-19, first emerged in China in December 2019, caused the third Coronavirus pandemic among humans in the 21st century (Unhale et al., 2020: 109).

On December 31, 2019, the World Health Organization China Office reported that an unidentified respiratory inflammatory disease was detected in Wuhan, Hubei Province, which is located at the center of the international transport network and is a major metropolis with a population of 11 million.

Table 1: Number of Cases and Deaths Caused by COVID-19 in Selected Countries

Country	Total Deaths	Total Number of Cases
US	301,536	16.446.844
Germany	24.125	1.406.161
Brazil	182,799	6.970.034
China	4.764	95.375
France	58.969	2.367.648
South Africa	23.827	883,687
India	144,451	9.956.577
Italy	66.537	1.888.144
Japan	2.739	187,103
Russian Federation	49.151	2.762.668
Turkey	17.121	1.113.827

Source: World Health Organization, December 17, 2020.

Within the first three days, national authorities identified this disease with an unknown cause in 44 people. In the following days, the said disease was found to have originated from a local seafood market in Wuhan, and on January 7, 2020, Chinese authorities announced that it was caused by a novel Coronavirus (WHO, 21.01.2020).

Due to the effects caused by the COVID-19 virus, the World Health Organization declared a global pandemic on March 12, 2020. Today (as of December 17, 2020), there are 72.851.747 confirmed cases, including 1.643.339 deaths. The number of cases by countries is as follows (Table 1):

COVID-19 continues to transmit between humans. Governments are trying to lower the rate of spread of the disease by adopting necessary measures. The most effective method to avoid COVID-19, which spreads via contact and respiratory droplets, is isolation (Laçinel Gürlevik, 2020: 47). Due to the uncontrollable surge in the number of cases, hospitals dedicated to COVID-19 treatment, as well as other hospitals, have had to restrict their services (such as reducing emergency services) to combat COVID-19 (Parodi and Liu, 2020: 1441). It is of great importance to contain the pandemic, as the sudden increase in the number of cases strain the existing capacities of healthcare institutions.

1.1. First Cases and Measures

The COVID-19 virus can easily transmit from person to person through droplets that carriers produce during coughing or sneezing. According to the World Health Organization, the virus can spread via coughing/sneezing, as well as by touching the mouth and face with hands that had contact with contaminated surfaces. Thanks to its high infectiousness, the virus spread all around the world in a very short period of time. Following the emergence of the outbreak, China informed the World Health Organization and the whole world was provided with information. After that, many countries began screening passengers arriving from China for signs of the disease. The goal for screening efforts was to prevent the spread of the disease by preventing the entry of individuals with symptoms of the disease (Unhale et al., 2020: 109). These measures could not prevent the disease from spreading to other countries, leaving the whole world having to face it (Quijin, 2020: 1).

The city of Wuhan, the starting point of the pandemic, was caught off guard by the growing number of cases. Thousands of people tried to reach doctors, and many people died waiting for an empty bed in hospitals. More than 30,000 healthcare workers were sent to Wuhan to fulfill the shortage of staff in hospitals. In Jingmen, another city in Hubei Province, strict measures were adopted the moment the outbreak was identified, resulting in a successful respond to COVID-19. On January 26, 2020, the Chinese government closed entrances to all cities (Quijin, 2020: 1–2).

The first Coronavirus case in Europe was detected in France on January 24, 2020. As of January 10, 2020, France strengthened its surveillance efforts for early diagnosis of cases, and put in place a risk classification. According to this classification, contact with 5 people was low risk, less than 18 people was medium risk, and more than 18 people was high risk. The first cases in the country were identified in three people arrived from China on January 24, 2020, followed by contact-tracing (Stoecklin et al., 2020: 1).

On February 5, 2020, 171 people on a cruise ship were found to have COVID-19 and were quarantined at an airbase in California. On March 2, 2020, the Governor of California announced a USD 20 million emergency aid package in response to COVID-19. As contact-tracing became more and more difficult due to a surge in cases, quarantine efforts were introduced (Parodi and Liu, 2020: 1441).

Increasing case numbers and the inability of medical services to respond to these cases led the focus to shift from preventive measures to mitigating measures. Otherwise, the already-strained healthcare systems would crash. In this context the measures below have been adopted and are still in place in many countries:

a. Reducing the spread of the disease
b. Reducing demand for healthcare services,
c. Focusing more on home isolation,
d. Increasing testing capacity and
e. Self isolation.

(Parodi and Liu, 2020: 1441).

2. COVID-19 Pandemic in Turkey

The first confirmed case of COVID-19 in Turkey, which began to spread rapidly around the world, was announced by the Minister of Health on March 11, 2020. A patient admitted to the hospital with a high fever and cough was diagnosed with COVID-19. It was noted that the patient arrived from Europe, and was isolated soon after diagnosis. All individuals close to the case were also considered suspected cases and put under monitoring (Ministry of Health, 11.03.2020).

The process that began with COVID-19 indicated a shift in the provision of public services. Digital services, which previously had an auxiliary function for public services, played a major role during the COVID-19 pandemic (Kostenbaum and Dener, 2020).

2.1. Administrative Measures Adopted

A variety of measures were adopted to contain the spread of the disease such as restricting social, cultural, and sports activities, shifting to distance education, tax and loan deferrals, curfews, calls to stay at home, travel restrictions between cities, and flexible working arrangements (Turan, Hamza, and Çelikyay, 2020: 14).

The first measure adopted in response to the COVID-19 pandemic in Turkey was the establishment of the Coronavirus Scientific Board by the Ministry of Health on January 10, 2020. The board, which is made up of experts of various branches, including the Ministry of Health, follows the course of the disease in the country and in other countries and offers recommendations (Ministry of Health, 2020). These recommendations are translated into policies under the coordination by the President and the ministers and adopted countrywide.

2.1.1. Administrative Measures Adopted in the Field of Health

The COVID-19 pandemic, which started out as a health crisis, claimed the lives of millions of people. Even though COVID-19 had a major impact on social and economic life, it posed the greatest threat to human health.

As in the world, numerous measures were adopted to combat the COVID-19 pandemic in Turkey. Measures adopted in the field were as follows:

a. Detection and treatment of those infected with the virus
b. Prevention of infection

(Güler and Aydınbaş, 2020: 17).

Turkey implemented a number of measures to prevent the spread of the disease in accordance with the recommendations of the Coronavirus Scientific Board, which convened on January 22, 2020. In this context, the COVID-19 virus was treated as a public health issue and a guide was published covering diagnostic, prevention, prevention and control measures (Ministry of Health, 2020).

COVID-19 Dashboard

The Ministry of Health announced that the total number of patients, the number of tests, the number of deaths, the number of patients in intensive care, the number of intubated patients, and the number of recovered patients would be shared with the public in order to present the data on the disease (Ministry of Health, 2020). Within this context, the COVID-19 Dashboard has been shared with the public daily (Table 2). The COVID-19 Dashboard has allowed the public to be presented with up-to-date data on a daily, and weekly basis.

TURKEY COVID-19 PATIENT TABLE 17 DECEMBER 2020	TODAY	THIS WEEK	TOTAL
	NUMBER OF TESTS	PNEUMONIA RATE IN PATIENTS	NUMBER OF TESTS
	26.102	%2,9	21.904.694
	NUMBER OF CASES	HOSPITAL BED OCCUPANCY RATE	NUMBER OF PATIENTS
	27.515	%55,8	1.955.680
		ADULT ICU OCCUPANCY RATE	
	NUMBER OF PATIENTS	%73,7	NUMBER OF DEATHS
	4.209	VENTILATOR OCCUPANCY RATE	17.364
	NUMBER OF DEATHS	%41,5	NUMBER OF CRITICALLY ILL PATIENTS
	243	AVERAGE DETECTION TIME OF CONTACTS OF POSITIVE PATIENTS 10 HOURS	5.803
	NUMBER OF RECOVERIES	FILIATION RATE	NUMBER OF RECOVERIES
	30.494	%99,9	1.721.607

Table 2: Turkey COVID-19 Dashboard, December 17, 2020
Source: Ministry of Health, December 17, 2020

Contact Tracing

As of March 10, 2020, the date when the first case was detected in Turkey, contact tracing efforts were kicked off, which aimed to contain the spread of the pandemic by screening the chain of contact. Efforts were made to prevent the spread of the disease by identifying individuals having close contact with patients diagnosed with COVID-19. The Ministry of Health was able to reach cases and contacts as soon as possible by allowing contact tracing teams on the field to enter data on the mobile application called the Contact Tracing and Isolation Tracking System in real time. As a result of the successful implementation of contact tracing, the rate of reaching those known to be a contact increased to 99.9 % (Ministry of Health, 2020).

The Life Fits Home Application

A digital application called "Life Fits Home" was developed to track patients who are required to be in isolation at home and to issue warnings if necessary. The Ministry of Health's Life Fits Home mobile app reached 10 million users as of May 13, 2020. Later on, the Life Fits Home code was introduced to identify high-risk passengers on intercity travels and their contacts (Ministry of Health, 2020).

Isolation and Quarantine

Isolation and quarantine efforts were kicked off thanks to their success in combatting outbreaks. Isolation and quarantine are the two best known measures to avoid the spread of pandemics. Isolation is the prevention of transmission of disease to healthy individuals by isolating the patient diagnosed with the disease from others. Quarantine is the cautionary separation of individuals suspected of disease from others. Quarantine ends when the infectiousness ends or the suspicion of the disease is eliminated, while individuals who are known to be ill are placed in isolation (Doğan and Bayraktar, 2020: 72).

During the COVID-19 pandemic, Turkish nationals returning from abroad to Turkey were quarantined for 14 days in dormitories of the Directorate of Credit and Dormitories of the Ministry of Youth and Sports, which were mostly empty with the temporary suspension of university education (Ministry of Youth and Sports, 2020). In addition, confirmed COVID-19 cases and their contacts were isolated at home. Information about people in home isolation was submitted to provincial/district pandemic control centers via the Contact Tracing and Isolation Tracking System and neighborhood audit teams conducted audits and reported the results to the Ministry of Health (Circular of the Ministry of Interior No. E.13429).

Curfews

One measure often resorted to during outbreaks is curfews. The first measure adopted was the curfew imposed upon those aged 65 and over and those with chronic diseases as of March 21, 2020 midnight by the circular on restriction/prohibition of leaving residence (Circular of the Ministry of Interior No. E.5762). The scope of this restriction was extended on April 3, 2020 to cover those born after January 1, 2000. Another circular imposed a curfew during April 10–12, 2020 weekend in 30 metropolitan provinces and Zonguldak (Circulars of the Ministry of Interior No. E. 6235 and E.6484). This was the first countrywide curfew introduced in the pandemic.

Compulsory Mask Wearing

The possibility of airborne transmission of the COVID-19 virus brought about measures relating to mask-wearing. As of April 3, 2020, mask-wearing was made compulsory for those working in public areas, such as markets, and administrative fines were introduced for failure to wear masks. A circular published on September 8, 2020, made it mandatory to wear masks at all places, except for residences, all across the country (Circulars of the Ministry of Interior No. E. 6235 and E. 14553).

Travel Restrictions

The circular published by the General Directorate of Provincial Administration of the Ministry of Health on April 3, 2020, all entry and exits to and from 30 metropolitan provinces and Zonguldak were suspended starting from April 3, 2020 midnight for 15 days, except for mandatory cases. Those who were to travel due to a force majeure had to obtain a "Travel Permit Document" from governorates/district governorates. Travel restrictions were repeated according to the course of the pandemic (Circular of the Ministry of Interior No. E.6235).

The effectiveness of the administrative measures adopted can be clearly seen during curfews. Table 3 shows the number of COVID-19 cases between November 30, 2020, when the curfew started, and December 17, 2020. Considering the 17-day data following November 30, 2020, when restrictions were introduced, there was a significant decrease in the number of cases and a significant increase in the number of recovered patients after December 10, 2020. Given the fact that the administrative measures cannot show immediate

Administrative Measures Adopted during COVID-19 Pandemic 183

Table 3: Turkey COVID-19 Dashboard Between November 30 and December 17, 2020

Date	Number of Patients	Number of Tests	Number of Deaths	Number of Recoveries
December 17, 2020	4.209	206.102	243	30.494
December 16, 2020	4.893	205.397	240	29.922
December 15, 2020	5.105	206.190	235	29.247
December 14, 2020	5.064	204.289	229	28.164
December 13, 2020	5.103	181.199	218	22.215
December 12, 2020	5.203	189.065	222	20.191
December 11, 2020	5.607	208.873	226	5.516
December 10, 2020	5.918	206.202	220	5.232
December 9, 2020	6.213	204.411	217	5.846
December 8, 2020	6.593	201.219	211	5.245
December 7, 2020	6.420	196.902	203	5.017
December 6, 2020	6.093	174.761	195	4.011
December 5, 2020	6.128	178.903	196	4.100
December 4, 2020	6.903	194.435	193	4.811
December 3, 2020	6.511	187.518	187	4.190
December 2, 2020	6.690	183,624	193	4.821
December 1, 2020	6.101	180.312	190	4.593
November 30, 2020	6.514	176.656	188	4.485

Source: COVID-19 Information Page, Ministry of Health, December 17, 2020.

results, it is safe to say that reducing social mobility in conjunction with curfews on weekends and between 9 pm and 5 am on weekdays was effective in the fight against COVID-19.

Contact tracing and the Life Fits Home application were measures towards the identification and treatment of patients while isolation, quarantine, mask use, curfews, and travel restrictions were measures towards the prevention of the spread of the disease.

2.1.2. Administrative Measures Adopted in the Field of Education

The Turkish national education system is made up of preschool (preschool and kindergarten), primary (grades 1 to 8), secondary (9 to 12), and higher education (associate, bachelor's, master's, and doctoral degrees) systems. There are over 18 million students and over 1 million teachers in preschool education, primary and secondary education (Ministry of National Education, 2020b). In addition, there are around 8 million higher education students in associate's, bachelor's, master's, and doctoral degree programs and 175 thousand faculty members (Higher Education Information Management System, 2020).

Given Turkey's 83 million population, we can see that 30 % of the population is in this educational network. Education-related social mobility brings people together indoors, increasing the risk of COVID-19 infection. For this reason, administrative measures targeting the educational system, which includes more than 27 million students, teachers, and faculty members, from preschool to graduate education, have led to consequences that will affect the entire society, considering also the relatives of these people.

Ministry of National Education

Following the detection of the first COVID-19 case in Turkey, the semester break, which was planned to take place between 6 and 10 April 2020, was pushed forward to 16–20 March 2020, and distance education started on March 23, 2020. In this process, the digital learning platform called the Education Information Network (EBA) was updating, laying the groundwork for students to receive distance education through the Internet and television. Due to the ongoing pandemic, distance education was decided to continue until May 31, 2020, ending the school year of 2019–2020. The school year of 2020–2021 began as distance education on August 31, 2020, and grades identified by the Coronavirus Scientific Committee shifted to face-to-face education gradually. Due to another surge in cases, it was decided that schools would shift to distance education from November 20, 2020 to January 4, 2021 (Ministry of National Education, 2020a).

Digitalization efforts prior to COVID-19 became a necessity after it. In a time when face-to-face education was abandoned, distance education came to be the most appropriate tool, and digital technologies previously used to only support education became a main element. In this context, the EBA infrastructure of the Ministry of National Education, previously used complementarily, became the main element of education (Buluk and Eşitti, 2020: 288).

Distance education gave the opportunity to maintain education without interruption during the pandemic, but also led to inequalities in opportunity for students. Due to differences in socioeconomic status, students' level of access to information and communication technologies such as mobile phones, TV, and computer also differs. There are significant discrepancies between the children of families that are unable to offer a proper learning environment for distance education and those who can (Sezgin and Fırat, 2020: 45). A study conducted on high school students found that distance education negatively affected them and led to educational anxiety. Even though school administrations and teachers seek the interest of students, there are many students living in rural areas with infrastructural problems, lacking adequate facilities, and having insufficient access to distance education systems, which lead to inequalities in education (Karaca and Kelam, 2020: 16).

Council of Higher Education and Universities

Higher education was suspended as of March 12, 2020 and then it was decided to shift completely to distance education for the spring semester of 2019–2020 school year (Council of Higher Education, 26.03.2020).

COVID-19's rapid transformation into a global pandemic, and the sudden shift to distance education by the decision of the Council of Higher Education, caught universities off guard, which led to Internet-related problems and lack of preparation for distance education (Telli Yamamoto and Altun, 2020: 30). The pandemic forced universities to improve their infrastructure so that they can continue education, and lecturers to increase their level of knowledge about how technological tools can be used for education and to communicate with students (Güneş, 2020).

Given COVID-19's infectiousness and the social mobility of more than 27 million people for education purposes, distance education both helped slow down the pandemic and relieved the burden of healthcare systems (Giannini and Albrectsen, 2020). However, administrative measures adopted will likely bring about negative consequences for students who lack a computer, mobile phone, or a suitable learning environment necessary for distance education. Research has shown that distance education deepens inequality in access to education (Gençoğlu and Çiftçi, 2020: 1648).

A study conducted on university students showed that 86 % of students were able to follow courses by promptly adapting to distance education. However, only 38.8 % of these students were satisfied with distance education (Buluk and Eşitti, 2020: 288–294). In another study, the satisfaction level of university students from distance education system was 23.1 %. Although students were satisfied with the opportunities offered by distance education, they criticized it due to the lack of face-to-face interaction (Genç and Gümrükçüoğlu, 2020: 419). Another study found that the inability to create a suitable personal work environment was the most common problem faced by students receiving distance education, which led to problems in concentration (Akbal and Akbal, 2020: 543).

The experience of universities, faculty members, and students in distance education also affects the efficiency of distance education. Low participation in live lessons and the fact that only a handful of students offer feedback during these lessons are examples of how distance education is not used efficiently. For this reason, aside from mandatory situations such as a pandemic, distance education may only be efficient for students with a high level of awareness. In addition, the efficiency of distance education also depends on the competence of the teaching staff on distance education systems (Kaysi, 2020: 21).

Given the need for social isolation to contain the pandemic, distance education practices have played major role, allowing the continuation of education.

2.1.3. Administrative Measures for Working Life

In response to the COVID-19 pandemic, those infected are identified and treated, while efforts are being made to prevent others from getting infected. Preventing the spread of the disease is made possible by social distancing, through which people are prevented from gathering (Güler and Aydınbaş, 2020: 17). Social distancing affected the economy as a whole by leading to major changes in working life and pushed businesses to shift their services or production activities.

COVID-19, which emerged as a global health crisis, took over the whole world in a very short period of time. Many economic activities were halted, health and food industries became more important while tourism and transport were adversely affected. These issues broke the supply and demand balance, contracting economies (Karakaya, 2020). In Turkey, various administrative measures were adopted to mitigate the impact of the pandemic and to reduce losses.

Economy

A number of economic measures adopted due to the COVID-19 pandemic. These were:

a. Supporting employment to prevent loss in businesses whose production activities slowed down due to the pandemic (unemployment benefit, short-time working allowance)
b. Incentive and support packages to maintain businesses (Economic Stability Shield) (Güler and Aydınbaş, 2020: 17).

It is anticipated that the pandemic may lead to an increase in unemployment and inflation rates, budget and payment balance may deteriorate, growth rate may go down and that external financing difficulties may emerge. Governments took measures such as restructuring loans and debts, offering liquidity to the market, and provided low-interest loan options in order to reduce the negative impact of the pandemic on the economy (Arabacı and Yücel, 2020: 196).

In Turkey, measures were adopted to mitigate the negative effects of the pandemic on the economy. A package of economic measures called the Economic Stability Shield was announced on March 18, 2020 to mitigate the negative effects of the Coronavirus pandemic on the economy. A total of TRY 494 billion (10 % of GDP) of economic support was offered to keep the labor market afloat, assist households and businesses affected by the pandemic, and sustain supply chains by ensuring the sustainability of the activities of essential sectors (Ministry of Treasury and Finance, 29.09.2020).

During COVID-19, many businesses reduced weekly working hours and some partially or completely suspended activities due to restrictions imposed upon restaurants, and cafes, reduction in number of orders brought about by a change of consumer consumption habits, lack of customers, and lack of raw material supply (Ocak, 2020:1). Short-work allowance support was introduced to mitigate these negative effects suffered by businesses. Short-time work allowance is defined as "the allowance paid in the event of a general economic, sectoral or regional crisis, force majeure (such as the COVID-19 pandemic), temporary and significant reduction of weekly working hours at the workplace or the temporary cessation of the activity in the workplace" (Yürekli, 2020: 36). As a result of short work allowance applications placed by employers whose work activities were completely or partially stopped due to the pandemic, income support was provided to the insured who could not work during that period, and employers were restricted in terms of layoffs (Ministry of Family, Labour and Social Services, 22.03.2020). The aim was to compensate for the loss of income not caused by workers themselves and to prevent workers from being laid off without any additional cost to employers (Topgül, 2020: 12).

The economic impact of the pandemic can be analyzed under two groups. The first group is public employees, those working in essential sectors, such as healthcare and food, and the second group is those who lost their jobs or businesses or are at risk. While those in the first group continued to earn income, thousands of small and middle-size businesses in the second group went bankrupt or were in the brink of bankruptcy (Karakaya, 2020). There is no doubt that these measures will support businesses that are experiencing economic difficulties, but the prolongation of the pandemic can bring about more problems in terms of sustainability of measures and increased economic risk for such businesses and employees.

Transport and Tourism

Flight bans were introduced worldwide, international events were cancelled or postponed and social gatherings were suspended. Turkey also took a number of measures in this context. On March 13, 2020, flights from Germany, Spain, France, Austria, Norway, Denmark, Sweden, Belgium, and the Netherlands, which were high-risk, were banned. Turkish nationals were also banned from traveling to these countries (Ministry of Transport and infrastructure, 2020).

The need to reduce social mobility to the lowest possible level to combat the COVID-19 pandemic impacted cultural and tourism activities. The pandemic and restrictions brought tourism to a standstill, leading to a decrease in the number of tourists and tourism revenues (İbiş, 2020: 86).

During the COVID-19 pandemic, people cancelled or postponed their travel plans, changed their preferences, and became more aware of their hygiene (Kabadayı and Kardeş, 2020: 3703). With the Safe Tourism Certification program initiated by the Ministry of Culture and Tourism, it was aimed to encourage tourism by adopting the necessary health measures in tourism enterprises and to revitalize the tourism sector. Controlled and healthy tourism is considered a requirement given the share of tourism in Turkey's GNP and the sectors from which tourism supplies goods and services (Bahar and Çelik İlal, 2020: 133).

Alternative Working Arrangements

The COVID-19 pandemic emerged at a time when technology and communication were developing and digital possibilities for communication were available. To reduce social mobility, flexible working arrangements such as working from home, alternate working, and remote working were introduced. In the process, both public institutions and businesses in private sector experienced various working arrangements.

The presidential decree published in the Official Gazette on March 22, 2020, about "Additional Measures for Public Servants during the COVID-19 Pandemic" allowed public institutions to adopt flexible working arrangements such as remote and alternate working (Legislative Information System, 2020).

Home isolation triggered digital transformation. Working life had to keep up with current developments using digital opportunities. Businesses that were afraid to use alternative working methods before the pandemic period began to make more use of remote working more to maintain their activities (Demirdöğmez, Taş and Gültekin, 2020: 130).

Remote working brought about a number of advantages and disadvantages for workplaces. It was found that the information and communication infrastructure, the competence of employees, and the working environment directly affect productivity and that remote working can increase workload and disrupt workplace discipline. Working from home also brought about some advantages such as saving time, flexible working arrangements, and increased productivity (Akbaş Tuna and Türkmendağ, 2020: 3246).

Working from home, which is independent of the physical limitations of the conventional form of working, has many aspects such as economic, employee psychology, occupational health and safety, and social security law. Considering the impact of employee psychology on productivity, remote working arrangements should be taken into consideration (Kabakçı Günay and Özer Tolgalöz, 2020: 410).

2.1.4. Administrative Measures for Disadvantaged Groups

Disadvantaged groups, defined as "people or groups who are partially or completely deprived of social life activities and job opportunities compared to other people in society" (Altan, 2007: 191), were also hit the hardest by the pandemic. For this reason, disadvantaged groups were at the center of measures more than the general public (Yolcu and Sezgin, 2020: 148). As it became more difficult to access medical services due to curfews, the elderly faced more challenges in receiving treatment for conditions such as cardiovascular disease, stroke, high cholesterol, and diabetes (Silberner, 2020).

During the pandemic, curfews were imposed upon those aged 65 and over on various dates. The circular on "restriction/prohibition of leaving from residence," which was submitted to provinces on March 22, 2020, imposed a curfew upon those aged 65 and over and those with chronic conditions starting from midnight on March 21, 2020 (E. 5762 and E. Circulars of the Ministry of Interior No. 13102, 2020).

Vefa Social Support Groups and the 199 Vefa social support line were created to meet the needs of citizens targeted by the ban and received incoming requests. Vefa social support groups made a significant contribution in meeting the needs of disadvantaged groups and consolidated the sense of trust, cooperation, and belonging. Vefa Social Support Groups, which were considered a reflection of the welfare state, strengthened the relationship between the public and the state (Yolcu and Sezgin, 2020: 151–162). Vefa social support application fulfilled the duties of a social state and demonstrated that such services can be offered without any strings attached. The fact that the application was named vefa (loyalty) demonstrates the approach towards the elderly (Gencer, 2020: 39).

Curfews imposed upon those aged 65 and over and those with chronic illnesses played an important role in preventing them from being in crowded places but also changed the perception towards old age in society. The elderly who went out during curfews were blamed, mocked, and excluded, to which they responded with physical reactions, disregard, sadness, fear, guilt, and denial. Curfews imposed upon the elderly prevented them from going out while negatively impacted the perception towards age in society by leaving them vulnerable to the discriminatory discourse (Yaşar and Avcı, 2020: 1271). Social media posts also confirmed that negative perceptions towards the elderly heightened during the pandemic (Uysal and Eren, 2020: 1159). Although curfews contributed to the protection of the health of the elderly, they adversely affected people aged 65 and over socially and psychologically.

Curfews and home isolation practices impose a heavier burden on those lack sufficient economic resources and who need protection. In addition, stress and anxiety caused by prolonged stay at home in an unsuitable environment can lead to psycho-social problems such as domestic violence and abuse (Karataş, 2020: 15). A "Psycho-social Support Call Center" was established under the Ministry of Education in order to reduce the anxiety and traumatic effects of the pandemic on young people and families. People were able to receive psycho-social support from special education and guidance counselors via phone (Ministry of National Education, 2020a).

Research has shown that administrative measures targeting disadvantaged groups can lead to a negative perception in society, especially towards the elderly (Yaşar ve Avcı, 2020: 1271; Uysal ve Eren, 2020: 1159; Taşdelen, 2020: 887). These administrative measures adopted to protect public health also laid the foundation for negative attitudes. However, efforts such as Vefa social support groups improved state-citizen relations, helping to better understand the measures adopted.

CONCLUSION

About three months after the emergence of the COVID-19 virus, the first case was detected in Turkey. Soon after that, face-to-face education was suspended, distance education was kicked off, curfews were imposed, and entry and exit to cities were restricted. Public areas such as shopping centers, marketplaces, and recreational areas were shut down and mass gatherings were postponed. Measures were adopted in public transportation vehicles to maintain social distance. Wearing masks was made mandatory everywhere. The recommendations produced by the Coronavirus Scientific Committee, which was established quite early on, following the developments in the world and the course of the disease within the country, were quickly transformed into policies under the coordination of the president and ministers.

The pandemic showed the important role of digital services in striking a balance between protecting public health and ensuring the continuity of public services. The setting caused by the pandemic allowed digital services to improve quickly, and progress that would normally take years took a very short time. Thanks to digitalization in health, data could easily be transformed, allowing the prompt adoption of necessary measures according to the course of the pandemic. People who were high-risk were prevented from accessing public areas via the Life Fits Home code. The Contact Tracing and Isolation Tracking System allowed experts working on the field to receive and share information rapidly.

In the face of a sudden shift to distance education, the Ministry of National Education, the Council of Higher Education, and universities promptly took part in distance education together with other stakeholders. The pandemic revealed the obstacles before the effective delivery of distance education.

In a process where social and economic life is restricted and the availability of public services is difficult, the government took steps to ensure the continuity of public services much faster than usual and introduced many services.

The COVID-19 pandemic is of great importance as it reminds us again of the importance of healthcare and social security systems and social state practices. Turkey, on the one hand, introduced administrative measures to treat patients, prevent the spread of the disease and contain the pandemic, and on the other hand, resorted to measures to support social and economic life, which have been deeply impacted. Thus, a balance point was sought between protecting public health and maintaining social and economic life.

REFERENCES

Akbal, H. and Akbal, H. İ. (2020). COVID-19 pandemisi sürecinde uzaktan eğitim ile ilgili yaşanan sorunların öğrenci bakış açısına göre ahp yöntemi ile incelenmesi. *Bartın Üniversitesi İktisadi ve İdari Bilimler Fakültesi Dergisi*, 11(22), 533–546.

Akbaş, T. and Türkmendağ, Z. (2020). COVID-19 pandemi döneminde uzaktan çalışma uygulamaları ve çalışma motivasyonunu etkileyen faktörler. *İşletme Araştırmaları Dergisi*, 12(3), 3246–3260.

Altan, Ö. Z. (2007). *Sosyal politika*. Eskişehir: Anadolu Üniversitesi Yayınları.

Arabacı, H. and Yücel, D. (2020). COVID-19 Pandemisinin Türk bankacılık sektörü üzerine etkisi. *Sosyal Bilimler Araştırma Dergisi*, 9(3), 196–208.

Bahar, O. and Çelik İlal, N. (2020). Coronavirüsün (COVID-19) turizm sektörü üzerindeki ekonomik etkileri. *International Journal of Social Sciences and Education Research*, 6(1), 125–139.

Buluk, B. and Eşitti, B. (2020). Koronavirüs (COVID-19) sürecinde uzaktan eğitimin turizm lisans öğrencileri tarafından değerlendirilmesi. *Journal of Awareness*, 5(3), 285–298.

Circular of the Ministry of Interior No. E. 5762 (2020, March 22). İkametten Ayrılma Kısıtlaması/Yasaklanması. İçişleri Bakanlığı İller İdaresi Genel Müdürlüğü, Ankara.

Circular of the Ministry of Interior No. E. 6235 (2020, April 3). Şehir Giriş/Çıkış Tedbirleri ve Yaş Sınırlaması. İçişleri Bakanlığı İller İdaresi Genel Müdürlüğü, Ankara.

Circular of the Ministry of Interior No. E. 6284 (2020, April 11). Sokağa Çıkma Yasağı. İçişleri Bakanlığı İller İdaresi Genel Müdürlüğü, Ankara.

Circular of the Ministry of Interior No. E. 13102 (2020, August 12). 65 Yaş ve Üzeri Vatandaşlarımızın Sokağa Çıkma Kısıtlamaları Hk. İçişleri Bakanlığı İller İdaresi Genel Müdürlüğü, Ankara.

Circular of the Ministry of Interior No. E. 13429 (2020, August 20). İl/İlçe Salgın Denetim Merkezleri. İçişleri Bakanlığı İller İdaresi Genel Müdürlüğü, Ankara.

Circular of the Ministry of Interior No. E. 14553 (2020, September 8). Covid Ek Tedbirler. İçişleri Bakanlığı İller İdaresi Genel Müdürlüğü, Ankara.

Circular of the Ministry of Interior No. E. 20076 (2020, November 30). Sokağa Çıkma Kısıtlamaları. İçişleri Bakanlığı İller İdaresi Genel Müdürlüğü, Ankara.

Council of Higher Education (2020, March 26). Basın Açıklaması. Retrieved November 10, 2020, from https://www.yok.gov.tr/Sayfalar/Haberler/2020/YKS%20Ertelenmesi%20Bas%C4%B1n%20A%C3%A7%C4%B1klamas%C4%B1.aspx

Demirdöğmez, M., Taş, H. Y. and Gültekin, N. (2020). Koronavirüs'ün (COVID-19) E-Ticarete Etkileri. *Uluslararası Toplum Araştırmaları Dergisi*, 16(29), 125–145.

Doğan, M. and Bayraktar, M. (2020). COVID-19 with a public health perspective: Measures taken in Turkey and public compliance with the measures. *Iran J Public Health*, 49(1), 67–75.

Gencer, N. (2020). Kovid-19 sürecinde yaşlı olmak: 65 yaş ve üstü vatandaşlar için uygulanan sokağa çıkma yasağı üzerine değerlendirmeler ve manevi sosyal hizmet. *Türkiye Sosyal Hizmet Araştırmaları Dergisi,* 4(1), 35–42.

Genç, M. F. and Gümrükçüoğlu, S. (2020). Koronavirüs (COVID-19) sürecinde ilâhiyat fakültesi öğrencilerinin uzaktan eğitime bakışları. *Turkish Studies,* 15(4), 403–422.

Gençoğlu, C. and Çiftçi, M. (2020). COVID-19 salgınında eğitim: Türkiye üzerinden bir analiz. *Tarih Okulu Dergisi,* 13(46), 1648–1673.

Giannini, S. and Albrectsen, A. B. (2020, March 31). COVID-19 School Closures around the World Will Hit Girls Hardest. Retrieved November 18, 2020, from https://en.unesco.org/news/COVID-19-school-closures-around-world-will-hit-girls-hardest

Güler, İ. and Aydınbaş, Y. E. (2020). Koronavirüs sürecinin Türkiye ekonomisine etkisi: koronavirüs vaka sayısı ve elektrik tüketimi ilişkisi. *Türkiye Yazarlar Birliği Akademi Dil, Edebiyat ve Sosyal Bilimler Dergisi,* 10(30), 11–32.

Güneş, A. (2020, May 9). Pandemic could be an opportunity for Turkish higher education. Retrieved September 7, 2020, from https://www.universityworldnews.com/post.php?story=20200506061559172

Heymann, David L. (2020). *COVID-19:* What is next for public health? *The Lancet,* 395(10224), 542–545.

Higher Education Information Management System (2020). Yükseköğretim Bilgi Yönetim Sistemi. Retrieved December 3, 2020, from https://istatistik.yok.gov.tr/

İbiş, S. (2020). COVID-19 salgının seyahat acentaları üzerine etkisi. *Safran Kültür ve Turizm Araştırmaları Dergisi,* 3(1), 85–98.

Kabadayı, M. and Kardeş, N. (2020). Kovid-19'un (koronavirüsün) yerli turist davranışı ve seyahat eğilimlerine etkileri. *Türk Turizm Araştırmaları Dergisi,* 4(4), 3703–3719.

Kabakçı Günay, E. and Özer Torgalöz, A. (2020). COVID-19 sürecinde Türkiye'de uzaktan çalışma ve istihdamdaki dönüşüm. *3. Uluslararası Akademik Araştırmalar Kongresi (ICAR)* içinde, 404–412.

Karaca, Ş. and Kelam, D. (2020). COVID-19 gölgesinde uzaktan eğitim hizmet kalitesinin incelenmesi. *Sivas Interdisipliner Turizm Araştırmaları Dergisi,* 3(5), 7–18.

Karakaya, E. (2020, April 25). COVID-19 Krizinin ekonomi, enerji ve emisyonlara etkileri: mevcut durum ve olası post-korona senaryoları. Retrieved December 17, 2020, from https://www.iklimhaber.org/COVID-19-krizinin-ekonomi-enerji-ve-emisyonlara-etkileri-mevcut-durum-ve-olasi-post-corona-senaryolari/

Karataş, Z. (2020). COVID-19 pandemisinin toplumsal etkileri, değişim ve güçlenme. *Türkiye Sosyal Hizmet Araştırmaları Dergisi*, 4(1), 1–17.

Kaysi, F. (2020). COVID-19 salgını sürecinde Türkiye'de gerçekleştirilen uzaktan eğitimin değerlendirilmesi. *5th International Scientific Research Congress (IBAD-2020)* (17–22) içinde.

Kostenbaum, S. and Dener, C. (2020, May 28). The importance of digital services during COVID-19. Retrieved August 23, 2020, from https://apolitical.co/en/solution_article/the-importance-of-digital-services-during-COVID-19

Laçinel, Gürlevik, S. (2020). Koronavirüsler ve yeni koronavirüs SARS-CoV-2. *Güncel Literatür*, 14(1), 46–48.

Legislative Information System (2020, September 20). Cumhurbaşkanlığı Genelgeleri. Retrieved October 5, 2020, from https://www.mevzuat.gov.tr/#cumhurbaskaniGenelgeleri

Ministry of Health (2020). Manşet Haberleri. Retrieved October 7, 2020, from https://www.saglik.gov.tr/Genel/MansetHaberListesi.aspx

Ministry of Health COVID-19 Information Page (2020, December 17). Genel Koronavirüs Tablosu. Retrieved December 24, 2020 from https://covid19.saglik.gov.tr/TR-66935/genel-koronavirus-tablosu

Ministry of National Education (2020a). Haberler. Retrieved December 7, 2020, from http://www.meb.gov.tr/meb_haberindex.php?dil=tr

Ministry of National Education (2020b, September 7). Resmî İstatistikler. Retrieved December 7, 2020 from http://sgb.meb.gov.tr/meb_iys_dosyalar/2020_09/04144812_meb_istatistikleri_orgun_egitim_2019_2020.pdf

Ministry of Family, Labour and Social Services (2020, March 22). Bakan Selçuk: "Kısa Çalışma Ödeneği Başvuruları Yarın Başlıyor". Retrieved December 15, 2020, from https://ailevecalisma.gov.tr/tr-tr/haberler/bakan-selcuk-kisa-calisma-odenegi-basvurulari-yarin-basliyor/

Ministry of Transport and Infrastructure (2020). Haberler. Retrieved September 13, 2020, from https://www.uab.gov.tr/haberler

Ministry of Treasury and Finance (2020, September 29). Hazine ve Maliye Bakanı Sayın Berat Albayrak Yeni Ekonomi Programı Sunumunu Gerçekleştirdi. Retrieved October 20, 2020, from https://www.hmb.gov.tr/haberler/hazine-ve-maliye-bakani-sayin-berat-albayrak-yeni-ekonomi-programi-sunumunu-gerceklestirdi

Ministry of Youth and Sports (2020). Haber Arşivi. Retrieved October 7, 2020, from https://gsb.gov.tr/HaberListesi/3/1

Ocak, S. (2020, December 12). Güncel değişiklikle koronavirüs (COVID-19) kısa çalışma uygulaması ve kısa çalışma ödeneği. https://drive.google.com/file/d/1tj-eBptO9JkcNKfAno9Cn4Ke0NoaFQIG/view?fbclid=IwAR3BgtEz2V94x2kNKZsBE0WAXTzU9iyMp-WF6PlY_2Gbm_PBIKuyijeIKWE adresinden edinilmiştir.

Parodi, Stephen M. and Liu, Vincent X. (2020). From Containment to Mitigation of COVID-19 in the US. *JAMA,* 323(15), 1441–1442.

Sezgin, S. and Fırat, M. (2020). COVID-19 pandemisinde uzaktan eğitime geçiş ve dijital uçurum tehlikesi. *Açıköğretim Uygulamaları ve Araştırmaları Dergisi,* 6(4), 37–54.

Silberner, J. (2020, March 28). In a time of distancing due to coronavirus, the health threat of loneliness looms. Retrieved October 26, 2020, from https://www.statnews.com/2020/03/28/coronavirus-isolation-loneliness-health/

Stoecklin, Sibylle Bernard and investigation team (2020, July 27). First cases of coronavirus disease 2019 (COVID-19) in France: surveillance, investigations and control measures, January 2020. Retrieved August 20, 2020, from https://www.eurosurveillance.org/content/10.2807/1560-7917.ES.2020.25.6.2000094

Taşdelen, B. (2020). COVID-19 salgın sürecinde yaşlılığa bakış: 280 karakter yaşlılar hakkında ne söylüyor? *Turkish Studies,* 15(6), 877–891.

Telli Yamamoto, G. and Altun, D. (2020). Coronavirüs ve çevrimiçi (online) eğitimin önlenemeyen yükselişi. *Üniversite Araştırmaları Dergisi,* 3(1), 25–34.

Topgül, S. (2020). COVID-19 salgını ile iş hukukundaki kısa çalışma uygulaması ve kısa çalışma ödeneğine ilişkin güncel gelişmeler. *Karatahta İş Yazıları Dergisi,* 17, 1–16.

Turan, A. and Hamza Çelikyay, H. (2020). Türkiye'de kovid-19 ile mücadele: politikalar ve aktörler. *Uluslararası Yönetim Akademisi Dergisi,* 3(1), 1–25.

Turkish Language Association (2020). Güncel Türkçe Sözlük. Retrieved July 5, 2020 from https://sozluk.gov.tr/

Unhale, Shrikrushna Subhash; Ansar, Quazi Bilal; Sanap, Shubham; Thakhre, Suraj; Wadatkar, Shreya; Bairagi, Rohit; Sagrule, Suraj and Biyani, K. R. (2020). A review on corona virus (COVID-19). *World Journal of Pharmaceutical and Life Sciences,* 6(4), 109–115.

Uysal, M. T. and Eren, G. T. (2020). COVID-19 salgın sürecinde sosyal medyada yaşlılara yönelik ayrımcılık: Twitter örneği. *Turkish Studies,* 15(4), 1147–1162.

Wang, Chen; Horby, Peter W.; Hayden, Frederick G. and Gao, George F. (2020). A novel coronavirus outbreak of global health concern. *The Lancet Journals*, 395(10223), 470–473.

Weston, S. and Frieman, Matthew B. (2020). COVID-19: Knowns, unknowns and questions. *American Society for Microbiology Journals*, 5(2), 1–5.

World Health Organization (2020, January 21). Novel Coronavirus (2019-nCoV) Situation Report-1. Retrieved July 20, 2020, from https://www.who.int/docs/default-source/coronaviruse/situation-reports/20200121-sitrep-1-2019-ncov.pdf?sfvrsn=20a99c10_4

World Health Organization (2020, December 17). WHO Coronavirus Disease (COVID-19) Dashboard. Retrieved December 18, 2020, from https://covid19.who.int/

Yaşar, Ö. and Avcı, N. (2020). Değişen yaşlılık algısı: COVID-19 ile damgalanan yaşlılar. *Turkish Studies*, 15(4), 1251–1273.

Yolcu, T. and Sezgin, A. A. (2020). Salgında sosyal sermayenin üretilmesinde kamu ve sivil toplum: vefa sosyal destek grubu ve ahbap. *Türkiye Yazarlar Birliği Akademi Dil, Edebiyat ve Sosyal Bilimler Dergisi*, 10(30), 143–164.

Yürekli, S. (2020). Çalışma hayatında koronavirüs (COVID-19) salgının etkileri. *İstanbul Ticaret Üniversitesi Sosyal Bilimler Dergisi*, 19(38), 34–61.

Zhao, Guangyu; Du, Lanying; Ma, Cuiqing, Li, Ye; Li, Lin; Poon, Vincent KM; Wang, Lili; Yu, Fei; Zheng, Bo-Jian; Jiang, Shibog and Zhou, Yusen (2013). A safe and convenient pseudovirus-based inhibition assay to detect neutralizing antibodies and screen for viral entry inhibitors against the novel human coronavirus MERS-CoV. *Virology Journal*, 10(266), 1–8.

Tekin Akdemir*

Public Financial Management Responses to the COVID-19: General Overview and Policy Practices in Turkey

Abstract The world faced an unpreceded crisis in 2020. Following the first COVID-19 case in China, many countries have closed their borders and introduced measures to prevent the spread of the virus. Nonetheless, the devastating effects of novel coronavirus spread across the globe. Many governments have endeavored to ensure accessibility of their health systems and sustain their health system. COVID-19 has had profound impacts and pressures on health systems. It has also led to severe social and economic risks. To protect public health and alleviate the risks posed by the COVID-19 on national economies, great many countries have adopted anti-covid policies. In this process, public financial management (PFM) systems and their components have been at the heart of anti-covid policies. While well-designed PFM systems have enabled the effective implementation of anti-covid policies, they have also prevented further deterioration in the financial structure. Thereby, PFM responses to the COVID-19 crisis have attracted considerable interest among both policymakers and academics. Given the fact that PFM systems may play an important role in easing unprecedented adverse effects of the COVID-19 crisis, this study focuses on PFM practices that is essential to minimize the adverse impacts of the COVID-19. To this end, it aims to evaluate what kind of solutions should be introduced in response to the COVID-19 Crisis by the governments, with a focus on Turkey's experience.

Keywords: public financial management, public financial management systems, budgeting for COVID-19, COVID-19 crisis, Turkey, discretionary fiscal measures

INTRODUCTION

After the discovery of the first coronavirus a century ago, the world has witnessed different coronaviruses (Yesudhas et al., 2020). While this virus generally caused diseases in animals, human coronaviruses were first characterized in 1965 (Kahn and McIntosh, 2005) and have become a major problem for human health in the 2000s. As of 2020, while 46 species are officially recognized

---

* Prof., Ankara Yıldırım Beyazıt University, Faculty of Political Sciences, Department of Public Finance, takdemir@ybu.edu.tr

by the International Committee on Taxonomy of Viruses (ICTV, 2020), Species like SARS, MERS, and the COVID-19 have recently come into prominence as they cause severe health problems.

The first novel coronavirus case was seen in China in December 2019. About three months after the first case, the novel coronavirus spread across the globe and was officially recognized by the WHO as a pandemic on March 13, 2020 (WHO, www.who.int).

After March 2020, with the coronavirus disease turning into a pandemic, many countries have announced restrictions to curb the spread of the COVID-19. The coronavirus measures and economic slowdown led to the deterioration in the world economies. More precisely, the novel coronavirus has not only brought about severe health problems and death cases but has also led to an enormous adverse impact on the global economy. That is to say, unlike other coronaviruses, the COVID-19 first turned into a health crisis and then an economic crisis. Almost all countries faced substantial economic disruption due to quarantines, home confinements, restrictions, and uncertainties.

With novel coronavirus, the world faced an unprecedented challenge like never before. Since economic actors are faced with a high degree of uncertainty, they have postponed their consumption and investment, which led to a drop-in economic activity and resulted in a delay in the recovery (Barrero and Bloom, 2020). Although the economic effects of coronavirus outbreaks have varied from country to country, as Kristalina Georgieva (2020) indicated that the world faced the worst economic crisis since the 1930s depression. Just as it is uncertain when the global economic recovery occurs, countries still continue to implement measures against the negative effects of the corona pandemic.

Today the COVID-19 pandemic has turned into an economic crisis. As noted by the UN (2020: 3), the COVID-19 pandemic is far more than a health crisis, as its effects are immensely felt in every sphere of life. The coronavirus lockdown measures and economic slowdown not only led to lower growth rates and job losses but also caused an increase in global poverty and inequalities in many countries. To provide the urgent needs of the health sector and to support the vulnerable households and firms affected by the COVID-19 pandemic, many countries introduced fiscal and monetary stimulus packages.

Due to a sharp economic slowdown, budget balances/fiscal positions have deteriorated in many countries. While significant declines in productivity and output decreased tax revenues, health problems and widespread unemployment increased public spending. Moreover, monetary and fiscal policy measures taken in response to the COVID-19 pandemic imposed an extra burden on fiscal balances. At this point, concerns about the sustainability of public finance have been raised all over the world. This situation paves the way for the question of how public financial management (hereafter PFM) systems should be designed in response to the COVID 19 pandemic.

Like many other countries, Turkey has also introduced fiscal and monetary stimulus packages to mitigate the negative impact of the COVID-19 pandemic on its economy. As a response to the COVID-19 pandemic, a number of discretionary fiscal measures, including additional spending, accelerated spending, and deferred revenue, have been implemented. In addition to the aforementioned fiscal measures, money and credit measures such as equity injections, asset purchases, and expanded debt facilities have been executed. Unlike some other countries, Turkey's fiscal space was limited, and the country was struggling with macroeconomic problems in the precrisis period. Therefore, the measures against the economic contraction resulted in further deterioration in the fiscal structure.

Today, the need for a strong budget to overcome the challenges posed by the COVID-19 pandemic is more obvious than ever, but that requires substantial improvements in PFM systems in many countries. To put it more explicitly, designing PFM systems in a responsive way to tackle health and economic problems arising from the COVID-19 pandemic requires a faster and more flexible response. It would not be wrong to say that sound and well-designed PFM systems are of great importance to maintain an effective struggle for the COVID-19 pandemic and not to endanger the sustainability of public finance systems in the post-pandemic period.

By taking into account PFM systems that may play a key role in tackling challenges induced by the COVID-19 pandemic, this study aims to assess what kind of solutions are offered by PFM systems to mitigate the immediate and ongoing challenges of the COVID-19 pandemic. It also attempts to provide insights for practitioners and policymakers on how PFM systems can be used to support an effective and efficient response to the COVID-19 pandemic. It particularly focuses on the Turkish evidence rather than a comparative analysis. To reveal this, firstly it provides a general clarification of PFM systems and then highlights how PFM systems are designed in response to the COVID-19 pandemic. Finally, it draws attention to PFM interventions in response to the COVID-9 pandemic in Turkey.

1. A Conceptual Framework for Public Financial Management

PFM is the central element of public administration and the foundation of a well-functioning economy. Today, there is a consensus among social scientists that improving the quality of the PFM is of great importance for sustainable public finance. Moreover, PFM reform is frequently a key pillar in reforms to build more capable, efficient, and accountable states in many countries (Fritz, et al., 2012). For this reason, several international organizations, like the IMF, World Bank, and OECD, have initiated efforts to introduce these reforms.

Although there has been an increasing worldwide focus on improving the quality of PFM following the global financial crisis, it is possible to say that reforms to improve the quality of PFM started in the second half of the 1980s with the reform of New Zealand's financial management system. These reforms, which emerged with the reflection of the new public administration approach in the public finance field, are generally perceived as an important component of public administration reforms (Kıral and Akdemir, 2020). PFM constitutes a fundamental building block for good public sector governance and is an essential tool for governments to achieve their public policy objectives. By and large, well-functioning PFM is crucial for effective and sustainable economic management (Alkaraan, 2018).

In the past 40 years, the scope of PFM has expanded, which made the issues covered by it more complex. Therefore, different definitions have been made about the concept of PFM. While PFM initially was defined in a narrow sense that included the central government's budget process and expenditure management, more recently, this definition has broadened to all aspects of managing public resources over time (Cangiano et al., 2013).

In the narrowest sense, PFM is defined as a system that deals with how governments manage the budget in its established phases. However, its definition has extended over time from budget-centered explanation to all aspects of managing public resources as so includes resource mobilization and debt management. In addition to that, a progressive extension in the medium to long term implications and risks for public finances of today's policy decisions have been taken into consideration (Allen et al., 2013; Cangiano et al., 2013). As argued by Andrews et al. (2014), the term denotes how a government manages its resources (revenue and expenditure alike) and the immediate and medium to the long-term impact of such resources on the economy or society. As such, PFM has to do with both process (how governments manage) and results (short, medium and long term implications of financial flows) (Andrews et al., 2014). In brief, PFM refers to the set of laws, rules, systems, processes, and procedures that are used by sovereigns to mobilize public revenues, to allocate public funds, to conduct public expenditures, to account for funds and audit results (Lawson, 2015).

As can be drawn from the definitions above, it is clear that PFM comprises a wider scope from the public expenditure management or budget stages. It comprises revenue management, expenditure management, budgeting, debt management, cash management, accounting, financial reporting, and auditing (Kıral and Akdemir, 2020).

Today, PFM systems cover highly complex and multiple interrelated but often separated issues (Moynihan and Andrews, 2010). Although there is no consensus on the appropriate definition of the PFM concept, there at least seems to be unanimousness on PFM objectives. In general terms, there are three broad objectives of PFM. These objectives are maintaining aggregate fiscal discipline, allocating resources to strategic priorities, and ensuring technical efficiency (Allen et al., 2013).

In a nutshell, while the components and importance of the PFM system have gradually expanded over the last 20 years, the tasks the PFM system has undertaken have become more complex with each passing day.

Although PFM systems still have some shortcomings, reforms in this field have promoted better government performance and public service delivery (Fritz et al., 2014). Open and orderly designed PFM systems have not only enabled the realization of the governments' policy objectives but have also contributed to the fiscal health of governments.

In line with this, there is general recognition that a well-designed PFM system would constitute a sound basis for public finance. The existence of sound PFM systems strengthens fiscal discipline by increasing transparency and accountability. In other words, a well-functioning PFM system based on comprehensive, transparent, and result-oriented budgeting, medium-term expenditure frameworks, accrual accounting, performance auditing, strong accountability mechanisms may prevent the overspending tendency and deficits in the public sector and thus strength fiscal discipline.

Bearing in mind from explanations throughout this paper that PFM is essential for fiscal sustainability, good governance, and macroeconomic stability. Since public revenues and expenditures are at the heart of mitigating immediate and on-going threats of the COVID-19 pandemic, the PFM responses against the COVID-19 pandemic might well play a critical role through effective implementation of public policies in tackling the problems arising from the COVID-19 crisis. Put it differently, it is possible to say that a strong and well-functioning PFM system is a prerequisite for setting up and executing efficient fiscal measures packages against the COVID-19 crisis.

The COVID-19 crisis has highlighted the need for better policies and well-designed anti-crisis mechanisms to address the adverse impact of the

COVID-19 pandemic. As countries faced unprecedented challenges following the COVID-19 pandemic, the role and importance of PFM have come to the spotlight once again during the recent pandemic. Considering the PFM as a crucial factor enabling anti-COVID measures to introduce, the next section of the study will focus on financial management responses to problems caused by the COVID-19.

2. Public Financial Management Responses to COVID-19

The coronavirus pandemic first emerged in China but soon after spread to almost all countries. Due to the uncontrollable spread of the virus, the world faced an unprecedented crisis in 2020. Following the first COVID-19 case in China, many countries closed their borders and introduced measures to prevent the spread of the virus. Nonetheless, the devastating effects of novel coronavirus spread across the globe.

Throughout 2020, the virus spilled rapidly over throughout other nations. Several countries have been heavily affected. Many governments have endeavored to ensure accessibility of their health services and to pursue sustainability in their health system. That is to say, the COVID-19 has had profound impacts and pressures on health systems. It has also led to severe social and economic risks.

The measures aimed at protecting public health and alleviating the risks posed by COVID-19 on public health have brought further burdens on the health systems, such as test, medicine, treatment, health personnel expenses. Due to the widespread closures introduced within the scope of policies to control the ripple effect of the epidemic, substantial losses have occurred in economic welfare. Following the COVID-19 outbreak, fiscal and monetary policies introduced by countries have focused on controlling the epidemic, mitigating income losses of households and businesses, and keeping aggregate demand alive.

In other words, with a global turn of the virus, many countries have adopted fiscal stimulus measures to ensure economic recovery and to tackle the spread of the pandemic. The COVID-19 crisis has forced governments to implement fiscal stimulus packages, reprioritize public expenditures, and undertake new fiscal responsibilities. Governments, accordingly, have implemented rapid remedial discretionary fiscal measures through their PFM systems. The measures have mainly included health-related emergency measures and support for jobless people, firms, and vulnerable households.

Just as PFM components and reforms generally originated in crisis conditions (Quak, 2020), they have become a core element of effective solutions to the crisis. That is why the role and importance of PFM gained prominence during the recent pandemic. More clearly, since the PFM systems constitute a general framework for how public resources are to be used to achieve public policy ends, they have played a crucial role in mitigating the damaging effects of the COVID-19 outbreak.

PFM interventions used to offset the contractionary effects of the COVID-19 pandemic have been composed of temporary and targeted measures. They mainly focused on supporting the most vulnerable ones. As shown in Figure 1, they comprised additional spending and foregone revenue in addition to equity, loans, and guarantees. The size of fiscal measures packages to alleviate the COVID-19 pandemic differed widely depending on country characteristics. The figure displays that the magnitude of fiscal measures packages ranges from 1 % of GDP to well over 44 % as of 2020. It can be explicitly stated that this difference stems from the development level of the countries, the degree to which countries are affected by the crisis and the fiscal space they had before the crisis. In this sense, the size, outcomes and effectiveness of anti-COVID measures have been shaped by the development level of countries, availability of the financial resource, the degree of exposure to the epidemic and the quality of the PFM system. Another point that should be emphasized regarding fiscal measures is that the ratio of the fiscal packages implemented by the advanced countries to the GDP is greater than that of the emerging and low-income countries. In the content of these measures, more emphasis is placed on expenditure increases and foregone revenues in advanced countries when compared to emerging and low-income countries. When the COVID-19 pandemic emerged, advanced economies enjoyed extremely low borrowing costs and used the opportunity to provide more financial support to ensure a permanent recovery. Unlike advanced countries, emerging markets and developing countries are faced with additional costs due to reversals in capital flows, currency pressures, and limited access to external funds. Due to existing resource constraints, their anti-COVID policies aimed at addressing the devastating economic fallout of the crisis were realized in the form of indirect supports.

As mentioned above, the COVID-19 crisis has forced governments to implement fiscal stimulus packages, reprioritize public expenditures, and undertake new fiscal responsibilities. As a response to this crisis, governments have adopted many distinct solutions through their PFM systems. In this context, several countries have launched a range of measures to alleviate the impact of coronavirus and to support households, employers, and businesses. Anti-COVID

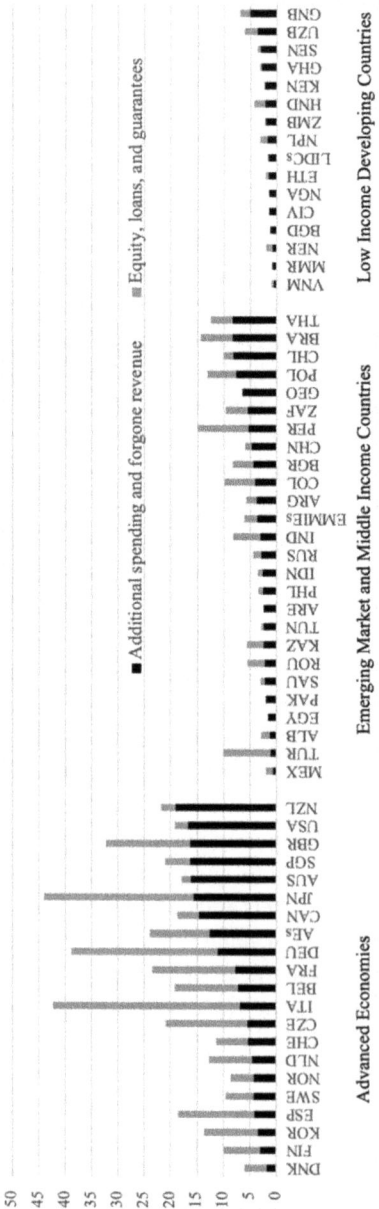

Figure 1. Discretionary Fiscal measures to the COVID-19 Crisis in Selected Economics (Percent of GDP)
Source: Adopted from IMF Sources (IMF, 2020a; IMF, 2021a).

PFM measures are targeted to employees, the most affected sectors, or vulnerable households. They encompassed, among the many others, revenue measures, expenditure measures, budget measures, borrowing-related measures and other measures.

The revenue and expenditure-based measures have been made up of contractionary and expansionary measures. Expansionary revenue-based measures aim at reducing the burden of taxpayers or providing temporary liquidity to them through the extension of a tax return and tax payment periods, temporary suspension of payments, amnesty from penalties, and rate reductions in tax and social security payments. As for the expansionary expenditure measures, they would primarily focus on expediting health-related spending, additional investments to priority areas,* the extension of unemployment benefits, creating subsidies, providing grants to entrepreneurs and firms, and assisting the poor or vulnerable households (IMF, 2020b).

To mitigate the negative impact of the ongoing pandemic, regulations ensuring faster and more flexible response to the COVID-19 pandemic have been put into effect. This is because the public procurement process can be notoriously slow and characterized by complex procedures. Countries have generally used the emergency provisions of their public procurement legislation to procure critical goods and services and to ensure the continued provision of public services. This provided flexibility while retaining accountability (Marchessault, 2020; OECD, 2020a). Public procurement procedures were loosened or suspended (in countries such as Central African Republic, Zimbabwe) to provide flexibility in the spending process and prevent delays in the implementation of anti-COVID-19 policies. To this end, regulations for accelerating the procurement process up have been put into practice in countries such as Mexico or Pakistan to ensure the supply of essential goods and services. In some countries such as Mauritania, Spain, and South Africa an emergency management process has been put in place to ensure the supply of essential goods. European Union countries adopted joint public procurement practices to secure equitable access to medical products at a proportionate price (McEvoy

---

* The priority areas cover the following three: (i) Increasing education spending to remedy the setback to human capital accumulation; (ii) Giving importance to digitalization to boost productivity growth; and (iii) focusing on green investment to enhance reliance on renewables and increase energy conservation. (see IMF, 2021b: 9).

and Ferri, 2020). In Chile, payments in government procurement have been accelerated (IMF, 2020b).

As with public procurement procedures, fiscal rules have also been relaxed or suspended. European Commission activated the general escape clause in the EU fiscal rules, West-Africa Economic and Monetary Union temporarily suspended growth and stability Pact criteria, Honduras and Jamaica increased fiscal deficit limits through approving the escape clause included in their Fiscal Responsibility Laws. Columbia temporarily suspended its fiscal rule. Temporary suspension of fiscal rules or other international convergence criteria allowed countries to raise their overall fiscal deficit temporarily. Thus, they had the opportunity to provide additional support to their households and firms (IMF, 2020b).

Suspension or relaxation of public procurement procedures or fiscal rules have increased the importance of auditing as public resources become more vulnerable to risks such as abuse and corruption. Since these measures were implemented through accelerated processes or were not subject to the same degree of scrutiny as annual national budgets, the public audit has become more critical to hold policy-makers accountable. Public auditors play a significant role in assessing whether not only public funds are appropriately used but also the impact of measures after implementation along with establishing accountability. Consequently, the COVID-19 has posed significant challenges and opportunities to internal and external audit institutions. In addition to maintaining their traditional role, internal audit units have tracked whether governments' aid programs serving the intended beneficiaries. They have also sought to prevent fraud. Most countries have avoided physical controls and face-to-face activities in the conducting of internal audit activities. Aforesaid activities have been executed in such a way that physical presence has been replaced with remote works by taking advantage of digital and electronic technologies (OECD, 2020b). Like internal audit units, the supreme audit institutions (SAIs) have also monitored the measures taken by their governments against the corona crisis. Alongside ongoing duties, the SAIs have had to perform the auditing of the national discretionary responses against the COVID-19 pandemic. The audit was conducted by SAIs to ensure that public funds are used as the intended increased their workload. Some supreme audit institutions, such as the UK National Audit Office established a COVID-19 program of work (OECD, 2020c). In combination with the increased workload, suspending and rescheduling of on-site inspections and the lockdown decisions are taken by national governments have hindered both the sustainability and continuity of the usual audit methods (World Bank, 2020). However, flexible working hours, working by turns, home office working system, the dissemination of digital technologies and electronic applications have made audit activities possible to carry out without substantial disruptions. External audits have generally carried out using home working and teleworking. The continuity of audit work has been ensured through video conferencing and other IT tools (OECD, 2020b).

Another aspect of the PFM response to the COVID-19 pandemic was contractionary measures. Due to the fall of public revenues or commodity prices or increased expenditures government budgets remained under pressure. So, some countries such as Paraguay, Uruguay, Vietnam, Kosta Rika, Belize turned to cuts in government pays or suspend wage increases (Garcia-Escribano and Abdallah, 2020). Apart from these countries, low-income countries, faced with resource constraints before the crisis, have also adopted contractionary measures such as reducing or prioritizing public spending, suspending wage increases or cutting personal expenditures, raising the excise tax, VAT and custom duties or imposing new solidary or corona tax. Additional fiscal space has also been generated through expenditure reprioritizations such as reallocations and budgetary virements or by the elimination of inefficient spending (IMF, 2020b). As a result, the financial maneuverability of developing, low-income, and resource-dependent countries has increased in the struggle against COVID-19.

Equity, loans, and guarantees constituted an important pillar of discretionary fiscal measures as a supportive policy initiative for revenue and expenditure-based policies. Among these kinds of measures, capital/equity injections, liquidity provisions, concessional credits, loan guarantees, debt service deferrals have come to the forefront.

PFM solutions have been generally implemented under the authority conferred on the executive branch with the budgetary laws and procedures. Due to unprecedented health-related challenges and economic uncertainties, conventional budgeting practices has transformed significantly. Governments primarily aimed at the continuity of public services and alleviating adverse economic and social effects of the COVID-19 through benefitting from expenditure prioritization, reallocations, and budgetary virements. To that end, they used existing budget appropriations, contingency appropriations, and supplementary appropriations. Apart from this, some countries also adopted an emergency budget or established new extra-budgetary funds. Supplementary budgets and emergency fund provisions allowed countries to spend more public funds than initial appropriations contained in their budget. These budgetary and extra-budgetary measures are supported by the acceleration of appropriation transfers and the establishment of strong transparency and accountability frameworks. In some countries, COVID-19 related spending measures have been flagged in the budget document and financial reports (OECD, 2020c).

PFM systems have come under considerable pressure due to the measures alleviating the economic contraction caused by the COVID 19. In other words, the measures introduced against the COVID-19 pandemic have created an extra burden on countries' budgets. The value and importance of efficient cash management have further increased as public institutions need to struggle more quickly to the crisis and channeling resources to priority areas such as urgently needed healthcare products without shortfall of cash and delay. More clearly, given the increased uncertainty during the COVID-19 crisis, ensuring the availability of funds to service delivery units and disbursing them efficiently was of great importance due to increasing volatility in government cash flows and balances. In addition to the normal transaction balance needed for smooth execution of the budget, governments around the world had to build or keep a strong cash buffer to meet short-term liquidity needs and direct funds to high-priority spending items (Hurcan et al., 2020; van Eden, 2020). Therefore, the existence of a well-structured government cash management cash preservation and cash generation has become even more important than before (Cangoz and Secunho, 2020).

The policy responses aiming to alleviate the negative consequences of the COVID-19 pandemic, along with economic slowdown and revenue losses, led to a rising budget deficit and resulted in a higher level of debt (debt-to GDP ratio). The COVID-19 pandemic posed substantial challenges on public debt management by driving up governments' financing requirements. Debt management units had to tackle some challenges arising from the unforeseen changes in borrowing requirements, raised market volatility, and increased operational risks (Hurcan et al., 2020). Some countries have authorized Central Banks to finance governments directly through the purchase of government securities in the primary market and to support the bondholders in the secondary market (Arslan et al., 2020). While advanced countries benefit from low-interest rates to meet their financing requirements, developing and low-income countries faced higher financing costs due to undeveloped domestic financial markets, constraints to accessing external financing, and increased risk aversion. As shown in Figure 2, fiscal balance as a share of GDP deteriorated in many countries. The projected ratio of general government budget deficit over GDP would reach 5,7 % in low-income countries, whereas this ratio would exceed 10 % in emerging market and middle-income countries and 13 % in advanced countries. Compared to 2019 average 2020 public debt-to-GDP levels are projected to rise by about 18 % in advanced countries, 9 % in emerging

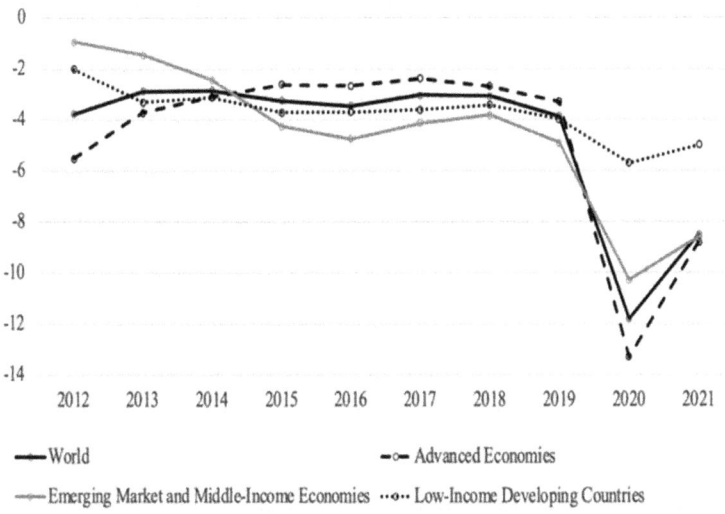

Figure 2: General Government Fiscal Balance (Percent of GDP)

countries, and 5 % in low-income countries (Figure 3). While the projected budget deficit-to-GDP ratio is expected to improve in 2021, it is also expected that the debt ratio over GDP will rise by approximately 2 %. Considering the uncertainties in vaccination and ambiguity about how long ongoing adverse effects of the COVID-19 will continue, the fiscal balances of governments will likely further worsen in 2021. Compared with previous years, these high rates of growth in public debt levels would drive up borrowing risks and constrain additional borrowing, particularly in developing and low-income countries and Thus, debt sustainability concerns will inevitably come to the forth. The requirement of devoting more resources to realize debt service payments would increase budget rigidity. This situation would undermine the public resource allocation mechanism and would lead to cut back on other expenditures such as growth-enhancing expenditures, health and social expenditures. Due to the increased interest burden, protecting existing spending composition would not be feasible in developing and low-income countries. Since fiscal space shrinks, policymakers would become interested in further PFM reforms. Given that PFM reforms have become common in the post-financial crisis, it seems that the corona crisis would require new generation PFM reforms.

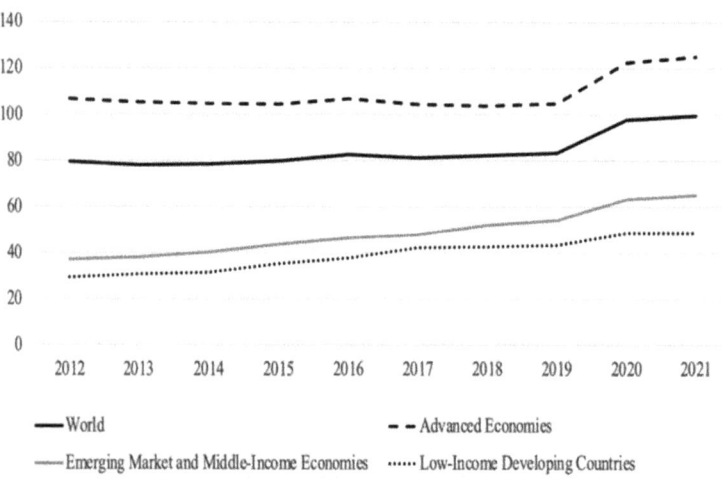

Figure 3: General Government Debt (Percent of GDP)
Source: Adopted from IMF Sources (IMF, 2020a; IMF, 2021a).

3. Public Financial Management Interventions in Response to the COVID-19 in Turkey

As in all other countries, COVID-19 has led to negative consequences in the health sector and the general welfare in Turkey. By January 31, 2021, the number of total confirmed coronavirus cases reached more than 2.4 million in Turkey.

Following the first confirmed coronavirus case, Turkey has introduced a range of measures including ensuring social distancing, mandatory mask-wearing, self-isolation, travel restrictions, allowing flexible working hours for employees, the week-end curfews, closures of educational institutions, and staying at home campaigns to curb the spread of the COVID -19.

Like many other countries in the world, the COVID-19 outbreak has heightened uncertainties in Turkey. Lockdowns and other coronavirus restrictions including travel bans, educational institutions closures, and stay-at-home orders exacerbated economic distortions such as lowering economic growth, increasing capital flows, and exchange rate pressures. They have caused public spending to increase and losses in public revenues or a decline in the rate of revenue growth. The widespread negative impacts of the COVID-19 outbreak on macroeconomic situations compelled the government to take severe measures against it.

Consequently, Turkey has put forward a range of measures including additional expenditure, forgone revenue, loans, and guarantees measures to ease the social and economic fallout of the virus. While the revenue-based fiscal measures, among many others, contained tax and social security premium deferral, tax breaks, the extension of tax filing and payment, tax relief, and restructuring of certain receivables,[†] the expenditure based-measures included additional healthcare-related expenditures, cash transfers to poor and vulnerable households, grants and rent subsidy for tradesmen, financial support to local governments, increased pension, the short-and term working allowance (see Figure 4).

The COVID-19 pandemic erupted when Turkey had just begun to implement its 2020 budget. The budget was prepared based on the conditions of the pre-COVID crisis period. So, measures against the negative effects of coronavirus on the health system and the overall economy have been implemented through the enacted budget. Since the coronavirus outbreak emerged in a condition that Turkey did not have enough budget flexibility, it has inevitably constrained options that the country may resort to against the crisis. Therefore, expenditure-based measures have been implemented, on the one hand, through the measures such as budget virements, reallocations of budget appropriations, and utilization of contingency funds practices and, on the other hand, through the use of unemployment insurance fund's resources.

With the addition of in and out-institution transfers, expenditures made from contingency appropriation amounted to 8.59 % of overall expenditures of the general budget for 2020. Besides, the ratio of the expenditures incurred from the contingency appropriation to the preceding year of that expenditures increased by 90 %. From the contingency appropriation, transfers were made to more than 150 administrations for personnel expenses, goods and services purchase expenses, capital expenses, current and capital transfer expenses. The 35.86 % of total budgetary virements from that appropriation were used for current transfer expenses (Ministry of Family, Labor and Social Services (23.74 %), Ministry of Treasury and Finance (9.91 %), General Directorate of Highways (2.21 %)), 27.27 % for capital expenses (General Directorate of Highways (19,70

---

† With law no:7256, the accrued public receivables were restructured, allowed the taxpayers to pay their debts in instalments, and the interest rates were recalculated at a low rate. Moreover, fines for some receivables in advance payments (e.g. tax) were completely written off. Thus, with this law, both markets were eased and revenue was provided to the public (see Official Gazette of Turkey, 2020).

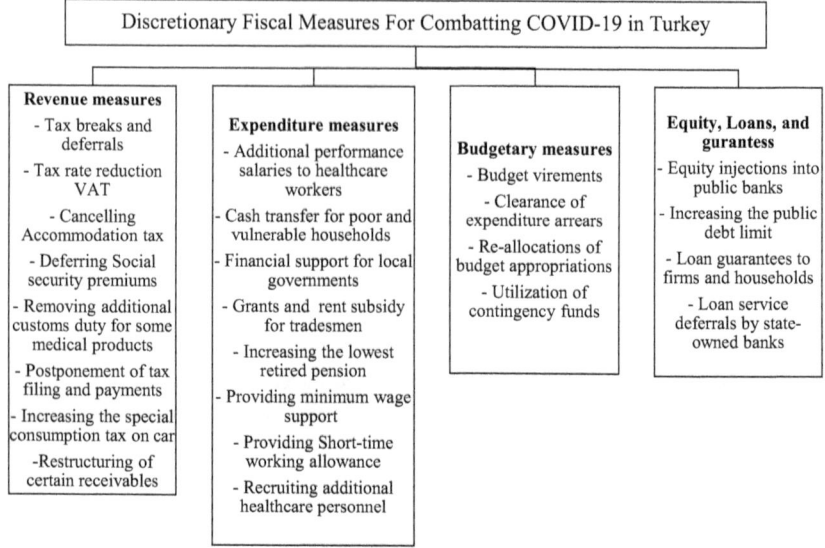

Figure 4: Discretionary Fiscal Measures for Combatting COVID-19 in Turkey

Source: Data were gathered from various sources. IMF (2020b), Policy Responses to COVID-19, Retrieved December 16, 2020, from https://www.imf.org/en/Topics/imf-and-covid19/Policy-Responses-to-COVID-19#E; TCCB (2020), *Turkey's Economic Stability* Shield *Package*, Retrieved March 25, 2020, from https://www.tccb.gov.tr/haberler/410/117037/-ulkemizin-maruz-kaldigi-virus-tehdidinin-en-kisa-surede-bertaraf-edilmesi-icin-devlet-olarak-tum-imk-nlarimizi-seferber-ettik-; GIB (2020), Announcement on Some Measures Taken within the Scope of Effective Combating with the New Coronavirus Disease, Retrieved April 30, 2020, from https://www.gib.gov.tr/koronavirus-salginindan-etkilenmeleri-nedeniyle-beyanlari-uzatilarak-odemeleri-ertelenen-mukellefler.

%), Ministry of Transport and Infrastructure (4,17 %), General Directorate of State Hydraulic Works (3.40 %)) and 7.96 % for purchase of goods and services (Ministry of Health (3.21 %), Ministry of National Defence (2.47 %), Ministry of Justice (2.28 %)) (TCA, 2020a; PSB, 2021).

When it comes to the support provided from unemployment insurance fund sources, short-time work allowance and cash wage support payments have been covered from unemployment insurance fund resources to protect workers' income and to support employers. To this end, As of December 2020, the aggregate amount of payments made from the unemployment insurance fund has exceeded $4.5 billion (Table 1). Although these payments provided temporary

Table 1: Unemployment Insurence Fund Balance (USD)

USD	2018	2019	2020
Total Revenues	6.545.417.068	6.783.297.427	5.148.928.788
Employer and employer contribution	2.623.171.345	2.780.685.129	2.182.954.108
State contribution	874.390.511	926.894.987	727.650.921
Interest revenues	2.855.752.575	2.828.581.175	2.118.977.357
Other revenues	192.102.826	247.136.135	119.346.402
Total Expenditures	4.480.700.312	6.128.267.431	8.960.295.048
Unemployment insurance benefits	1.108.688.782	1.681.550.574	1.128.092.752
Short term working allowance	159.342	32.337.708	3.685.823.994
Cash wage support	-	-	879.364.027
Active labour programs	926.989.131	1.105.630.094	397.607.464
Job shadowing programs	350.055.949	510.700.926	361.938.461
Incentive and support payments	2.024.275.588	2.698.526.224	2.433.650.894
Other expenditures	70.531.330	99.521.737	73.817.186

Source: Turkish Employment Agency, Unemployment Insurence Fund Bulletin, December 2020, p. 6, https://www.iskur.gov.tr/yayinlarimiz/issizlik-sigortasi-bulteni/

relief in the labor market and partially protected the worker and employer from the adverse effects of the crisis, they deteriorated the asset balance of the fund.

In addition to revenue and expenditure-based measures, a considerable number of additional measures have also been taken. For instance, equity injections were made into public banks, concessional loans provided to the private sector, loan service payments deferred by public banks, the limit of special category state domestic borrowing notes, and public debt limits were raised.

As has been the case in many other countries, control and audit of on-budget and off-budget measures has been of great importance in ensuring the effectiveness of anti-COVID policies as well as in making/holding the government more accountable. However, COVID-19 has had a great impact on carrying out these activities just like in every sphere of life. Due to the lockdowns and remote work measures, while digital technologies were firmly used in the execution and continuation of internal audit activities in some institutions with adequate institutional capacity, these activities were reduced in others. Most internal audit units rescheduled their audit programs and some others cancelled local audits because of the restrictions on travel. Turkish Court of Accounts (TCA) has switched to working by turns and allowed its staff to work from home to minimize the impact of the COVID-19 pandemic on the auditors, except for those who have to work on the premises due to compelling reasons. In addition to this, a series of measures such as making the TCA Audit Management Program suitable for remote access and the establishment of the TCA File Sharing System, and providing distance working equipment have been introduced to facilitate the home office working system and to ensure the continuation of the audit (TCA, 2020b). In remote audit process, the audit data have been mainly gathered through the Data Analysis System (VERA). The analyses have been performed using this system. All auditors have had access to VERA and have attained analysis results and financial data of the auditees. Thus, the auditors had the opportunity to analyze the data dynamically, which they would use in the audit (TCA, 2021: 21). Despite these positive steps in external audit, the TCA has not yet reported the expenditures related to COVID and the risks arising from the use of COVID-19 resources.

When compared to other emerging markets and developing countries, Turkey's anti-COVID PFM reforms consisted of extending loans and guarantees facilities rather than revenue and expenditure measures. The reason why Turkey did not allocate sufficient resources to combat the corona outbreak may well be associated with both its relatively weak fiscal position and its exposure to the COVID-19 crisis at a time when the country was struggling with the ongoing economic crisis. In other words, since Turkey was faced with substantial financing constraints before the COVID-19 crisis, its budgetary measures were relatively small.

More precisely, the macroeconomic situation has substantially worsened since 2018. The measures have been taken to tackle economic difficulties and to stabilize the economy between 2018 and 2020 reduced the government's fiscal maneuver in designing and enforcing comprehensive anti-COVID policies. In addition, they also constrained the government's ability to respond to the COVID-19 crisis. Put it differently, in Turkey, the elevated budget deficit and debt stock have constrained revenue and expenditure-based anti-COVID measures. Therefore, different policy options such as equities, loans, and guarantees have been put into effect to alleviate the crippling effect of the novel pandemic. The economic downturn and a decline in tax revenue exerted an additional burden on public finance.

Despite the sharp contraction seen in many countries, the economic slowdown was relatively moderate in Turkey. Policy responses to the pandemic have contributed to a relative rebound in GDP. However, macroeconomic vulnerabilities have been exacerbated by these policy responses. Although the growth rate was expected to contract in 2020, the downturn in economic activity did not affect budget revenues to the same extent. While the budget revenues increased by 17 % compared to the previous year, the increase in tax revenues was 23.6 %

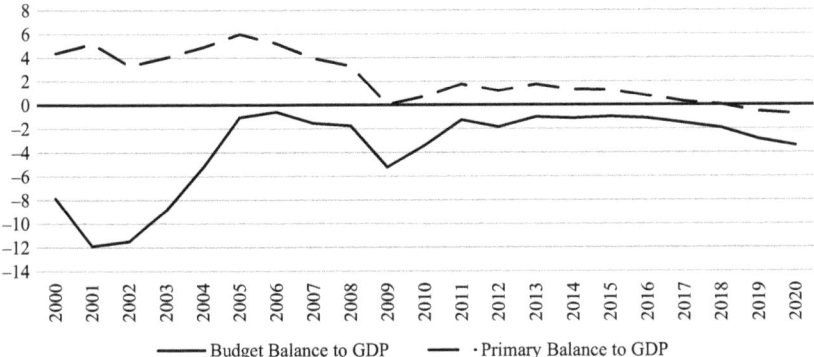

Figure 5: The Ratio of Budget Balance to GDP in Turkey
Source: Author's calculations based on the figures provided from Ministry of Treasury and Finance (2021a), Treasury Cash Realizations, https://www.hmb.gov.tr/kamu-finansmani-istatistikleri

despite a decrease in the ratio of tax receipts to tax accruals. In addition, enterprise, property, and capital revenues fell behind the budget targets, whereas Excise Duty, VAT and Corporate Tax revenues preceded the targets (Ministry of Treasury and Finance General Directorate of Accounting, 2021). As a result, the proportion of indirect taxes in total taxes rose.

Figure 5 illustrates the historical development of the central government budget balance over the past 20 years. As a result of the COVID-19 response and economic slowdown, the budget deficit to GDP ratio reached 3.42 % of GDP on average this year (Figure 5). In addition to that, the primary deficit increased by 38 % compared to the previous year, while the increase in the budget deficit was 56.3 % in the same period. Although budget revenues increased by 17 % compared to the previous year, as overall expenditures exceeded revenues, the ratio of revenues in covering expenses declined and thus both the budget deficit and the primary deficit increased evidently. The deterioration of the central government budget balance largely resulted from expenditure increases. In 2020, the size of the deviation central government total budget expenditure realizations from initial budget appropriations was more than 10 %. This deviation was the highest since 2006. When looking at the deviations by sub-items of expenditures, there was a very high deviation in goods and service purchase expenses (27 %), capital expenses (64 %) and capital transfers (123 %) (Ministry of Treasury and Finance General Directorate of Accounting, 2021).

As discretionary fiscal policies were primarily composed of equity, loan, and guarantees, the ratio of the budget deficit to GDP remained relatively moderate (see Figure 6). Another reason why Turkey's budget deficits were low compared to countries with similar development levels can be explained by the implementation of relatively small scale on-budget measures against the COVID-19 and fulfillment of additional health capacity and investment needs through off-budgetary sources. Although the acceleration and completion of health investments made with public-private partnership (PPP) meet the need for additional capacity and ensure the sustainability of health services, an increase occurred in potential risks and costs due to guaranteed liabilities provided to these investments. Moreover, concessional loans, loan guarantees, and other quasi-fiscal expenditures that were implemented to curb the COVID-19 pandemic raised conditional liabilities. Therefore, it has become more critical than ever to measure and publishing conditional liabilities to boost the long-term credibility of PFM. In Turkey, an accrual basis accounting, implementation of international public sector accounting standards, and independent external audit have enabled the government's financial performance and position were determined in a timely and accurate manner. Timely, comprehensive and reliable tracking, accounting, and reporting of the funds used for combating COVID-19 have helped policymakers make informed decisions and take timely corrective actions as well contributed to greater transparency and accountability. However, most of the public sector liabilities under PPPs contracts are not exactly reported. Given that fiscal transparency has become crucial during the COVID-19 pandemic in preventing misuse of public funds and strengthening accountability, to fully identify the financial obligations of the public sector and to accurately assess its financial risk especially those arising from PPPs, should be periodically reported and announced to the public.

The low level of on-budget pandemic expenditures and increased tax revenues have enabled the deterioration in the budget balance to be lower than in countries with similar development levels, as of 2020 in Turkey (see Figure 6). The policies based on credit expansion in combatting the COVID-19 increased domestic demand and imports, they also increased budget revenues through taxing increasing consumption and import. Hence, the share of indirect taxes in total tax revenues increased. Turkey was able to achieve minimizing the burden of the pandemic on public finance through quasi-fiscal expenditures (OECD, 2021: 37). Whilst these policies have limited Turkey's budget deficit, they have brought the debt stock to higher levels, in contrast to countries with a similar level of development with Turkey.

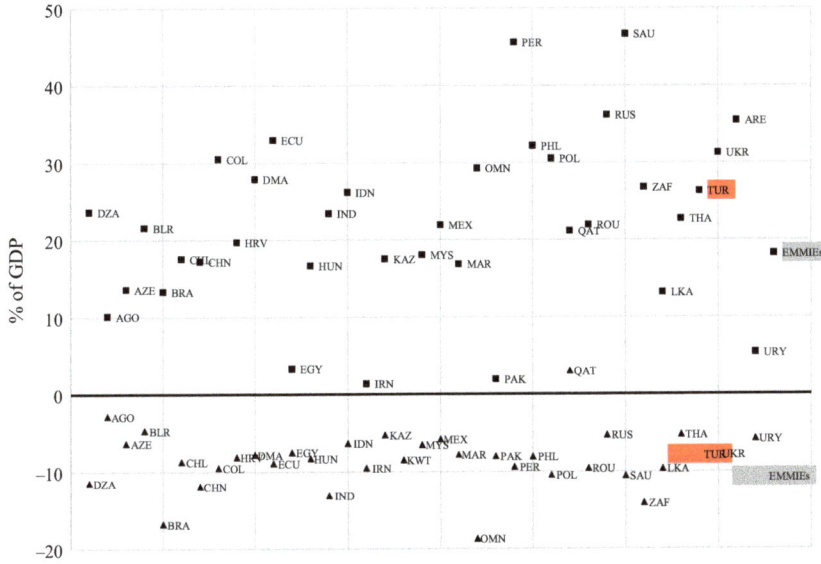

Figure 6: General Government Debt and Fiscal Balance in EMMICs in 2020
Source: Adopted from IMF, 2020a

As discussed earlier, Turkey's anti-COVID measures have not only been limited to on-budget measures. Concessional credits provided by state-owned banks to the private sector, including households during the ongoing pandemic have rised quasi-fiscal expenditures and amplified contingent liabilities of the government (OECD, 2021: 10). To meet increased liquidity requirements of public banks resulting from the losses of privileged loans and increased credit demand, the upper limit of special category state domestic borrowing notes was raised from 3 % to 5 %. In addition to the increase in borrowing arising from off-budget operations, a substantial increase also occurred in borrowing to meet the budget deficit.

What is more, the introduction and pursuing of anti-COVID measures to reduce the potential adverse impact of the COVID-19 pandemic on the economy have triggered the Treasury's cash deficit and borrowing requirement. Thanks to the New Extended Treasury Single Account system, Turkey easily managed to observe and monitor its cash flow and balance during the COVID crisis.

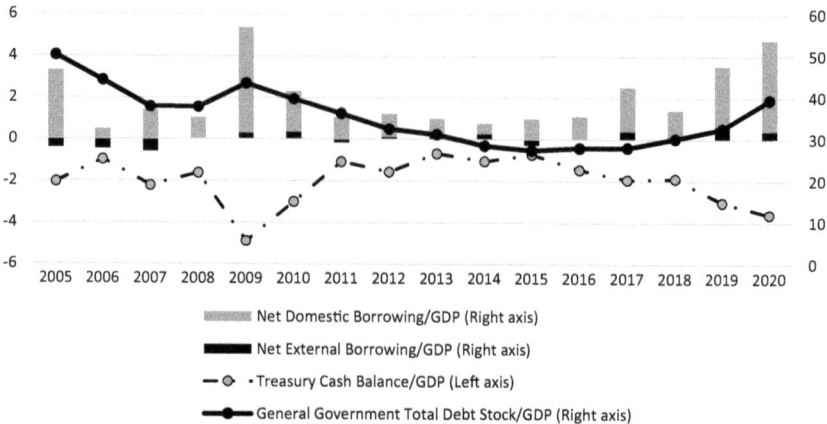

Figure 7: Treasury Cash Balance, General Government Total Debt Stock and Net Borrowing (as percent GDP)
Source: Author's calculations based on Ministry of Treasury and Finance, Treasury Cash Realizations, https://www.hmb.gov.tr/kamu-finansmani-istatistikleri

Reliable and timely cash forecasts enabled great easiness in directing quickly and sufficient resources to areas in need of cash. Encountering the dramatically increased cash needs during the outbreak, required additional action. Ministry of Treasury and Finance pursued a policy that aims to keep a strong level of cash reserve to reduce the liquidity risk associated with cash and debt management. Borrowing costs decreased when compared to the previous year. However, the cost of Turkish bonds, compared to the countries with a similar level of development, was presented substantial variations (Ministry of Treasury and Finance, 2021b: 10). In this sense, meeting the increasing financing need of the central government budget through borrowing drove up the net debt revenue, which represents the difference in receipts and payments of debt within the year, approximately by 58 % compared to the previous year. Moreover, public sector debt stock increased by 20 % compared to the previous year, reaching approximately $258.035 million as of September 2020. The ratio of general government debt to GDP has jumped from 32.6 % to 39.5 %, almost reaching its level that was in the global economic and financial crisis of 2008–2009. Thus, public debt stock has approximately risen by 7 % of GDP (Ministry of Treasury and Finance, 2021b: 2, 18).

Borrowing policies are not performed out by strategic benchmarks. While the share of floating rate and foreign currency-denominated debt in domestic public debt has risen, the weighted average cost of fixed-rate TL denominated domestic borrowing has soared as of the second half of the year. Due to the higher cost of external borrowing, uncertainties in global markets, and difficulties in securing and accessing external sources, there has been no favorable change in the outlook of the net external debt stock of Turkey. However, the share of debtors in the total external debt stock has changed. As the share of the private sector gross external debt stock in the total gross external debt stock declined by 5 %, the central government gross external debt stock moved up by 2.9 %, and the public sector gross external debt stock increased by 2.1 % (Ministry of Treasury and Finance, 2021c).

CONCLUSION

The world has witnessed a global pandemic in 2020 and has faced unprecedented challenges that we have never witnessed before. Although strict economic and health-related measures were introduced in response to the pandemic, its adverse effects could not be eliminated. As of the first quarter of 2021, countries are still in the middle of the crisis. The COVID-19 crisis has heavily impacted nearly every aspect of our lives. It severely affected all facets of social life, from education to health, and decreased employment, growth and public revenues. It also put additional burdens on the national economies. So, the COVID-19 crisis has raised not only concerns about the efficacy of countries' health systems and policies but also significantly endangered fiscal sustainability by exacerbating budget deficit and debt level.

It probably will not be wrong to say that the magnitude of the COVID-19 crisis on national economies has changed depending, to a large extent, on the number of COVID-19 cases and the capacity to introduce economic and fiscal measures against the crisis.

This process, on the one hand, forced countries to spend more to protect the health of the population and to provide financial and monetary support for the most affected portion of the coronavirus, on the other hand, highlighted the need for the importance of an efficient, transparent, and accountable PFM.

More or less similar measures have been taken by countries in terms of their content, albeit with differences between countries in the number of cases and the impact of the crisis on countries. These measures have composed of temporary and targeted fiscal and monetary measures. While discretionary monetary measures have consisted of, inter alia, ensuring additional liquidity, reducing the statutory cash reserve requirements, lowering the interest rate, fiscal measures have mainly included revenue and expenditure-based measures. Moreover, one facet of the measures was revenue-based discretionary fiscal measures encompassing the extension or postponement of tax filing and payment periods in addition to the reductions or complete cancellations of taxes and social security premiums, and rent reliefs, whereas others were expenditure-based measures including additional health-related spending, unemployment benefits, social aid, grants, and additional investments in sectors such as education, green technologies, and infrastructure.

The limited fiscal capacities and inadequate coordination mechanisms have been the main factors of reducing the effectiveness of anti-COVID measures. The crisis, therefore, caused a contraction in economic activity in many countries. As mentioned earlier, the COVID crisis brought about a contraction in economic activity in many countries. Due to the unexpected decline in public revenues and rapidly increasing spending requirements, many countries have re-prioritized their expenditures, and used their contingency appropriations or enacted supplementary budget to implement discretionary fiscal measures. However, some resource-dependent or low-income countries have faced implementation measures that aiming at increasing revenues or casting down their low priority expenditures.

Discretionary fiscal and monetary precautions taken to reduce the harmful effects of the COVID-19 pandemic has contributed to the continuity of health services and saving lives. They have also alleviated the effects of the corona crisis on consumption and output to some extent. In this sense, it is possible to say that while strong PFM systems played a paramount role in addressing the COVID-19 crisis. Nevertheless, it should be noted that the weak PFM systems and lack of fiscal space undermined the realization of desired outcomes. Although these measures helped circumvent a severe crisis caused by COVID-19, they have also exacerbated macroeconomic vulnerabilities and led to an increase in public debt and deficits.

As of the first quarter of 2021, although the ultimate effect of the corona crisis on national economies remains vague, almost all countries are under increasing economic and financial pressure due to the uncertainty caused by the COVID-19. Country experiences have shown that the policies that aim to overcome the COVID-19 crisis not only caused deterioration in the financial structure but also hindered efforts to provide a permanent recovery in the economies.

Like many other developing countries, Turkey has faced remarkable challenges in the mobilization and generation of public funds for providing additional support to households and the business sector or in covering health-related expenses.

Due to ongoing economic problems since 2018, the Turkish economy has limited financial maneuverability when the corona crisis emerged. Therefore, unlike many other countries, Turkey's discretionary fiscal measures against the COVID-19 have focused on equity, loan guarantees rather than revenue, and expenditure-based measures. With the effect of these policies, although the limited increase occurred in the budget deficit, the COVID-19 crisis has resulted in a substantial increase in public debt stock.

The introduction and pursuing of anti-COVID measures to reduce the harmful impact of the COVID-19 pandemic on the economy have triggered the Treasury's cash deficit and borrowing requirement.

Meanwhile, revenue generation from external borrowing has been constrained by global uncertainties, currency instability, higher external borrowing costs, and limited availability of foreign resources. The adverse effects of external borrowing conditions triggered domestic borrowing to finance the treasury's cash deficit and borrowing requirement.

Domestic borrowing increased significantly compared to previous years due to policies that aimed at expanding the investor base in domestic borrowing, offering investors alternative borrowing instruments, and reducing dollarization. With the effect of the increase in the exchange rate, the domestic debt stock increased by 40 % compared to the previous year. This situation, which caused both the ratio of total debt to GDP and the debt rollover ratio to increase, increased the cost of debt rollover and budget rigidity. This will create problems for the functioning of the central government budget in the coming years. And consequently, fiscal consolidation will become inevitable in the post-covid period. Herein, it will be of great importance to report the risks caused by the COVID transparently and regularly to ensure citizens' support for the post-crisis steps.

What's more, although the adverse effects of the pandemic were intense in 2020 and the global relief is likely to occur in the second half of 2021, uncertainties about whether mass vaccination will be applied successfully, how much the vaccine will protect against the virus, and the effectiveness of vaccines against the mutated virus may delay the economic recovery. Problems in the supplies of coronavirus vaccines to countries and the referral chain may cause a continuing burden on the healthcare system. This situation may bring about lockdown measures to be continued for a while, and may restrict social mobility. The fact that the vaccine is not the ultimate solution and the necessity to continue vaccination at regular intervals may put countries, particularly low-income and developing ones, under a burden that they cannot handle. Considering that health or vaccine are global issues, developing efficient solutions against the

COVID-19 entails broader partnerships and joint struggle. This situation also requires the strengthening of PFM systems to improve the effectiveness of potential fiscal consolidation steps to be introduced in the post-pandemic recovery period.

REFERENCES

Alkaraan, F. (2018). Public Financial Management Reform: An Ongoing Journey Towards Good Governance. *Journal of Financial Reporting and Accounting*, 16 (4), 585–609.

Allen R., Hemming R., and Potter B.H. (2013). Introduction: The Meaning, Content and Objectives of Public Financial Management. In: The International Handbook of Public Financial Management (Eds: Allen R., Hemming R., and Potter B.H.), Palgrave Macmillan, London. pp. 1–12, https://doi.org/10.1057/9781137315304_1.

Andrews, M., Cangiano, M., Cole N., De Renzio P., Krause P., and Seligmann R. (2014), "This is PFM." CID Working Paper Series 2014.285, Harvard University, Cambridge, MA, pp. 1–13.

Arslan, Y., Drehmann, M., and Hoffmann, B. (June 2020) "Central Bank Bond Purchases in Emerging Market Economies." BIS Bulletin No. 20.

Barrero, J. M., and Bloom, N. (2020), Economic Uncertainty and the Recovery, Unpublished manuscript, Retrieved October 15, 2020, from https://www.kansascityfed.org/~/media/files/publicat/sympos/2020/20200806bloom.pdf

Cangiano, M., Curristine, T., and Lazare, M. (2013). Public Financial Management and Its Emerging Architecture. International Monetary Fund, Washington, DC.

Cangoz, M. C., and Secunho, L. (2020). Cash Management: How Do Countries Perform Sound Practices? World Bank Publications, Wahington, DC.

Fritz, V., Fialho Lopez, A. P., Hedger, E., Tavakoli, H., and Krause, P. (2012). Public Financial Management Reforms in Post-Conflict Countries. *Synthesis Report*. WorldBank, Washington, DC. Retrieved December 17, 2020, from http://documents.worldbank.org/curated/en/945231468340162289/pdf/699640WP0P1206070023B0PFM0Web0Final.pdf

Fritz V., Sweet S., and Verhoeven M (2014), Strengthening Public Financial Management; Exploring Drivers and Effects, *Policy Research Working Paper*, No: 7084. Washington (DC): World Bank, pp.1–55.

Garcia-Escribano, M., and Abdallah, C. (2020). Cutting Government Pay during a Crisis: Key Issues, Retrieved September 20, 2020, from https://blog-pfm.imf.org/pfmblog/2020/07/-cutting-government-pay-during-a-crisis-key-issues-.html

Georgieva, K. (2020), The Great Lockdown: Worst Economic Downturn Since the Great Depression, Retrived March 25, 2020, from https://www.imf.org/en/News/Articles/2020/03/23/pr2098-imf-managing-director-statement-following-a-g20-ministerial-call-on-the-coronavirus-emergency

GIB. (2020). Announcement on Some Measures Taken within the Scope of Effective Combating with the New Coronavirus Disease, Retrived April 30, 2020, from https://www.gib.gov.tr/koronavirus-salginindan-etkilenmelerinedeniyle-beyanlari-uzatilarak-odemeleri-ertelenen-mukellefler

Hurcan, Y., Koc, F., and Balibek, E.B. (2020). Responding to COVID-19 Challenges: Cash Buffers for a Rainy Day, Retrieved October 10, 2020, from https://blog-pfm.imf.org/pfmblog/2020/04/-COVID-19rethinking-treasury-business-continuity-plans-1.html

ICTV. (2020). International Committee on Taxonomy of Viruses, Virus Taxonomy: 2019 Release, Retrieved August 10, 2020, from https://talk.ictvonline.org/taxonomy/

IMF. (2020a). Fiscal Monitor Database, Retrieved January 31, 2021, from https://www.imf.org/en/Publications/FM/Issues/2020/09/30/october-2020-fiscal-monitor

IMF. (2020b). Policy Responses to COVID-19, Retrieved December 16, 2020, from https://www.imf.org/en/Topics/imf-and-covid19/Policy-Responses-to-COVID-19#E

IMF. (2021a). Fiscal Monitor Update, January 2021, Washington, DC: IMF Publications

IMF. (2021b). World Economic Outlook Update, Washington, DC: IMF Publications.

Kahn, J. S., and McIntosh, K. (2005). History and Recent Advances in Coronavirus Discovery, *The Pediatric Infectious Disease Journal*, 24 (11), 223–227.

Kıral, H., and Akdemir, T. (2020), Introduction. In: *Public Financial Management Reforms in Turkey: Progress and Challenges, Volume 1. Accounting, Finance, Sustainability, Governance & Fraud: Theory and Application* (Eds: Kıral, H., and Akdemir, T.), Springer, Singapore. https://doi.org/10.1007/978-981-15-1914-7_1

Lawson, A. (2015). Public Financial Management. *GSDRC Professional Development Reading Pack*, No. 6. GSDRC, University of Birmingham, Birmingham, UK. pp. 1–6.

Marchessault, L. (2020) Efficient Public Contracting for Emergency Responses, Retrieved December 25, 2020, from https://blog-pfm.imf.org/pfmblog/2020/05/-efficient-public-contracting-for-emergency-responses-.html

McEvoy, E., and Ferri, D. (2020). The Role of the Joint Procurement Agreement during the COVID-19 Pandemic: Assessing Its Usefulness and Discussing Its Potential to Support a European Health Union. *European Journal of Risk Regulation*, 11(4), 851–863.

Ministry of Treasury and Finance General Directorate of Accounting. (2021). Central Government Budget Statistics, Retrieved February 5, 2021, from https://muhasebat.hmb.gov.tr/merkezi-yonetim-butce-istatistikleri

Ministry of Treasury and Finance. (2021a). Treasury Cash Realizations, Retrieved January 15, 2021, from https://www.hmb.gov.tr/kamu-finansmani-istatistikleri

Ministry of Treasury and Finance. (2021b). Public Debt Management Report January 2021, Number: 186, Retrieved January 30, 2021, from https://ms.hmb.gov.tr/uploads/2021/01/Kamu_Borc_Yonetimi_Raporu_Ocak_2021.pdf-2018377

Ministry of Treasury and Finance. (2021c). External Debt Statistics of Turkey, Retrieved February 15, 2021, from https://www.hmb.gov.tr/kamu-finansmani-istatistikleri

Moynihan, D. P., and Andrews, M. (2010). Budgets and Financial Management. In: *Public Management and Performance: Research Directions* (Eds: Walker, R. M., Boyne, G. A., and Brewer, G. A.), Cambridge University Press, Cambridge, UK. pp. 60–88.

OECD. (2020a July). Public Procurement and Infrastructure Governance: Initial Policy Responses to the Coronavirus (COVID-19) Crisis, Retrieved August 11, 2020, from http://www.oecd.org/coronavirus/policy-responses/public-procurementand-infrastructure-governance-initial-policy-responses-to-the-coronavirus-COVID-19-crisis-c0ab0a96/

OECD. (2020b). Public Administration: Responding to the COVID-19 Pandemic. Support for Improvement in Governance and Management (SIGMA), a Joint Initiative of the OECD and the European Union, Retrieved September 30, 2020, from http://www.sigmaweb.org/publications/SIGMA-mapping-public-administration-responseEU-members-coronavirus-COVID19.pdf

OECD. (2020c). Government Financial Management and Reporting in Times of Crisis. OECD Publishing, Paris, France, Retrieved March 15, 2021, from https://read.oecd-ilibrary.org/view/?ref=433_433120-4x64f30lbd&title=Government-financial-management-and-reporting-in-times-of-crisis

OECD. (2021). OECD Economic Surveys: Turkey 2021, OECD Publishing, Paris, France.

Official Gazette of Turkey. (2020). The Law on the Restructuring of Certain Receivables and Amendments to Certain Laws, No. 7256, Promulgated on the Official Gazette No. 31307 on November 17, 2020.

Presidency Strategy and Budget. (2021). Realization of Contingency Appropriations in the 2020 Central Government Budget Law, Retrieved January 16, 2021, from https://www.sbb.gov.tr/2020-yili-merkezi-yonetim-butce-kanunundaki-yedek-odeneklerin-kullanimi/

Quak, E. (2020). Lessons from Public Financial Management (PFM) Reforms after a Financial Crisis. K4D Helpdesk Report No. 810. Institute of Development Studies, Brighton, UK, p. 1.37.

TCCB. (2020). *Turkey's Economic Stability* Shield *Package*, Retrieved March 25, 2020, from https://www.tccb.gov.tr/haberler/410/117037/-ulkemizin-maruz-kaldigi-virus-tehdidinin-en-kisa-surede-bertaraf-edilmesi-icin-devlet-olarak-tum-imk-nlarimizi-seferber-ettik-

TCA. (2020a), General Comformity Report of the Year 2019, Retrieved December 18, 2020, from https://www.sayistay.gov.tr/tr/?p=2&CategoryId=96

TCA. (2020b), Measures Taken fo Providing Business Contuinity of TCA, https://www.sayistay.gov.tr/en/Upload/files/Measures%20Taken%20For%20Providing%20Business%20Continuity%20of%20the%20TCA(1).pdf

TCA. (2021), Activity Report-2020, Retrieved February 22, 2021, from https://www.sayistay.gov.tr/tr/?p=2&CategoryId=61

Turkish Employment Agency. (December 2020). Unemployment Insurance Fund Bullutein, p. 6, https://www.iskur.gov.tr/yayinlarimiz/issizlik-sigortasi-bulteni/

UN. (April 2020). A UN Framework for The Immediate Socio-economic Response to COVID-19, Available at: https://unsdg.un.org/sites/default/files/2020-04/UN-framework-for-the-immediate-socio-economic-response-to-COVID-19.pdf.

Van Eden, H. (2020), Memo from Bangkok: Cash Management and COVID-19, Retrieved November 20, 2020, from https://blog-pfm.imf.org/pfmblog/2020/04/bangkok-cash-management-covid.html

WHO. (2020). WHO Timeline – COVID-19, Retrieved September 17, 2020, from https://www.who.int/news/item/27-04-2020-who-timeline---COVID-19

World Bank. (2020). *Role of Supreme Audit Institutions in Governments' Response to COVID-19: Emergency and Post Emergency Phases.* World Bank,

Washington, DC. © World Bank. https://openknowledge.worldbank.org/handle/10986/33901 License: "CC BY 3.0 IGO", pp. 1–16.

Yesudhas, D., Srivastava, A., and Gromiha, M.M. (2020). COVID-19 Outbreak: History, Mechanism, Transmission, Structural Studies and Therapeutics. Infection, 1–15, https://doi.org/10.1007/s15010-020-01516-2.

www.ingramcontent.com/pod-product-compliance
Ingram Content Group UK Ltd.
Pitfield, Milton Keynes, MK11 3LW, UK
UKHW021834210426
5322IPUK00018B/261